FINANCE AND INVESTMENT FOR SUSTAINABILITY

宝库山精选：面向可持续性的金融与投资

Digital editions

Finance and Investment for Sustainability is available through most major ebook and database services (please check with them for pricing). Special print/digital bundle pricing is also available in cooperation with Credo Reference; contact Berkshire Publishing (info@berkshirepublishing.com) for details.

For information, contact:
Berkshire Publishing Group LLC
122 Castle Street
Great Barrington, Massachusetts 01230-1506 USA
www.berkshirepublishing.com
Printed in the United States of America

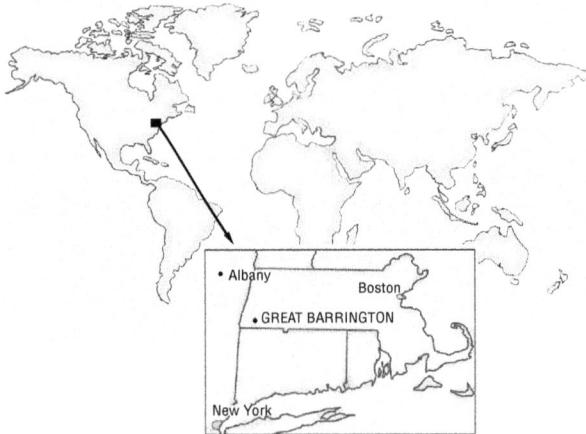

Library of Congress Cataloging-in-Publication Data

Finance and investment for sustainability / Ray C. Anderson, general editor, Chris Laszlo, volume editor.
    pages cm. — (Berkshire essentials)
    Includes bibliographical references and index.
    ISBN 978-1-61472-964-8 (alk. paper)
    1. Finance—Environmental aspects.   2. Finance—Social aspects.   3. Investments—Environmental aspects.
    4. Investments—Social aspects.   5. Sustainable development.   I. Anderson, Ray C.   II. Laszlo, Christopher.
    HG101.F53 2016
      338.9—dc23   2016030035

BERKSHIRE 宝库山
Essentials

FINANCE AND INVESTMENT FOR SUSTAINABILITY

宝库山精选：面向可持续性的金融与投资

Editors: Ray Anderson (series editor), Chris Laszlo, Karen Christensen, Daniel S. Fogel, Gernot Wagner, Peter Whitehouse

└┘ BERKSHIRE
Knowledge for our common future

About *Finance and Investment for Sustainability*

Finance and Investment for Sustainability, a Berkshire Essential, explores how a green economy can be created and sustained—using sustainability in both the environmental and financial sense of the word. Forty expert authors explain topics such as green-collar jobs, energy and foreign investment law, public-private partnerships, the World Bank, smart growth, the financial services industry, the "base of the pyramid," (i.e., the world's poor), social enterprise, green taxes, and the concept of the triple bottom line, sometimes described as "people, planet, and profit." This concise handbook offers a broad view of positive steps being taken to make responsible investment a priority around the globe, and is designed for use in classrooms at the high school and college level. The book will be helpful to engaged citizens as well as to investors, policy makers, and environmental professionals. Complex topics such as green GDP and "true cost" economics are explained clearly and impartially, with a view to promoting thoughtful discussion and informed decision-making.

THE **BERKSHIRE** *Essentials* SERIES

Berkshire Sustainability Essentials, distilled from the *Berkshire Encyclopedia of Sustainability*, take a global approach to environmental law, energy, business strategies and management, industrial ecology, and religion, among other topics.

- Religion and Sustainability
- Business Strategies and Management for Sustainability
- Community and Sustainability
- Energy Industries and Sustainability
- Ecosystem Services for Sustainability
- Environmental Law and Sustainability
- Industrial Ecology and Sustainability

Distilled for
the classroom
from Berkshire's
award-winning
encyclopedias

BERKSHIRE ESSENTIALS from the *Berkshire Encyclopedia of China* and the *Berkshire Encyclopedia of World History, 2nd Edition* also available.

Contents

Financial Services

Applications

About Berkshire Essentials

For more than a decade, Berkshire Publishing has collaborated with a worldwide network of scholars and editors to produce award-winning academic resources on popular subjects for a discerning audience. The "Berkshire Essentials" series are collections of concentrated content, inspired by requests from teachers, curriculum planners, and professors who praise the encyclopedic approach of Berkshire's reference works, but who still crave single volumes for course use.

Each Essentials series draws from Berkshire publications on a big topic—world history, Chinese studies, and (in the case of this book) environmental sustainability, for instance—to provide thematic volumes that can be purchased alone, in any combination, or as a set. Teachers will find the insightful articles indispensable for stimulating classroom discussion or independent study. Students, professionals, and general readers all will find the articles invaluable when exploring a line of research or an abiding interest.

These affordable books are available in paperback as well as ebook formats for convenient reading on mobile devices.

Introduction to *Finance and Investment for Sustainability*

The relationship between the business world and people with environmental and social concerns is evolving. Business leaders are increasingly concerned about the environment, and environmentalists are less inclined to see business as the enemy—and even to see some businesses as an important force for good. In designing this handy compilation, derived from a much larger academic work, our fundamental question was, how do humans promote environmental sustainability while ensuring that business (and the economy) doesn't collapse in the process? This is another way to define *sustainable business*—businesses that will grow, create jobs, and promote the common good.

The concepts and examples included here should serve to build a knowledge base for those who want to work toward a sustainability transition in any area of business. Chapters cover key concepts, areas, and directions, and have been written by many of the world's best-known authors, providing a compelling explanation of the business of sustainability.

New metrics continue to be implemented in an effort to balance the environment with the social, economic, and political movements of the twenty-first century. As contributors Jianguo Wu and Tong Wu write in "Green GDP," despite the various flaws in that first attempt to quantify the price of environmental degradation in China, it was an important opportunity to identify the true cost of the country's breakneck rate of development.

In the "Triple Bottom Line," John Elkington discusses an integrative way of doing business that examines how economic gain, humanity's varied needs, and the environment are connected. William Rees delves into the subject of hidden costs and the value of nature in "True Cost Economics."

Some industries, such as the financial sector, are so gigantic and far-reaching that their every move has wide-ranging repercussions for the sustainability movement, as pointed out by Daniel S. Fogel in "Financial Services Industry." Other industries, such as construction and cement, forestry, steel, and mining, have made strides in recent years that may surprise those who think there is nothing that can be done—or at least nothing that can be done profitably—to improve the environmental impacts of such industries.

As Steve Rhyne points out in "Climate Change Disclosure," publicly traded businesses in the United States must disclose to the Securities and Exchange Commission the potential risks their businesses face from climate change and legislation stemming from climate change—even when the legislation hasn't yet been passed, or indeed even thought of.

Carbon disclosure is especially relevant to companies such as coal-fired power plants, which may be affected by the availability and costs of raw materials in the event that legislation is enacted that puts a price on greenhouse gas emissions. Many companies are making the best of the situation by ensuring they are in the vanguard of disclosure, thus giving them an edge over their competitors as the public becomes ever more aware of the activities of the business world. The theme is further explored by Aarti Gupta in her article on "Transparency." Clearly, the more knowledgeable a company is about environmental issues, the better positioned it will be to deal with twenty-first-century issues such as climate change and resource depletion.

We hope this small book, with its many suggestions for further reading, will inspire business students, busy professionals, and policy makers in all levels of government in their good—and profitable—endeavors.

Chris Laszlo
Karen Christensen
Peter Whitehouse
Daniel Fogel

Core Concepts

True Cost Economics

Traditional economics doesn't account for prevailing business practices' collateral damage to the health and well-being of humankind and ecosystems; critics think the free market / cost-price system is detached from these realities and undermines sustainability. True cost economics attempts to incorporate environmental and health damage into product pricing, which could influence consumption patterns and allow the burden to be borne more equitably.

As prepared by the anti-consumerist, not-for-profit organization AdBusters, the "True Cost Economics Manifesto" begins: "We, the Undersigned, make this accusation: that you, the teachers of neoclassical economics and the students that you graduate, have perpetuated a gigantic fraud upon the world" (Bauwens 2009). The alleged fraud consists of conjuring the illusion of perpetual progress and endless growth from theoretical abstractions that obscure a real world of accelerating ecological decay and widespread human misery. One possible wake-up call is the reality check implicit in true cost economics.

The theoretical debate around true cost economics has been simmering for decades but has now begun to boil over. Its proponents believe that the neoclassical (or neoliberal) economics that has dominated the world for at least the past fifty years is hopelessly flawed. Neoclassical free-market models are detached from physical or social realities. They float disdainfully above the ecological, cultural, and ethical contexts within which the real economy is embedded and thus undermine the quest for sustainability.

Neoclassical economists have traditionally been content to allow the prices of goods and services to be determined solely by the law of supply and demand. However, in unregulated markets, only direct producer costs (for rent, labor, resources, and capital, for example) are reflected in consumer prices. The prevailing cost-price system does not account for the collateral damage to ecosystems, human communities, or population health caused by many production processes. These external (outside the market) costs are born disproportionately by third parties or society at large—and, of course, the ecosphere. Because negative externalities represent real costs, the goods and services inflicting them enter the marketplace at prices below their true cost of production. Such underpricing leads to overconsumption, inefficient resource use, and pollution—all classic symptoms of market failure.

True Cost Pricing

By contrast, in a true cost economic system, consumer prices would incorporate environmental, health, and other welfare damage costs of production. When prices "tell the truth" about costs, consumers adjust their consumption patterns accordingly, purchasing fewer ecologically costly goods. Markets would operate more efficiently, producers would innovate and adopt cleaner production processes, total production/consumption would decline (a good thing in a resource-stressed world), pollution and health costs would be would be reduced to insignificance, and third parties would be relieved of an unfair burden.

With so much going for it, why hasn't true cost economics become standard economics? As we shall see, the answer is complicated but, for starters, consider that the true cost approach would result in steep increases in prices for many goods and services that are today within reach of even lower-income groups. For example, some analysts suggest that true cost economics would raise the price of an average car by many thousands of dollars at current production practices. Who would vote for that? Ours is a global consumer culture accustomed to getting more and more for less and less. Correcting for market failure requires government intervention, and any policy that spawned dramatic price increases would spell electoral disaster for the governing party.

Incentive-Based Instruments

Economists have long argued about how best to internalize wayward external costs. By the 1960s, two main schools of thought had coalesced around the competing theories of Arthur Cecil Pigou and Ronald Harry Coase.

Pigovian Taxes

The English economist Arthur Cecil Pigou (1932) argued in *The Economics of Welfare* (first published in 1920) that the existence of externalities justifies government action. He advocated that pollution charges or taxes be applied to offending activities, to better reflect their true social costs and reduce consumption of the relevant goods. (Pigou also suggested that government subsidize private activities generating positive externalities. This would encourage private engagement in those activities and enhance the gains to society at large.)

The mechanics are simple. Imagine an economy in which a number of polluting industries are imposing unaccounted "pollution avoidance costs" on other industries (such as extra expenses for air and water treatment) as well as various "welfare damage costs" on the public (health costs, aesthetic losses, and forgone recreational opportunities, for example). A reasonable public policy objective would be to "internalize these externalities," keeping in mind that, in a total social-cost framework, any solution that imposes pollution-prevention costs on the polluters greater than the anticipated benefits (avoided costs) to other firms and the public would be inefficient.

Government could, in theory, meet this objective through a flat pollution tax per unit of contaminant emitted. The tax would force each polluting firm to decide between treating its wastes and paying the tax. Acting rationally, firms would opt to treat their emissions to the point where their rising, marginal unit-treatment costs just equal the tax. Beyond that, it would be cheaper to pay the tax.

Since different firms have differing "marginal cost of treatment" curves, each will treat a different proportion of its wastes. However, since the tax is uniform, the marginal cost at which firms switch to paying the tax will be the same for all. This ensures that low-cost polluters do most of the cleanup and minimizes the total costs of treatment (a necessary condition for maximum efficiency).

Note that pollution taxes bring the maximum amount of private information to bear on cleanup strategies. Government need not know the internal processes or cost structures of affected firms. Taxes also pay for their own administration and enforcement. But there is a major problem: in the absence of perfect knowledge, setting the tax rate is just an educated guess. If set too low, the tax will not induce sufficient waste treatment; if too high, firms will inefficiently overtreat their emissions (that is, marginal treatment costs will exceed welfare gains). Subsequent corrective adjustments to the tax are both materially—and politically—costly.

Coasian Bargaining

Despite such drawbacks, the logic of Pigovian taxes charmed most economists until 1960, when it was seriously challenged by the economist Ronald Coase, who argued that if property rights to resources (including sink capacity, or nature's ability to absorb humanity's output and wastes) were clearly defined, then government intervention to correct for externalities was unnecessary, and society could avoid the administrative and enforcement costs of antipollution taxes.

In the absence of significant transaction costs, both polluters and affected parties have a financial incentive to reach an efficient solution through bargaining, regardless of who owns the contested resource. Suppose you, as a papermaker, hold the right to pollute a stream from which I, as a food processor, draw my water. Then I have an incentive to pay you to treat your waste water as long as the cost to me is less than the cost of treating my intake water. Similarly you have an incentive to accept payment because you can profit from treating your wastes. This is because the marginal cost to you of decontaminating your relatively concentrated wastewater is less than the marginal cost to me of cleaning up my more diluted intake water. Of course with more intensive treatment your marginal costs rise to the point where I would save money by shifting to treating my intake water. We bargain around this point—you to maximize receipts, me to minimize pollution avoidance costs.

Now assume I hold the rights to the stream. You have an incentive to pay me to let you pollute as long as my unit price is less than your marginal wastewater treatment costs; I would profit by selling you pollution rights, but only to the point where your payments just cover the cost of treating my now-contaminated intake water. Again, we negotiate an agreement that internalizes costs with no government involvement.

But what if there are thousands of competing firms and myriad other social entities with interests in the negotiated outcome? In the real world, the initial allocation of property rights does matter, and total transaction costs (for research and information, negotiation, administration, and so on) balloon astronomically. Moreover, it is naïve to think that any collection of narrowly "self-interested utility maxi-mizers" will arrive at a solution that is optimal for nature or society at large. As ecological economist Herman Daly constantly reminds us, the "self" in which we are primarily interested is not an isolated atom, but is defined by its relationships in community and by diverse biophysical connections that are affected, but not acknowledged, in economic transactions. This negates any possibility of achieving an efficient or effective solution through private bargaining alone—community (or government) must be involved.

Cap-and-Trade Systems

Government does have one attractive policy option that capitalizes on financial incentives and the allocative efficiency of competitive markets to take the guesswork out of pollution pricing. So-called cap-and-trade schemes also combine fixed emission levels with tradable pollution rights and thus separate the public-policy issue of what constitutes acceptable environmental quality from the legitimate economic question of efficient allocation. The U.S. Clean Air Act was based, in part, on caps and tradable permits, as is the early Obama administration's proposed climate change policy (the Waxman-Markey bill).

In an ideal cap-and-trade scenario, government solicits scientific advice and public opinion to set desirable environmental quality objectives and place a firm limit (cap) on allowable emissions that reflects regional assimilation capacity. The allowable emissions are then divided into a fixed number of shares or permits and distributed by some fair means to existing polluters. After initial distribution, subsequent allocation is determined by trading in an open market. The price per share is thus set by the usual law of supply and demand, except that supply is fixed. If demand increases, prices rise, inducing market participants to invest in more efficient (cheaper) production or waste-treatment processes and reduce their need for pollution rights. New businesses, or firms needing additional shares, purchase them from businesses that no longer require their full quota. Inefficient players are forced out of the market.

In theory then, a tradable permit scheme could achieve ecological and social objectives with certainty, using multiple sources of public and private information to set limits and prices while internalizing erstwhile externalities with market efficiency. And if government charged for the initial distribution of permits or demanded a royalty on subsequent trades (environmental capacity is, after all, a public good), the system would pay for its own implementation and monitoring.

Invisible and Intangible Costs

We have already shown that, despite their theoretical appeal, standard Pigovian and Coasian approaches have serious practical weaknesses. We now consider a fundamental problem that plagues all formal instruments for true cost economics—identifying and monetizing intangible and invisible costs.

Direct production costs and external property damage costs are readily determined from current market prices. But there are no markets for numerous indirect use, non-use, option, and existence values associated with ecosystems and communities. The market price for a truckload of logs, for example, is mute about the flood control, water purification, biodiversity, carbon sink, and aesthetic and spiritual values sacrificed in clear-cutting the forest. This is why the consumer purchasing a board foot of lumber—or just about anything else—doesn't come close to paying the full social cost of production.

One problem is that assigning a valid money price to something assumes the ability to compress all the values associated with that thing into a single metric. Arild Vatn and Daniel Bromley (1994) identify three theoretical obstacles to such inclusive pricing of environmental (or social) entities:

- A *cognition problem* always exists in the absence of perfect knowledge, and the simple fact is that many critical functions of species and ecosystems are cognitively invisible. This "functional transparency" means that the cost of losing any important element of an ecosystem may be unknowable until that element has been destroyed. We obviously cannot place any value on that which we cannot know.
- An *incongruity problem* exists when the values associated with an ecologically significant good are incongruous or incommensurable with dollar values. How can we conflate the market price of duck breast with the sheer aesthetic rush experienced from witnessing a wedge of mallards in full flight over the marsh?
- A *composition problem* arises because in ecosystems the whole may be dependent on each of its fundamental parts. This means that value of any single component (for example, a species or nutrient) cannot be interpreted independently of the value of the whole.

These and related barriers mean that mainstream efforts to derive accurate, unambiguous *money* values for complex ecological entities (such as contingent valuation) are doomed to failure—we cannot compute costs. Our assumed ability to commoditize nature and basic life support is an arrogant fiction (and in any event, may not be such a good idea).

Transcending Benefit-Cost Analysis

All important decisions involve weighing the relative gains and losses associated with the various options under consideration. As we have seen, pollution charges, one-on-one bargaining, and cap-and-trade schemes all force the affected parties to compute private self-interested benefit-cost ratios as the basis for their internal waste management decisions ("Do we treat our wastes or pay the tax?").

More generally, formal benefit-cost analysis (BCA) purports to provide a comprehensive comparison of the discounted future benefits and costs associated with different development options. The efficiency goal is to maximize any positive difference between gains and losses. Because of its conceptual simplicity and theoretical elegance, many economists regard BCA as the definitive tool for both private and public policy decision making. In an ideal world BCA would therefore be critical to true cost economics.

But this is not an ideal world—there are practical flies in the theoretical ointment. Missing data and irreducible uncertainty combined with limited resources and ideologically tainted analyses explode any claim that BCA produces a socially optimal true cost outcome. The fact is that comprehensive true cost economics is beyond our analytic reach.

This is no minor glitch. Ignorance of critical ecological and social costs has arguably long biased modern society toward endless growth even as the ecosphere slowly implodes. It is entirely possible that if we could subject the global economy to a valid BCA, we would find that the ecological and social costs of growth at the margin now exceed the benefits. We may have entered an era of what Herman Daly calls "uneconomic growth"—growth that makes the world poorer, not richer. True cost economics may well mean no-growth economics. The fact that the world's rich and powerful reap most of the benefits of growth, while the poor and the global commons bear most of the unaccounted costs, undoubtedly contributes to present policy paralysis.

Such conclusions are not cause for despair but rather should liberate society from the dictates of oppressively wrong-headed economic models. Governments, the private sector, and nongovernmental organizations must learn to eschew "crackpot rigor." We all share this single planet and cannot afford to be blinded by faulty theory and vacuous analysis. By all means, use BCA for those tangible things to which we can legitimately ascribe a dollar value. This may bring us closer to the efficient market economy to which we aspire. But both business and ordinary citizens must recognize that the results are not in themselves a sufficient basis for decision making.

In the end, sustainability is mainly a political, not an analytic, goal. Society must recognize that even as we strive for true cost economics, the most critical ecological and social choices must be made "without prices, without apologies" (Vatn and Bromley 1994). Given the scale of the problem, multiple conflicting values, gross distributive inequity, and a deepening well of uncertainty, there is no

substitute for informed, cautiously practical political judgment, all for the common good.

William E. REES
University of British Columbia

See also in the *Berkshire Encyclopedia of Sustainability*: **Accounting; Cap-and-Trade Legislation; Consumer Behavior; Development, Sustainable; Ecolabeling; Ecosystem Services; Energy Efficiency; Green GDP; Human Rights; Investment, Socially Responsible (SRI); Natural Capitalism; Performance Metrics; Triple Bottom Line**

FURTHER READING

Baumol, William J., & Oates, Wallace E. (1988). *The theory of environmental policy* (2nd ed.). New York: Cambridge University Press.

Bauwens, Michel. (2009, August 9). True cost economics manifesto. Retrieved August 26, 2009, from http://blog.p2pfoundation.net/the-true-cost-economics-manifesto/2009/08/09

Coase, Ronald H. (1960). The problem of social cost. *Journal of Law and Economics, 1*(3), 1–44. Retrieved August 31, 2009, from http://www.sfu.ca/~allen/CoaseJLE1960.pdf

Dales, John. (1968). *Pollution, property and prices: An essay in policy-making and economics.* Toronto: University of Toronto Press.

Daly, Herman E. (1981). *Steady-state economics* (2nd ed.). Washington, DC: Island Press.

Daly, Herman E., & Cobb, John B., Jr. (1989). *For the common good: Redirecting the economy toward community, the environment, and a sustainable future.* Boston: Beacon Press.

Daly, Herman E. & Farley, Joshua. (2004). *Ecological economics: Principles and applications.* Washington, DC: Island Press.

Daly, Herman E., & Townsend, Kenneth N. (1993). *Valuing the Earth: Economics, ecology, ethics.* Cambridge, MA: MIT Press

Hahn, Robert W. (1989). *A primer on environmental policy design.* Chur, Switzerland: Harwood Academic Publishers.

Jacobs, Michael. (1991). *The green economy: Environment, sustainable development, and the politics of the future.* London: Pluto Press.

Lave, Lester B., & Gruenspecht, Howard K. (1991). Increasing the efficiency and effectiveness of environmental decisions: Benefit-cost analysis and effluent fees—a critical analysis. *Journal of the Air and Waste Management Association, 41*(5), 680–693.

Manno, Jack P. (2000). *Privileged goods: Commoditization and its impact on environment and society.* Boca Raton, FL: Lewis Publishers.

O'Neill, John. (2006). *Markets, deliberation and environment.* London: Routledge.

O'Neill, John; Holland, Alan; & Light, Andrew. (2008). *Environmental values.* London: Routledge.

Pearce, David W. (1993). *Economic values and the natural world.* Cambridge, MA: MIT Press.

Pigou, Arthur C. (1932). *The economics of welfare* (4th ed.). London: MacMillan,

Prugh, Thomas; Costanza, Robert; Cumberland, J. H.; Daly, Herman E.; Goodland, Robert; & Norgaard, Richard B. (1995). *Natural capital and human economic survival.* Solomons, MD: ISEE Press.

True cost economics. (n.d.). Retrieved November 10, 2009, from http://www.investopedia.com/terms/t/truecosteconomics.asp

Themes, Brendan. (2004, August 26). True cost economics. Retrieved August 26, 2009, from http://www.utne.com/2004-08-01/TrueCostEconomics.aspx

Vatn, Arild, & Bromley, Daniel W. (1994). Choices without prices without apologies. *Journal of Environmental Economics and Management, 26*(2), 129–148.

Victor, Peter A. (2008). *Managing without growth: Slower by design, not disaster.* Cheltenham, U.K.: Edward Elgar.

Triple Bottom Line

Triple bottom line reckoning is a form of business reporting that accounts not only for return on investment (the traditional reporting model) but also for environmental and social values. It has become an important tool for businesses pursuing sustainable growth.

The late 1990s saw the rise of the concept of the triple bottom line (TBL). The TBL underscores the fact that companies and other organizations create value in multiple dimensions. Given the nature and focus of modern accounting, the financial bottom line is generally an inadequate (and often misleading) expression of total value. In addition, the TBL concept aimed to help business people think through the question of how to make corporations more sustainable in the context of major emerging economic, social, and environmental challenges, among them corruption, human rights, and climate change.

TBL and the Three Ps

The term *triple bottom line* was coined in 1994 by John Elkington, countering the narrower focus on the then-fashionable term *eco-efficiency*, which focused on the financial and environmental dimensions of performance. TBL thinking, by contrast, extended to social impacts and to the wider economic impact issues rarely captured in the traditional financial bottom line.

The TBL approach was introduced in detail in *Cannibals with Forks* (Elkington 1997) and has been further elaborated in hundreds of company reports aligned with the Global Reporting Initiative (GRI) and in a growing number of books. A linked phrase, "People, Planet, Profit," or, alternatively, "People, Planet, Prosperity" was also coined by Elkington. This phrase was adopted by Shell in its early public sustainability reporting, following the company's Brent Spar and Nigerian crises in 1995. Known as the three Ps, it became central to the sustainable development discussion in countries such as the Netherlands. It sparked debate about the double bottom line (combining social and financial performance, as in social enterprise) and, variously, quadruple and quintuple bottom lines, in which issues such as ethics and governance were added.

Corporate Lifecycles

The average life expectancy of a company is relatively short. When the oil crises of the 1970s spotlighted the finite nature of fossil fuels, for example, Shell wondered whether there would be life—or at least industrial life—after oil. It investigated how other long-lived firms had addressed earlier market discontinuities. In most cases companies simply died or disappeared. They merged, were taken over, or went out of business. Of the original thirty constituents of the *Financial Times* Ordinary Share Index, an indicator of stock prices on the London Stock Exchange launched in 1935, just nine had survived more or less intact by the late 1990s. And the U.S. corporate death rates turned out to be even higher. Nearly 40 percent of the 1983 *Fortune* 500 companies had dematerialized, as had 60 percent of those so designated in the 1970s, and of the twelve companies making up the Dow Jones Industrial Index in 1900, General Electric (GE) was the only substantial survivor (Visser et al. 2008).

Although the average corporate life expectancy might be in the region of forty to fifty years, there may be several hundred companies around the world that have been operating between 100 and 150 years. This imbalance among the broad mass of companies and the long-winded few is a reflection of many factors, but perhaps the most important is the fact that in a capitalist world, companies that fail to deliver stockholder value are starved of capital and die. To date, sustainability factors have only rarely affected capital availability, but understanding of the relevant linkages is likely to grow rapidly.

Corporate Sustainability Challenges

Corporate sustainability is probably better understood not so much as the discipline by which companies ensure their own long-term survival—though that is clearly part of the equation—but as the field of thinking and practice by which companies and other business organizations work to extend the life expectancy of ecosystems and the natural resources they provide; societies and the cultures and communities that underpin commercial activity; and economies that provide the governance, financial, and other market context for corporate competition and survival. By paying attention to such wider issues, it is often argued, companies are better placed to ensure that their own business models remain valid and adaptable.

As for the corporate sustainability agenda, recent decades have seen sustainability issues gradually forced up through corporate hierarchies. They started on the fringes, handled (if at all) by professionals in such areas as site security, public relations, and legal affairs. Through the 1970s, as new techniques such as environmental impact assessment evolved, new groups of professionals became involved, among them project planners, process engineers, and site managers. Then, during the late 1980s, the spotlight opened out to illuminate new product development, design, marketing, and lifecycle management. As the triple bottom line agenda of sustainable development spread through the 1990s, with an inevitable growth in the complexity and political impact of key issues, the agenda was driven up to top management and boards. In the next round, in addition to those already involved, expect to see new ventures people—chief financial officers, investment bankers, and venture capitalists—included.

Over time, the agenda has opened out profoundly, increasingly embracing challenging issues such as transparency, corporate and global governance, human rights, bribery and corruption, and global poverty. The key text in this area has been 1987's Brundtland Commission report, *Our Common Future.* Its definition of sustainable development is now widely accepted. It was brought into greater focus in 1994 with the introduction of the TBL concept, which has subsequently been widely adopted—for example by the GRI. The concept has also been adopted by leading companies, most strikingly perhaps by Denmark's Novo Nordisk (2009).

As the agenda has morphed, several other factors have conspired to increase the challenge for business. First, business has increasingly been expected to do things that governments would once have done, if they were done at all. Second, the processes of globalization have enormously extended the areas and timescales over which companies are held accountable while the processes of outsourcing and "offshoring" mean that corporate value chains have become increasingly extensive, complex, and vulnerable to challenge. (Examples are Nike and Gap.) And third, the spread of the Internet and the introduction of search engines such as Google have subjected business to ever-growing levels of scrutiny.

The Impact of Globalization

The TBL agenda played into a period of intense globalization, with growing concerns about the lack of governance and regulatory systems at the global level. As sustainability and corporate citizenship agendas have evolved, the calls on the time and resources of business have increased almost exponentially. In 1999, for example, U.N. secretary-general Kofi Annan called on business leaders "to join the United Nations on a journey." He commented that business was already well down the road with a journey of its own, globalization. At the time, globalization appeared like "a force of nature," seeming to "lead inexorably in one direction: ever-closer integration of markets, ever-larger economies of scale, ever-bigger opportunities for profits and prosperity" (Annan 1999).

Ten months before the Seattle protests against the World Trade Organization (WTO), however, the secretary-general also felt it necessary to warn that globalization would only be as sustainable as its social foundations. "Global unease about poverty, equity and marginalization," he stressed, "is beginning to reach critical mass" (Annan 1999). These issues are no less important today, although some focus has shifted to political and security concerns in the wake of 9/11, the war in Iraq, and the Madrid train bombings of 2004, all of which, some would argue, are intimately connected to unresolved problems of poverty and inequity. In tackling such challenges, business is being told it must pay more attention to the need for new forms of global governance.

"Governance" became a buzzword in the 1990s. "Corporate governance," although not a new concept, began its rise in the public agenda in 1992, for example, with the publication of the Cadbury Report in the United Kingdom. That same year the United Nations held its Earth Summit in Rio de Janeiro, spotlighting the urgent need to shift the global economy toward more sustainable forms of development, and the World Bank released its report *Governance and Development,* making the case that governance failures lie behind the poor progress of development efforts to date. A decade later the spotlight had opened out, with those seeking "responsible globalization" now calling for further meaningful "global governance."

But there is a paradox here, and it has two main dimensions. First, the voluntary corporate responsibility (CR) movement has evolved as a pragmatic response to pressing environmental, community, or human rights issues. Companies are asked to address problems and even deliver public goods because governments have been unable or unwilling to do so. But second, because of the weakness—or absence—of appropriate governance systems, CR initiatives are generally disconnected from wider frameworks. As a result, they are at risk of amounting to little more than drops in the ocean when compared to the scale of the challenges. At worst, they may even undermine long-term solutions.

Progress Report

Nevertheless, huge progress has been made. From the defensive stances adopted in the heyday of government-driven responses, companies have begun to explore ways forward with an expanding range of external stakeholders. There has been acknowledgment of the legitimate—and critical—role of companies. While there are still skeptics, there is also an emerging consensus among civil society, government, and business that, in principle, companies play an important role in developing and implementing solutions to pressing sustainable development problems.

In addition, there has been engagement of a significant number of leading multinationals. For example, some 180 companies are members of the World Business Council for Sustainable Development. Nearly 1,000 companies use part or all of the GRI guidelines to report on their social and environmental performance. Business in The Community, a U.K. business association focused on CR, reports a membership accounting for one in five private-sector employees in the United Kingdom and a global workforce of more than 15.7 million people. Similarly, membership of Brazil's Ethos Institute accounts for more than a quarter of the country's gross national product (GNP). A key question remains: how can this potential critical mass be used to drive forward sustainable development even more powerfully?

Finally, there has been a clearer understanding of the "business case" (and its limits). The business case clearly has limits in driving CR to scale. But the extent of the business case for CR and the links with investment value drivers such as reputation, risk management, corporate governance, and management quality are increasingly recognized both by business and key stakeholder groups (e.g., government and the investment community).

While these certainly reflect accomplishments and progress, and individual companies can also claim substantial performance improvements, the fundamental question is whether the CR movement as a whole has made a real difference in addressing longer-term sustainability issues. The conclusion must be that current CR initiatives will increasingly run up against system limits. As former president Bill Clinton argued at a World Economic Forum summit, the scale of the challenges the world faces is such that systematic change will not be enough. Instead, he said, systemic change is needed, changes to the system itself.

But these problems are not new. Professor John Ruggie, responsible for Harvard's Corporate Social Responsibility Initiative and a key architect of the Global Compact, explains: "We in the industrialized world were slow to learn the lesson that markets must be embedded in broader frameworks of social values and shared objectives if they are to survive and thrive. Before we got to that point, we had struggled through the collapse of the Victorian era of globalization, a world war, the rise of the left wing revolutionary forces in Russia, right wing revolutionary forces in Germany and Italy as well as the Great Depression." When the lesson did finally sink in, Ruggie continues, "we called the new understanding by different names: the New Deal, the social market economy and social democracy" (Ruggie 2004, 2). The basis of these social bargains was that all actors agreed to open markets, but they also agreed to "share the social adjustment costs that open markets inevitably produce." And governments played a central role in the process, "moderating the volatility of transaction flows across borders and providing social investments, safety nets and adjustment assistance—but all the while pushing liberalization" (Ruggie 2004, 2).

One of the most striking recent trends has been the formation of new forms of partnerships and alliances, linking business with nongovernmental organizations (NGOs) and other civil society actors. But if future corporate efforts and alliances are to bridge the challenge–response gap, the scaling issue will need to be addressed more seriously and effectively. More thought also needs to be given on how to scale geometrically where the challenges are particularly serious. One answer here is to change market conditions to favor particular outcomes, which is where governments have a key role to play.

That is why two additional challenges evolving in the corporate sustainability space have to do with lobbying and tax policy. On corporate lobbying, there is growing concern that companies that give every surface sign of being committed to sustainability are often—directly or indirectly—lobbying behind the scenes to slow progress. The question here is not only how to make such lobbying more transparent but also how, over time, corporate lobbying can be swung around to support initiatives designed to tackle major problems such as climate change. Second, given the growing importance of government in dealing with so many of the challenges that have landed on the business agenda in the early twenty-first century, there is a real question about how government can be properly funded. As a result, the ability of companies in a globalizing world to manage down their tax burdens is coming under growing scrutiny.

The Four Bs

Work on implementing the TBL agenda has shown that there are many points at which it potentially engages with and influences business thinking, strategy, investment, and operations. TBL-oriented organizations, such as the Global Reporting Initiative (2009) and the Dow Jones Sustainability Indexes (2009), provide insights into current practice. Meanwhile, the corporate work of organizations such as SustainAbility (2009) and Volans (2009) have suggested that a potentially powerful way of approaching TBL-focused corporate change is to think in terms of four Bs.

This often starts with external challenges targeting *brands*, often led by activists, NGOs, and the media. Few things stimulate corporate action faster than threats to brand value, with the result that the TBL agenda cross-cuts the world of brand management. Over time, corporate leaders are then encouraged to adapt their management, accounting, disclosure, communication, and external engagement strategies (*balance sheets*). Some companies can hold the challenge at this level, but, increasingly often, the issues have a sufficiently intense political spin so that they are forced up to *boards*, cross-connecting with the world of corporate governance. If the pressures are sustained, presenting new forms of risk and opportunity, then we may see companies adapting their *business models,* as General Electric (already mentioned as a long-term corporate survivor) has begun to do with its ecomagination strategy. This turn of the wheel brings us back to branding, a point underscored by the success of GE's initiative (2009).

The TBL agenda has spawned a broad range of management tools, ranging from auditing and reporting processes to new thinking about how to blend the different dimensions of value creation. (See, for example, the blended thinking of Jed Emerson—the foundation fund manager famous for popularizing the concept that the value of an organization is based on economic, social, and environmental criteria—and other like-minded analysts, at the Blended Value [2009] website.) In the end, however, there are few drop-in TBL solutions. Indeed, GE founder Thomas Edison's comment about his protracted efforts to find a workable electric lightbulb may be a good way to think of the intense period of experimentation that business is embarking on in pursuit of something like sustainability. Faced with yet one more failure, Edison said something to the effect of, well, now I know 10,000 things that don't work. Given that single-dimensional solutions to complex problems are more likely to fail, the hope is that TBL and blended value mind-sets will shorten the odds of hitting gold with the 10,001st attempt.

John ELKINGTON
SustainAbility; Volans Ventures

See also in the *Berkshire Encyclopedia of Sustainability*: **Corporate Citizenship; CSR and CSR 2.0; Development, Sustainable; Equator Principles; Global Reporting Initiative (GRI); Human Rights; Investment, Socially Responsible (SRI); Natural Capitalism; Social Enterprise; Stakeholder Theory; True Cost Economics**

FURTHER READING

Annan, Kofi. (1999). Press release SG/SM/6881: Secretary-General proposes global compact on human rights, labour, environment, in address to World Economic Forum in Davos. Retrieved November 10, 2009, from http://www.un.org/News/Press/docs/1999/19990201.sgsm6881.html

Blended Value. (2009). Retrieved May 11, 2009, from http://www.blendedvalue.org

Dow Jones Sustainability Indexes. (2009). Retrieved May 11, 2009, from http://www.sustainability-index.com

Elkington, John. (1997). *Cannibals with forks: The triple bottom line of 21st century business.* Oxford, U.K.: Capstone/John Wiley & Sons.

General Electric. (2009). Retrieved May 11, 2009, from http://www.ecomagination.com

Global Reporting Initiative. (2009). Retrieved May 11, 2009, from http://www.globalreporting.org

Henriques, Adrian, & Richardson, Julie. (Eds.). (2004). *The triple bottom line: Does it all add up?* London: Earthscan.

Novo Nordisk. (2009). Retrieved May 11, 2009, from http://www.novonordisk.com

Ruggie, John. (2004, March 15). *Creating public value: Everybody's business.* Address to Herrhausen Society, Frankfurt, Germany. Retrieved November 10, 2009, from http://www.unglobalcompact.org/docs/news_events/9.6/ruggie_160304.pdf

SustainAbility. (2009). Retrieved May 11, 2009, from http://www.sustainability.com

Visser, Wayne; Matten, Dirk; Pohl, Manfred; & Tolhurst, Nick. (Eds.) (2008). *The A to Z of corporate social responsibility: A complete reference guide to concepts, codes and organizations.* Chichester, U.K.: John Wiley & Sons.

Volans. (2009). Retrieved May 11, 2009, from http://www.volans.com

Green GDP

Traditional measurements of performance, such as gross domestic product (GDP), account for economic development but do not accurately reflect human or environmental well-being. Since the 1990s several new metrics have been proposed, including green GDP, which attempts to provide a more accurate accounting that considers both the positive transactions that benefit well-being and the negative economic activities that diminish it.

The concept of "green GDP" arose in the early 1990s in reaction to the deficiencies of the traditional gross domestic product (GDP) to account for the economic costs of depleted natural resources and incurred pollution, which in turn affect human welfare. GDP is usually defined as the total market value of all final goods and services produced within a territory in a given period of time (usually a year), including exports minus imports (net exports). It has been used as a standard measure of the size of an economy in national accounting and is often mistakenly regarded as a proxy for progress in the public discourse. A closely related term is *gross national product* (GNP), which is GDP plus international income transfers. The term *gross* means the exclusion of capital depreciation from the accounting. Infrastructural wear and tear, for instance, do not make their way into the GDP. When such considerations are taken into account, *net domestic product* (NDP) and *net national product* (NNP) are used.

Limits of Traditional GDP

Ecosystem services such as climate regulation, carbon sequestration, and nutrient cycling, while indispensable for human survival, are not part of traditional economic accounting. Some have estimated the economic value of

the world's ecosystem services to be US$33 trillion per year on average, mostly outside the market and almost twice as much as the global GDP total (Costanza et al. 1997). Valuing ecosystem services, however, has been controversial to some economists and ecologists for methodological and other reasons. GDP omits many of the important goods and services that we derive from nature because its scope is delimited completely by the market. Thus, despite its prominent position in economic analysis and public policy, GDP has become the target of increasing criticism in recent decades. In GDP accounting, no distinction is made between activities that contribute to well-being and those that detract from it. A classic example is an oil spill, which is counted as a positive addition to the GDP because it warrants expenditure on cleanup. In this way, many environmental damages are vindicated as contributions to economic progress. For the environmentally conscious, this is an affront to both intuition and ethics as pollution (especially of such a magnitude) is detrimental to both human and environmental health.

Also, GDP does a poor job of reflecting actual human well-being because it neither accounts for social sustainability nor future consequences of present consumptions. In fact, recent studies suggest that, for a number of countries, the positive correlation between human well-being and GDP breaks down after GDP values reach a certain threshold—known as the "threshold hypothesis" (Max-Neef 1995). A rising GDP merely signals an increasing level of market transactions, without regard for whether these activities are beneficial to humans and nature in the long run. Thus, a fixation on the temporally narrow scope of traditional economic accounting can lead to dangerously myopic policies. The absence of ecosystem services and environmental damages (known

as "externalities" in economic parlance) from monetary valuation potentiates the vicious cycle of economic shortsightedness and environmental misuse. It is widely accepted now that GDP significantly undervalues the contributions of nature to human well-being and is ill-suited for measuring sustainable development. Green GDP (also green NNP), therefore, has been proposed to explicitly estimate these missing costs by subtracting the economic penalties imposed by natural resource depletion and pollution from national accounting. As a result, the green GDP is meant to advance a more inclusive view of "natural capital" and promote more sustainable management practices.

Alternatives to GDP

The notion of "greening" GDP has gained some momentum in both academia and public policy since the early 1990s. One of the most noteworthy attempts to implement the concept was carried out by the People's Republic of China. In 2006, the Chinese government released its environmentally adjusted GDP—its green GDP, prepared jointly by the State Environmental Protection Agency and the National Bureau of Statistics (SEPA and NBS 2006). Included in the calculation were assessments of air, water, and solid-waste pollution as well as the costs of depleting various natural resources. The report concluded that the economic loss of environmental damages amounted to 3 percent of the country's GDP in 2004. Nearly as soon as the figures were released, however, it became clear that there still remained major defects in the accounting procedures. A large number of concerns were not factored into the analysis, and there were also myriad methodological obstacles that impeded a thorough economic analysis of environmental damages. For instance, only half of potentially more than twenty pollution costs were estimated in China's green GDP report. Concerns such as soil and groundwater contamination, as well as the entire categories of natural resource depletion and ecological damage, were not included in the accounting. Thus, the 3 percent diminution fell short of what many analysts believed the actual costs were. It is now evident that green GDP, for China and elsewhere, is still theoretically appealing but practically formidable.

In addition, several other development metrics similar to green GDP have also been developed as a part of a larger group of sustainable development indicators. For example, the Index of Sustainable Economic Welfare (ISEW) was developed in the late 1980s to address the flaws in GDP. ISEW accounts for both conventional economic transactions and nonmarket natural and social benefits, and its value is determined by the balance between positive transactions that benefit human well-being and negative economic activities that diminish it. Genuine Progress Indicator (GPI), developed later in 1994 by Redefining Progress (a nongovernmental organization focused on public policy), includes essentially the same measures as ISEW. The main differences between the two are related mostly to data availability and users' preferences for valuation methods. ISEW and GPI have widely been used by international organizations, governmental agencies, and academic researchers. Another common development metric is Genuine Savings (GS), proposed by the World Bank in 1999. Taking into account both natural and human capital, GS estimates the domestic savings less the value of resource depletion and environmental degradation. A relatively new metric, Happy Planet Index (HPI), was introduced by the New Economics Foundation (NEF) in 2006. HPI bypasses traditional monetary approaches and focuses on the efficiency with which countries translate natural resource use into human and societal well-being. Specifically, HPI is the ratio of happy life years (the product of life satisfaction and life expectancy) to environmental impact (measured by ecological footprint).

The Future of Green GDP

Despite the mounting criticisms of its irrelevance and the emergence of alternatives, GDP's deeply entrenched position in the mainstream discourse will likely ensure its continued prominence in both economics and public perception. It is important, therefore, to clearly understand what GDP measures and what it does not. Meanwhile, efforts for valuating the depletion of natural resources and the impacts and mitigations of pollution will continue. The environment must be part of national accounting. The United Nations has published a set of accounting guidelines in the *Handbook of National Accounting: Integrated Environmental and Economic Accounting* (known as SEEA 1993 and SEEA 2003), which provide a common framework for valuating environmental contributions to economies and economic impacts on the environment. Such efforts promote methodological standardization that in turn facilitates applications and cross-country comparisons. They also represent a continued operationalization (the process of strictly defining variables into measurable factors) of the ideas behind green GDP. Although it remains implausible that GDP will soon be displaced as the hallmark indicator of economic fitness, attempts to "green" it, despite various shortcomings, constitute a positive movement in the direction of environmental consciousness. Complementary

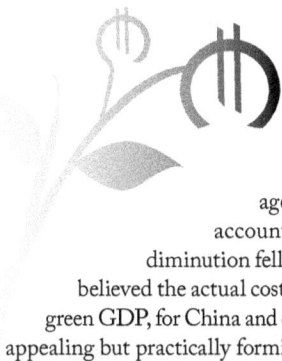

indicators and indices are also needed if we are to adequately measure our true economic wealth and health: the sustainability of human–environmental systems.

Jianguo WU
Arizona State University

Tong WU
Northern Arizona University

See also in the *Berkshire Encyclopedia of Sustainability*: **Development, Sustainable; Ecological Economics; Ecosystem Services; Natural Capitalism; True Cost Economics**

FURTHER READING

Abdallah, Saamah; Thompson, Sam; Michaelson, Juliet; Marks, Nic; Steuer, Nicola; & New Economics Foundation. (2009). *The happy planet index 2.0: Why good lives don't have to cost the Earth*. Retrieved October 1, 2009, from http://www.happyplanetindex.org/public-data/files/happy-planet-index-2-0.pdf

Boyd, James. (2007). Nonmarket benefits of nature: What should be counted in green GDP? *Ecological Economics 61*(4), 716–723.

Cobb, Clifford; Goodman, Gary Sue; & Wackernagel, Mathis. (1999, November). *Why bigger isn't better: The genuine progress indicator—1999 update*. Retrieved October 1, 2009, from http://www.rprogress.org/publications/1999/gpi1999.pdf

Costanza, Robert, et al. (1997). The value of the world's ecosystem services and natural capital. *Nature, 387*, 253–260.

Costanza, Robert. (2008). Stewardship for a "full" world. Current *History*, 107(705), 30–35.

Max-Neef, Manfred. (1995). Economic growth and quality of life. *Ecological Economics* 15(2), 115–118.

Qiu, Jane. (2007, August 2). China's green accounting system on shaky ground. *Nature*, 448, 518–519.

State Environmental Protection Administration of China (SEPA) and the National Bureau of Statistics of China (NBS). (2006). China's green national accounting study report 2004. Retrieved November 25, 2009, from http://www.gov.cn/english/2006-09/11/content_384596.htm

United Nations; European Commission; International Monetary Fund; Organisation for Economic Co-operation and Development; & World Bank. (2003). *Handbook of national accounting: Integrated environmental and economic accounting 2003*. Retrieved August 11, 2009, from http://unstats.un.org/unsd/envaccounting/seea2003.pdf

CSR and CSR 2.0

Despite its good intentions, corporate social responsibility (CSR) has largely failed to make a significant positive impact on the world's most serious social, environmental, and ethical challenges over the past fifty years. The CSR 2.0 model presents an evolution of CSR concept and practice that is connected, scalable, and responsive—one that hopes to make a real, measurable difference in how business is conducted.

The concept of corporate social responsibility, or CSR as it is commonly known, has existed in one form or another for more than four thousand years. Several world religions have taught the immorality of usury, or the charging of excessive interest, as well as the morality of caring for those who are less fortunate. The modern concept of CSR can be traced to the last few decades of the 1800s, when industrialists and philanthropists began setting a charitable precedent that is echoed more than a hundred years later in figures such as Bill Gates of Microsoft and Warren Buffett of Berkshire Hathaway.

CSR's Recent History

CSR entered the popular lexicon in the 1950s with the U.S. economist and college president Howard Rothmann Bowen's landmark 1953 book, *Social Responsibilities of the Businessman*. The concept took further shape in the 1960s with the birth of the environmental movement, following the U.S. environmental scientist Rachel Carson's 1962 critique of the chemicals industry (in particular the widely used pesticide DDT) in *Silent Spring*. The consumer movement took shape with the activities of the U.S. consumer advocate (and subsequent presidential candidate) Ralph Nader's social activism, most famously over General Motors's safety record.

The 1970s saw the first widely accepted definition of CSR emerge in the form of the U.S. business and management ethicist Archie Carroll's four-part concept of economic, legal, ethical, and philanthropic responsibilities, later depicted as a CSR pyramid. It also was implemented in the first CSR code, the Sullivan Principles, named for the Reverend Leon H. Sullivan. He successfully challenged U.S. businesses with South African ties to deal more forcefully with apartheid in South Africa. The 1980s brought the application of quality management to occupational health and safety and the introduction of CSR codes like Responsible Care, an initiative of the global chemical industry with the stated aim of improving health, safety, and environmental performance.

In the 1990s, CSR became institutionalized with standards like ISO 14001 (part of the International Organization for Standardization's system of voluntary industry standards for particular products and for environmental management issues) and SA8000 (overseen by Social Accountability International, a nonprofit affiliate of the Council on Economic Priorities). Guidelines like the Global Reporting Initiative (GRI) and corporate governance codes like the Cadbury and King reports (from the United Kingdom and South Africa, respectively) brought attention to the importance of stakeholders (as opposed to shareholders), among other issues.

The twenty-first century has spawned a multitude of CSR guidelines, codes, and standards addressing the industry sector and climate change variations. (*The A to Z of Corporate Social Responsibility* by George Visser et al. [2007], for instance, lists more than a hundred standards.)

An understanding of where CSR has come from is important in seeing where it is headed and what it might become in the twenty-first century. Because the term is used by such a variety of people and organizations there is a risk that it will cease to be meaningful, in the same way that the word "green" loses its luster when seemingly every product under the sun is marketed as being green.

CSR is a dynamic movement that has been evolving over decades, if not centuries, but despite this seemingly impressive progress, some would argue that CSR has failed and that we are witnessing its decline. Those who make this claim say that the concept needs to be reborn and rejuvenated. They make this claim because although CSR has had many positive impacts for communities and for the environment, it should be judged by the total impacts of business on society and the planet. Viewed this way, on every measure of social, ecological, and ethical performance that is available, the negative impacts of business (with a few notable exceptions) have been disastrous. CSR has not averted or even substantially moderated these impacts. The reasons CSR fails are threefold:

1. The incremental approach of CSR has not made any impact on the massive sustainability crises that the world faces, many of which are worsening at a pace that far outstrips any CSR-led attempts at improvement.
2. CSR is usually a peripheral corporate function, even when a company has a CSR manager or a CSR department. Shareholder-driven capitalism is pervasive, and its goal of short-term financial measures of progress contradicts the long-term stakeholder approach to capitalism that is needed for CSR to have any meaningful results. (In shareholder-driven capitalism, a company's primary purpose is to generate profits for its shareholders.)
3. Despite the rhetoric about the "business case for CSR," as practiced at the beginning of the twenty-first century, CSR remains uneconomical. Most of the difficult CSR changes that are needed to reverse the misery of poverty and mass species extinction require strategic change and massive investment. These necessary changes may be lucrative in the long term and economically rational over a generation or two, but the financial markets do not work this way—at least not yet.

A fourth point might be the old adage, "the path to hell is paved with good intentions." Although no one could possibly accuse the original framers of CSR of ill will, the fact remains that numerous corporations have used CSR to highlight their good points—providing jobs to communities or cheap goods to the consumer—in the hopes of playing down their less desirable points: environmental degradation or the promotion of an unsustainable, consumption-based economy. A classic example is Walmart, which has made significant environmental progress recently, but still leaves many questions on labor and social issues unanswered. Another is Exxon, which has strong social programs, but has a poor reputation on environmental and climate change issues. A new model of CSR that will actually work—one that is measurable and grounded in environmental sustainability—is being delineated and developed by those who would like to avoid the mistakes made by the misguided application of CSR.

CSR 2.0

The CSR 2.0 model, first suggested by the business author and CSR expert Wayne Visser in 2008, proposes keeping the acronym CSR but rebalancing the "scales." In this new model, CSR stands for "corporate sustainability and responsibility." This change acknowledges that *sustainability* (with roots in the environmental movement) and *responsibility* (with roots in the social activist movement) are really the two main components that we should care about. A cursory look at companies' nonfinancial reports will rapidly confirm this: they are mostly either corporate sustainability reports (which typically adopt a "triple bottom line" approach of reporting social and environmental impacts along with economic performance) or corporate responsibility reports (which typically reflect a stakeholder approach).

CSR 2.0, however, also proposes a new interpretation on these terms. Like two intertwined strands of DNA, sustainability and responsibility can be thought of as different, yet complementary, elements of CSR. Hence sustainability can be conceived as the destination (challenges, vision, strategy and goals, i.e., what we are aiming for), while responsibility is more about the journey (solutions, responses, management, actions, i.e., how we get there).

If we admit the failure of previous CSR efforts at tackling our most pressing social, environmental, and ethical challenges, then the world may find itself on the cusp of a revolution, in much the same way as the Internet transitioned from the static Web 1.0 technology to the interactive Web 2.0. The emergence of social media networks, user-generated content, and open-source approaches are a fitting metaphor for the changes CSR will have to undergo if it is to redefine its contribution and make a serious impact on the social, environmental, and ethical challenges the world faces.

For example, Web 1.0 moved from a one-way, advertising-push approach to a more collaborative Google–Facebook–Twitter mode. In the same way, CSR 2.0 is starting to move beyond the outmoded approach of CSR as philanthropy or public relations (which has been widely criticized as "greenwashing") to a more interactive, stakeholder-driven model. Similarly, Web 1.0 was dominated by standardized hardware and software, but Web 2.0 encourages co-creation and diversity. So too in CSR, we are beginning to realize the limitations of the generic CSR codes and standards that have proliferated in the past ten years. The similarities between Web 1.0 and CSR 1.0 are illustrated in table 1.

If this is where we have come from, where do we need to go to? The similarities between Web 2.0 and CSR 2.0 are illustrated in table 2.

Embracing the Future

Let us explore in more detail this revolution that will, if successful, change the way CSR is talked about and practiced and, ultimately, the way business is conducted. Five principles make up the "DNA" of CSR 2.0: connectedness to multiple stakeholders; scalability for expanding projects; responsiveness to the beneficiaries' needs; duality for balancing local concerns with larger principles; and circularity for closing the production loop so that there is no waste. Table 3 on the following page summarizes some of the shifts in these principles that are occurring between CSR 1.0 and CSR 2.0.

Hence, paternalistic relationships between companies and the community that are based on philanthropy give way to more equal partnerships. Defensive, minimalist responses to social and environmental issues (e.g., implementing carbon reductions only when climate legislation forces this action) are replaced with proactive strategies and investment in growing responsibility markets (e.g., investing in clean technology, as General Electric is doing with its ecomagination program). Image-conscious, public-relations approaches to CSR are no longer credible, and so companies are judged on actual social, environmental, and ethical performance (i.e., are things improving in absolute, cumulative terms?).

Although CSR specialists still have a role to play, each dimension of CSR 2.0 performance is embedded and integrated into the core operations of companies. Standardized approaches remain useful as guides to consensus, but CSR is implemented at the small-scale, local level. CSR solutions, including responsible products and services, go from niche "nice-to-haves" to mass-market "must-haves." And the whole concept of CSR loses its Western conceptual and operational dominance, becoming a more culturally diverse and internationally applied concept.

TABLE 1. Web 1.0 Compared with CSR 1.0

Web 1.0	CSR 1.0
Characterized as a vehicle for companies to connect to customers and use a new medium to present information and advertising	Characterized as a vehicle for companies to establish relationships with communities, channel philanthropic contributions, and manage their images
Saw the rise to prominence of innovators like Netscape, but these were quickly outmuscled by corporate giants like Microsoft, with its Internet Explorer browser	Included as a component of many start-up pioneers like Traidcraft, which is both a trading company and charity, but ultimately turned into a strategy for large multinational corporations like Royal Dutch Shell
Focused largely on the standardized hardware and software of the PC as its delivery platform, rather than on multilevel applications	Followed a "one size fits all" standardization through codes, standards, and guidelines to shape its offering

TABLE 2. Web 2.0 Compared with CSR 2.0

Web 2.0	CSR 2.0
Is being defined by watchwords like *collective intelligence, collaborative networks*, and *user participation*	Is being defined by terms like *global commons, innovative partnerships*, and *stakeholder involvement*
Includes tools such as social media, knowledge syndication, and beta testing	Includes mechanisms such as diverse stakeholder panels, real-time transparent reporting, and new-wave social entrepreneurship
Is as much a state of being as a technical advance—is a new philosophy or a way of seeing the world differently	Is recognizing a shift from centralized to decentralized power; a change in scale from a few large initiatives to many small ones; and a change from single, exclusive applications to multiple, shared ones

Table 3. Shifting CSR Principles

CSR 1.0	CSR 2.0
Paternalistic	Collaborative
Risk based	Reward based
Image driven	Performance driven
Specialized	Integrated
Standardized	Diversified
Marginal	Scalable
Western	Global

How might these shifting principles manifest as CSR practices? Table 4 summarizes some key changes to the way in which CSR would be implemented.

Table 4. Shifting CSR Practices

CSR 1.0	CSR 2.0
Premium markets	"Base of the Pyramid" (i.e., the poor) markets
Charity projects	Social enterprise
CSR indexes	CSR ratings
CSR departments	CSR incentives
Ethical consumerism	Choice editing
Product liability	Service agreements
CSR reporting cycles	CSR data streams
Stakeholder groups	Social networks
Process standards	Performance standards

CSR would no longer manifest as luxury products and services (like many green and fair trade options) but as affordable solutions for those who most need quality-of-life improvements. Investment in self-sustaining social enterprises would be favored over donations, or "checkbook charity." CSR indexes, which rank the same large companies over and over (often revealing contradictions between indexes), would make way for CSR rating systems. These systems would turn social, environmental, ethical, and economic performance into corporate scores (A+, B–, etc., similar to credit ratings) that analysts and others could compare and integrate into their decision making.

Reliance on CSR departments would disappear or disperse as responsibility and sustainability are increasingly built into corporate performance appraisal and market-incentive systems. Whether consumers choose, or self-select, ethical products would become irrelevant, as CSR 2.0 companies would begin to "choice edit." In choice editing, companies stop offering implicitly "less ethical" product ranges, thus allowing guilt-free shopping. Liability at the end of products' lifecycles would become obsolete, as the service-lease and take-back economy becomes mainstream. Annual CSR reporting would be replaced by online, real-time CSR performance data flows. Feeding into these live communications would be Web 2.0–connected social networks, instead of periodic meetings of rather cumbersome stakeholder panels. And typical CSR 1.0 management systems standards like ISO 14001 would be less credible than new performance standards that set absolute limits and thresholds, such as those emerging in climate change.

The Purpose of Business

CSR 2.0 comes down to one thing: clarification and reorientation of the purpose of business. It is inaccurate to believe that the purpose of business is to be profitable or to serve shareholders. These are simply means to an end. Ultimately the purpose of business is to serve society by providing safe, high-quality products and services that enhance our well-being without eroding our ecological and community life-support systems.

Making a positive contribution to society is the essence of CSR 2.0—not just as a marginal afterthought, but as a way of doing business. It is not about bailing out the *Titanic* with a teaspoon—which is the effect of CSR 1.0—but about turning the whole ship around and heading back to port for a structural overhaul. CSR 2.0 is about designing and adopting an inherently sustainable and responsible business model. That business model is supported by a reformed financial and economic system that makes creating a better world the easiest and most natural and rewarding thing to do.

Wayne VISSER
CSR International

See also in the *Berkshire Encyclopedia of Sustainability*: **Activism–NGOs; Climate Change Disclosure; Fair Trade; Global Reporting Initiative; Greenwashing; Information and Communication Technologies (ICT); Investment, CleanTech; Investment, Socially Responsible (SRI); Stakeholder Theory; United Nations Global Compact**

FURTHER READING

Achbar, Mark; Abbot, Jennifer; & Bakan, Joel. (2009). *The corporation* [Video clip]. Retrieved September 3, 2009, from http://www.thecorporation.com/

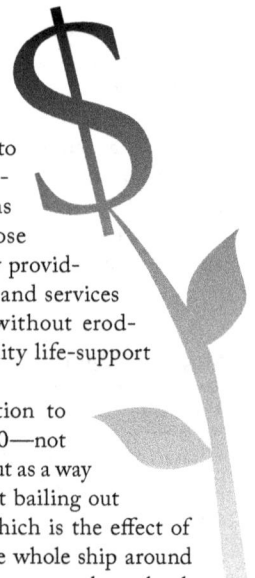

Bakan, Joel. (2004). *The corporation: The pathological pursuit of profit and power*. New York: Free Press.

Benyus, Janine M. (2002). *Biomimicry: Innovation inspired by nature*. New York: Harper Perennial.

Biomimicry Institute. (2009). Retrieved September 3, 2009, from http://www.biomimicryinstitute.org/

Bowen, Howard Rothmann. (1953). *Social responsibilities of the businessman; with a commentary by F. Ernest Johnson*. New York: Harper.

Carroll, Archie B. (1979). A three-dimensional conceptual model of corporate social performance. *Academy of Management Review, 4*, 497–505.

Carroll, Archie B. (2008). A history of corporate social responsibility: Concepts and practices. In Andrew Crane; Abagail McWilliams; Dirk Matten; Jeremy Moon; & Donald S. Siegel (Eds.), *The Oxford handbook of corporate social responsibility* (pp. 19–46). Oxford, U.K.: Oxford University Press.

Carson, Rachel. (1962). *Silent spring*. New York: Houghton Mifflin.

CSR International. (2009). *Welcome to CSR International—the incubator for CSR 2.0*. Retrieved September 3, 2009, from www.csrinternational.org

Elkington, John, & Hartigan, Pamela. (2008). *The power of unreasonable people: How social entrepreneurs create markets that change the world*. Boston: Harvard Business School Press.

Hawken, Paul; Lovins, Amory; & Lovins, L. Hunter. (1999). *Natural capitalism: Creating the next industrial revolution*. Boston: Little, Brown.

Henriques, Adrian. (2003, May 26). Ten things you always wanted to know about CSR (but were afraid to ask): Part 1: A brief history of corporate social responsibility (CSR). Retrieved November 4, 2009, from http://www.ethicalcorp.com/content.asp?ContentID=594

Leon H. Sullivan Foundation. (2005). *The global Sullivan principles*. Retrieved November 11, 2009, from http://www.thesullivanfoundation.org/gsp/principles/gsp/default.asp

McDonough, William, & Braungart, Michael. (2002). *Cradle to cradle: Remaking the way we make things*. New York: North Point Press.

McDonough Braungart Design Chemistry. (2009). *Transforming industry: Cradle to cradle design*. Retrieved September 3, 2009, from http://www.mbdc.com/c2c_home.htm

Natural Capitalism Solutions. (2009). Retrieved September 3, 2009, from http://www.natcapsolutions.org/

Skoll Foundation. (2009). Retrieved September 3, 2009, from http://www.skollfoundation.org/

United States Environmental Protection Agency. (2009). *Voluntary environmental management systems/ISO 14001*. Retrieved November 11, 2009, from http://www.epa.gov/OWM/iso14001/isofaq.htm

Visser, Wayne. (forthcoming). CSR 2.0: The evolution and revolution of corporate social responsibility. In Manfred Pohl & Nick Tolhurst (Eds.), *Responsible business: How to manage a CSR strategy successfully*. Chichester, U.K.: John Wiley & Sons.

Visser, Wayne. (forthcoming). *The age of responsibility*. London: John Wiley & Sons.

Visser, Wayne; Matten, Dirk; Pohl, Manfred; & Tolhurst, Nick (Eds.). (2007). *The A to Z of corporate social responsibility: A complete reference guide to concepts, codes and organisations*. Chichester, U.K.: John Wiley & Sons.

Visser, Wayne, & McIntosh, Alastair. (1998). A short review of the historical critique of usury. *Accounting, Business & Financial History, 8*(2), 175–189.

Yunus, Muhammad, & Weber, Karl. (2007). *Creating a world without poverty: Social business and the future of capitalism*. New York: PublicAffairs.

Global Approaches

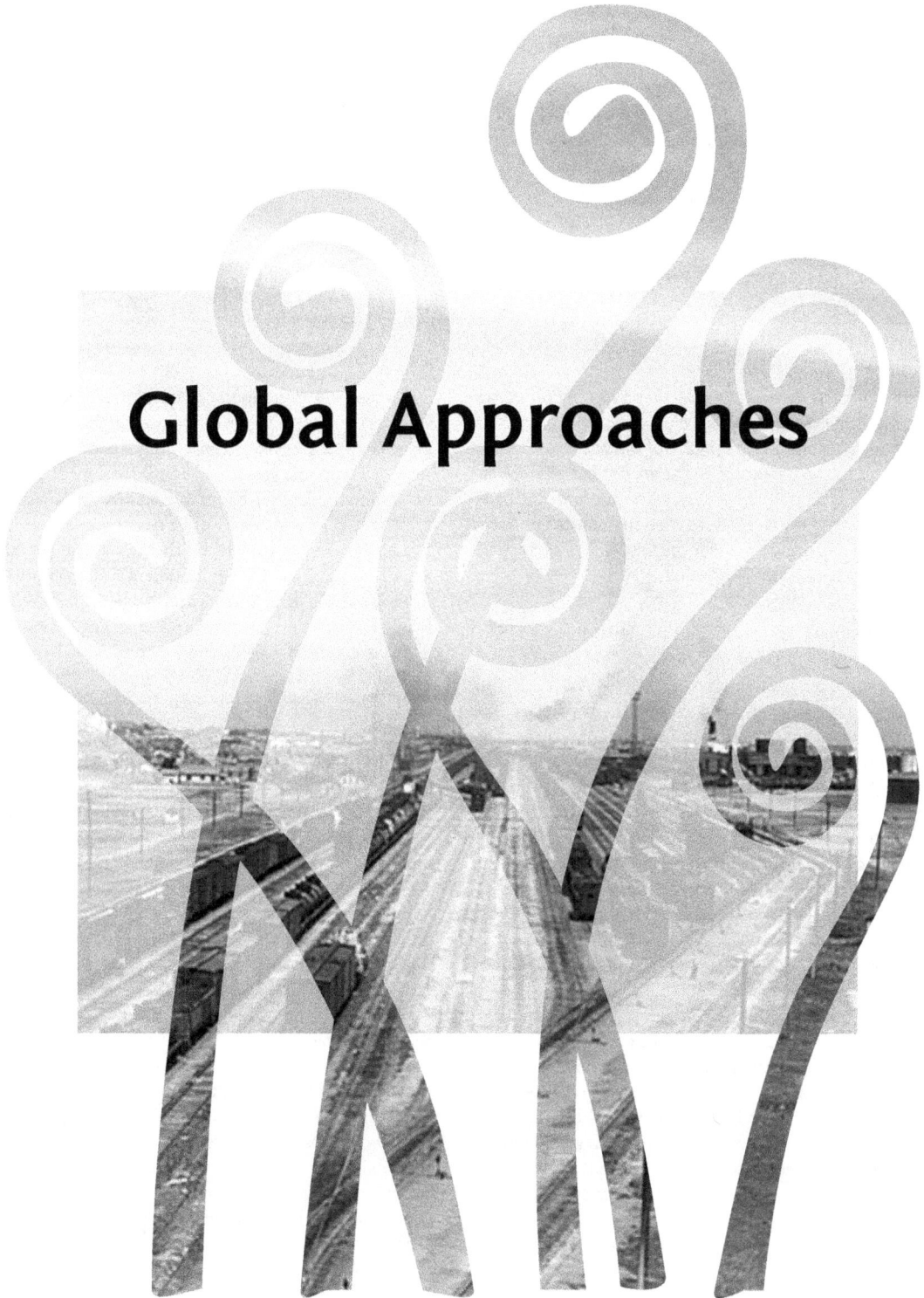

Equator Principles

Created in 2003 by ten international private-sector banks, the Equator Principles serve, according to the website, as "a benchmark for the financial industry to manage social and environmental issues in project financing." Since their inception, more than sixty-five financial institutions around the world have become signatories to the revised set of principles. It was the first global, sectorwide set of voluntary codes of conduct.

At the official launch of the Equator Principles (EPs) for financial institutions on 4 June 2003, ten leading international project finance banks (led by ABN AMRO, Barclays, Citi, and WestLB) adopted ten principles as a framework to ensure that projects funded by participants use socially and environmentally responsible practices. Upon publication of the first revision of the EPs on 6 July 2006, more than fifty-five banks and financial institutions (including two export credit agencies, which implied governmental support and appreciation of this initiative) from twenty-one countries were signatories. This represented more than 85 percent of the world's project finance institutions, which indicates that EPs have become a true global standard applied by banks, seriously taken into account by their clients, and actively monitored and from time to time challenged by leading nongovernmental organizations (NGOs). They have proven to be fit for the purpose—banks have started to take these issues more seriously and also have intensified dialogue with respect to challenges of the banks' performances by NGOs. In addition, an increasing number of banks have started to develop internal policies that incorporate many of the principles underlying the EPs in their nonproject-related lending and advisory business. Hence, the impact of the EPs has been quite significant in scale and scope.

Moreover, as a business-initiated, practitioner-written, voluntary initiative to set a common, global baseline, the Equator Principles have been a catalyst and benchmark for similar sectorwide projects by leading companies in other industries. It raises the bar of competition: competition on price, structure, and quality of service but not on some fundamental values or principles. The EPs are generally seen as a turning point in the application of sustainability in the financial sector. The Principles for Responsible Investment (PRI) for long-term asset owners (such as pension funds) and investment managers, sponsored in 2006 by the U.N. Global Compact and the U.N. Environment Programme's (UNEP) Finance Initiative, were inspired by the EPs.

Origins of the Equator Principles

According to the preamble of the Equator Principles, project financing is "a method of funding in which the lender looks primarily to the revenues generated by a single project both as the source of repayment and as security for the exposure." Project finance plays a major part in funding global development.

The Equator Principles were triggered by credit and reputational risks that banks increasingly faced in their project finance practice: self-interest was a driving factor. The reason why banks were deemed more complicit by civil society organizations (affected communities, labor organizations, and environmental and social advocacy groups) in the financing of projects was related to the large size of these projects ($50 million to sometimes billions of dollars); the public nature and demonstrable impact thereof (extractive industries, infrastructure); the high loan-to-cost ratio (sometimes as high as 90 percent); and limited recourse to the industrial project sponsors. Thus criticism was rising; in 2002 leading international NGOs adopted a broader vision of sustainable finance with the Collevecchio Declaration for Financial Institutions. These factors caused banks to improve their due diligence; tighten their credit requirements beyond just financial/economic issues; and require broader, stricter monitoring of social and environmental factors.

ABN AMRO's Herman Mulder and Peter Woicke of the International Finance Corporation (IFC) took the initiative in October 2002 and hosted a meeting in London of twelve leading project finance banks to discuss the challenges they were facing. At the beginning of this meeting (which was attended by loan officers from the banks, not public relations officials) there were twelve different causes; at the end of the day there was one common purpose. Initially called the Greenwich Principles, they later were renamed the Equator Principles, reflecting the global ambition of the participating banks. It took only nine months of intensive cooperation and consultation with leading industrial companies, official development agencies, and NGOs to agree to the EPs.

The implementation of the EPs is supported by training and toolkits (screening procedures with attention points to be addressed while evaluating a project). Although the commitment by the bank is individual, participating banks meet at least twice per year to share experiences and review the EPs. A leadership committee is rotating.

Content of the Equator Principles

The EPs are based on the Performance Standards on Social and Environmental Sustainability of the International Finance Corporation (IFC), a member of the World Bank Group. The second version of the EPs, published in July 2006, took into account a revision of these standards, as well as commentaries on the initial 2003 EPs from several NGOs, which have been actively engaged in the drafting and execution of the document. The scope of the EPs is global, and they apply to projects in all sectors—both new projects and upgrades or expansion of existing projects—costing more than $10 million. The EPs cover advisory, arranging, and lending operations.

Each of the participating banks commits itself to the following principles:

- Principle 1: Review and Categorization. Projects are categorized in relation to social and environmental impact and risks, with category A indicating the highest impact or risk and category C the lowest.
- Principle 2: Social and Environmental Assessment. For each project in categories A and B, the borrower must conduct a social and environmental assessment.
- Principle 3: Applicable Social and Environmental Standards. The assessment process must address compliance

with relevant host-country laws, regulations, and permits.
- Principle 4: Action Plan and Management System. For projects in categories A and B, the borrower must prepare an action plan that addresses the issues raised in the assessment, including mitigation measures, corrective actions, monitoring measures to manage impacts and risks, and decommissioning.
- Principle 5: Consultation and Disclosure. For all category A and many category B projects, the borrower must have disclosed the project plan and consulted with affected people (in local language and a culturally appropriate manner) before project construction commences.
- Principle 6: Grievance Mechanism. For category A projects and many category B projects, the borrower ensures ongoing consultation, disclosure, and community engagement throughout construction and operations, allowing facilitation and grievances to be addressed.
- Principle 7: Independent Review. The financing banks will be advised by an expert, independent from the borrower, to assess compliance with the assessment, the plan, and the consultation process.
- Principle 8: Covenants. The borrower pledges to incorporate several social and environmental covenants linked to compliance with the Action Plan; if they do not, it may constitute a default under such agreement and result in cancellation of the loan.
- Principle 9: Independent Monitoring and Reporting. The borrower is to retain external experts to verify its monitoring information, which will be shared with the banks.
- Principle 10: Equator Principles Financial Institution (EPFI) Reporting. Banks will report publicly about their EP implementation at least once a year.

Issues and Concerns

There are some relevant issues and criticisms, many coming from various NGOs, in relation to the EPs:

- Although the number of participating banks is increasing, there are still a number of absentee (nonparticipating) banks, including many from Asia.
- NGOs have criticized the EPs for vagueness; absence of enforcement mechanisms; limited coordination among the banks; indirect (or no) coverage of project bonds; consultation only (not consensus) with affected communities; and the implicit, indirect reference to human rights (just "socially responsible"). NGOs also have questioned the fact that inactive and even noncompliant

banks ("free riders") may still call themselves an Equator bank or an EPFI.

- Because the EPs are individual commitments on principles, each bank uses its own discretion in project selection. It is possible that one bank considers a project or structure EP compliant, while another may not.
- Not all banks apply the same standards, and some banks have even stricter policies than EPs require, especially in areas such as agriculture, fisheries, forestry, natural resources, dams, biodiversity, climate change, human rights, toxic substances, and taxes.
- With the growing importance of significant local capital markets in emerging countries, the question is how these principles may be made applicable for domestic infrastructure projects.

Implications

The Equator Principles are a good example of how even in a highly competitive, diverse environment like the financial sector, leading competing practitioners are able to agree to adhere to a common baseline in an effective and credible way and raise the bar for the entire sector. It also shows that external pressure may work in the interest of the sector, as initial "pain" inflicted on all banks from challengers may become "gain" for EP-adhering banks; governments, partners, and (affected) communities prefer a bank that has made certain public commitments.

The financial crisis that began in 2007, however, has clearly shown how important business principles, good governance, and transparency are. Moreover, the environment-social-governance agenda is gaining importance. Governments and society increasingly insist on a greater commitment by companies and banks to traditional voluntarism (like the Equator Principles), more forceful mandatory self-regulation, and greater public disclosure on environmental, social, and ethical issues, including standards, targets, and performance.

Herman MULDER
Independent ESG Advisor & Board Member

See also in the *Berkshire Encyclopedia of Sustainability*: **Activism—NGOs; Corporate Citizenship; CSR and CSR 2.0; Financial Services Industry; Global Reporting Initiative (GRI); Transparency**

FURTHER READING

BankTrack. (2007). The silence of the banks: An assessment of Equator Principles reporting. Retrieved October 30, 2009, from http://www.banktrack.org/download/the_silence_of_the_banks_1/0_0_071203_silence_of_the_banks.pdf

BankTrack. (2008). Retrieved June 18, 2009, from http://www.banktrack.org

Baue, William. (2004, June 4). Are the Equator Principles sincere or spin? Retrieved October 30, 2009, from http://www.socialfunds.com/news/article.cgi/1436.html

The Equator Principles. (n.d.). Retrieved June 18, 2009, from http://www.equator-principles.com

Esty, Benjamin C. (2005). The Equator Principles: An industry approach to managing environmental and social risks. HBS publishing case No. 9-205-114; Teaching note No. 5-205-115; Technical note No. 205-065. Retrieved October 30, 2009, from http://ssrn.com/abstract=759985

Forster, Malcom; Watchman, Paul; & July, Charles. (2005a). The Equator Principles—Towards sustainable banking? Part 1. *Journal of International Banking and Financial Law*, 46(6), 217–222.

Forster, Malcom; Watchman, Paul; & July, Charles. (2005b). The Equator Principles—Towards sustainable banking? Part 2. *Butterworths Journal of International Banking and Financial Law*, 46(7), 253–258.

Leading banks announce adoption of Equator Principles. (2003, June 4). Retrieved October 30, 2009, from http://www.equator-principles.com/pr030604.shtml

Watchman, Paul. (2006). Banks, business, and human rights. *Journal of International Banking and Financial Law*, 46(2). Retrieved October 30, 2009, from http://www.equator-principles.com/documents/IB_02.2006_Paul%20Watchman.pdf

Watchman, Paul; Delfino, Angela; & Addison, Juliette. (2007). EP 2: The revised Equator Principles: Why hard-nosed bankers are embracing soft law principles. *Law and Financial Markets Review*, 1(2), 85. Retrieved October 30, 2009, from http://www.equator-principles.com/documents/ClientBriefingforEquatorPrinciples_2007-02-07.pdf

Base of the Pyramid

The Base of the Pyramid refers to the huge proportion of humanity who are mired in poverty, as well as to the business strategies that are evolving to connect this segment of the population into the formal global economy as consumers, suppliers/producers, and entrepreneurs.

A concept developed in the late 1990s, the Base (bottom) of the Pyramid, or BOP, refers simultaneously to the socioeconomic demographic representing the 3–4 billion poorest people inhabiting the globe and to the private-sector business models meant to address the poverty of these people. The idea of the BOP as a business opportunity came about as a convergence of two streams of thought within strategic management. The first is premised on a new model of global economic expansion within international business that uses innovation and technology management. This perspective challenges assumptions regarding the source of innovation and creativity—shifting it from home offices and headquarters based in developed nations to subsidiaries and competitors based in developing countries. The second stream of thought is a model of the global economy that emerged from work on organizations and sustainability. This view describes the global economy as consisting of three distinct demographic categories (the layers of the pyramid) that transcend geographic boundaries, organized by the sustainability challenges that each faces (Hart and Milstein 1999).

Three Layers of the Pyramid

The first demographic category, the tip of the pyramid, is composed of the "mature" economy made up of the world's wealthiest individuals who represent about 15 percent of the global population. These individuals are able to afford all the goods and services they need as well as any or most of what they might want. Although these individuals tend to be found mostly in developed countries, a good percentage exist in less-developed countries as well. The challenge and opportunity for business is to develop goods and services that reduce the large environmental footprint that occurs through consumption in this market. Business can achieve this by applying renewable forms of energy, "green" building and design, and other advancements that offer significant reductions in energy usage, toxicity, and emissions.

The second demographic group represents the aspiring middle class that makes up approximately 20 percent of the global population. While found in many countries throughout the world, the majority of this demographic reside in China, India, Brazil, and other countries undergoing rapid economic transformation. These individuals are able to afford most goods and services they need and some of those they want. The challenge for businesses here is to develop innovative products and services that prevent further contributions to environmental degradation as the aspiring economy develops. Most efforts by companies to penetrate emerging economies are attempts to adapt the mature economy's expensive products and services to make them more affordable. They often do this by introducing earlier-generation technologies or stripped-down product offerings into the marketplace. Such products—for example, cars without catalytic converters—may be cheaper, but they are also dirtier. The incremental revenue generated from sales of such products is often lower than expected, and the impact on the environment can be high.

The third group represents the "survival economy" made up of the nearly two-thirds of humanity, living all over the globe, who earn between $1 and $3 a day. (It should be noted that poverty lines set by specific income levels suggest definitive levels at which poverty does and does not occur; such figures tend to conceal the variety of circumstances affecting the human condition.) Demographically, this is the BOP. These individuals are barely able or unable to meet their most basic needs, such as clean water, health care, education, housing, and nutrition. For the most part, the economic system has overlooked, ignored, or even exploited this market segment. Existing business models, products, and services have little relevance in this market because the logistical, cultural, technical, and political characteristics are so different from the mature economy for which the products were developed. What goods do exist are usually more expensive and of lower quality than comparable items available to the wealthy. The *poverty penalty* is a term used to describe the premium the poor have to pay for basic services—such as water, electricity, and sanitation—that are often of inferior quality to those available at lower costs to the rich (Prahalad and Hammond 2002).

BOP as a Business Opportunity

While the term BOP itself refers to the socioeconomic demographic of the world's poorest, the paradigm of the BOP that is being taught in many management education programs refers to private-sector activity where poverty is addressed when low-income markets become engines for entrepreneurship and business growth. This view is very contentious for those suspicious of the motivations of companies, such as Unilever and Procter & Gamble, who have been pursuing BOP initiatives. The concern is that such initiatives are simply another way to sell unnecessary goods to poor people in a way that extracts what little wealth exists in those markets. Other concerns are that successful BOP strategies will lead to increased consumption patterns that place even more pressure on critical ecosystem services and further environmental decline.

Another viewpoint, however, promotes BOP ventures as a way to unlock the latent vitality and ingenuity of robust, informal markets, thus releasing the poor from economic imprisonment. This view rejects the idea of the poor simply as a source of revenue for new business growth and instead sees the poor as capable partners and resources for technology development and innovation. The BOP is not advocated as simply the opportunity for increasing sales through the marketing of existing products and services in forms that are smaller and cheaper than their upmarket cousins (e.g., sachets and single servings of products such as shampoo or detergents). Instead, the BOP is conceptualized as a holistic, long-term investment process in business

model innovation. It is based on partnerships and need-based product and service development as articulated by the poor themselves and built on the local resource base, infrastructure, and cultural institutions. The most progressive concepts of BOP business are premised on the idea that the poor can provide markets for commercializing next-generation technologies that offer social, environmental, and economic value. For example, high-tech cookstoves can allow people to use the sun's energy to prepare meals rather than requiring the poor to further deplete vital wood supplies or breathe in noxious fumes from dung, kerosene, or coal.

Mark B. MILSTEIN, Erik SIMANIS,
Duncan DUKE, Stuart HART
Johnson Graduate School of Management,
Cornell University

This article is adapted from the article "Base of the Pyramid (BOP) Model" that appears in Wayne Visser, Dirk Matten, Manfred Pohl, & Nick Tolhurst (Eds.), *The A to Z of Corporate Social Responsibility: The Complete Reference of Concepts, Codes and Organisations*, Chichester, U.K.: John Wiley and Sons.

See also in the *Berkshire Encyclopedia of Sustainability*: **CSR and CSR 2.0; Development, Sustainable; Fair Trade; Investment, Socially Responsible (SRI); Poverty; Social Enterprise; Triple Bottom Line; United Nations Global Compact**

FURTHER READING

Hart, Stuart L. (2005). *Capitalism at the crossroads: The unlimited business opportunities in solving the world's most difficult problems*. Philadelphia: Wharton School Publishing.

Hart, Stuart L., & Christensen, Clayton M. (2002). The great leap: Driving innovation from the bottom of the pyramid. *Sloan Management Review, 44*(1), 51–56.

Hart, Stuart L., & Milstein, Mark B. (1999). Global sustainability and the creative destruction of industries. *Sloan Management Review, 41*(1), 23–33.

Prahalad, C. K. (2004). *The fortune at the bottom of the pyramid: Eradicating poverty through profits*. Philadelphia: Wharton School Publishing.

Prahalad, C. K., & Hammond, Allen. (2002). Serving the world's poor profitably. *Harvard Business Review, 80*(9), 48–57.

Prahalad, C. K., & Hart, Stuart L. (2002). The fortunate at the bottom of the pyramid. *Strategy+Business, 26*, 2–14.

Simanis, Erik, & Hart, Stuart L. (2009). Innovation from the inside out. *Sloan Management Review, 50*(4), 77–86.

Simanis, Erik; Hart, Stuart L.; & Duke, Duncan. (2008). The Base of the Pyramid protocol: Beyond "basic needs" business strategies. *Innovations, 3*(1), 57–84.

Free Trade

Free trade is the movement of goods, services, labor, and capital between countries, without government-imposed trade barriers. It also refers to the efforts of the World Trade Organization and various international agreements to liberalize, or reduce barriers to, trade. Free trade's effect on economic and environmental sustainability is unclear, and trade liberalization methods must balance the needs of developed and developing countries to achieve sustainability.

The term *free trade* refers generally to the free movement of goods, services, labor, and capital across national borders without the interference of government-imposed economic or regulatory barriers. Although it is often considered an antagonist to the goals of sustainability, many economists and policy makers view fully implemented free trade as the end goal of international economic relations. But free trade in the purest sense is far from a reality, especially on a global scale.

Free trade, more specifically, refers to the multilateral efforts at the World Trade Organization (WTO) to liberalize trade by reducing import taxes (tariffs) and removing nontariff barriers globally. It also refers to the bilateral and regional agreements that liberalize trade between trading partners. Some critics blame these concrete trade liberalization efforts for aggravating the inequalities between nations and putting additional strain on the environment through rapid industrialization (Stenzel 2002). Others claim that only free trade can promote worldwide sustainable growth and development.

Origins of Free Trade

The economist Adam Smith wrote in 1776 that "it is the maxim of every prudent master of a family never to attempt to make at home what it will cost him more to make than to buy. . . . What is prudence in the conduct of every private family can scarce be folly in that of a great kingdom" (Smith 1904, 2:11–12). This logic became the foundation for the nineteenth-century economist David Ricardo's theory of comparative advantage, which encouraged countries to specialize in certain products while trading for others. By the 1930s, economists began to embrace free trade as a way to promote both peace and prosperity (Bhagwati 2008).

After World War II, economists and policy makers rebuilding the global economic system proposed creating the International Trade Organization (ITO) to regulate trade between nations. Because the ITO was never founded, the interim General Agreement on Tariffs and Trade (GATT) became the "de facto institution" for governing international trade in the postwar era, until the WTO replaced it. (Bhagwati 2008, 8).

These early efforts at liberalizing trade sought to promote development and economic growth. They were reactions against the "beggar thy neighbor" economic policies that characterized the 1930s. During that time, countries devalued their currencies and increased import tariffs to give their goods a price advantage over other countries. Economists blame such protectionist policies, in part, for exacerbating the Great Depression and the resulting global economic downturn. Under the various negotiations of GATT, more countries began to liberalize trade in the latter half of the twentieth century.

In 1995, 123 countries formed the World Trade Organization. The WTO governs trade in services, goods, intellectual property, agriculture, textiles, and many other issues related to trade. In addition, the WTO established the Committee on Trade and the Environment (CTE) to examine the relationship between trade and environmental policies. The committee recommends modifications where trade liberalization measures do not promote sustainable development and protect the environment.

The Doha Round of WTO negotiations (named for Doha, Qatar, the location of the first meeting) marks the first time that environmental commitments were open for negotiation. The Doha Development Agenda (DDA) ambitiously advocates liberalizing trade in sensitive areas, such as agriculture and intellectual property, while promoting sustainable development and increasing incomes for less developed countries (WTO 2001). Although optimism surrounded the beginning of the Doha Round in 2001, many false starts have contributed to uncertainty about the future of the WTO as a forum for trade liberalization. Increasingly, countries are turning to bilateral and regional agreements to remove trade barriers.

Aims of Trade Liberalization

Since the 1980s, countries have been interested in the relationship between trade and sustainable development. Although the trade–sustainability relationship is largely indirect, the WTO argues that free trade leads to environmental sustainability through economic development, institutional stability and predictability, increasing innovation, more-efficient resource allocation, and increased incomes (WTO 2006). Trade liberalization, however, has not had a completely positive effect on environmental (or even economic and social) sustainability.

Since the mid-1990s, when bilateral and multilateral trade liberalization increased, the resulting industrialization often led to environmental degradation. The North American Free Trade Agreement (NAFTA), for example, worsened air and water pollution by encouraging the establishment of hundreds of export-focused *maquiladoras* (foreign-owned factories in Mexico that employ lower-paid workers; Stenzel 2002). Furthermore, gaps between rich and poor countries have actually widened since that time. Still, many policy makers view piecemeal bilateral and multilateral agreements as building blocks to attaining the promised benefits of fully implemented free trade.

Most countries see the market access provided by free trade as a benefit to their citizens. Market access includes access to goods, cross-border services, capital, and intellectual property (trademarks or patents, for example). Unfortunately, provisions that promote market access for one country may discourage it for another. Even fully implemented free trade cannot improve every person's or every country's welfare simultaneously. Instead, in theory, it would reallocate resources so that the "winners" would gain more than the "losers" would lose, thus leading to an overall average increase in global welfare.

Since no one country, sector, or industry wants to become the loser, each economic actor (i.e., seller, consumer, worker, or investor) has different goals for trade liberalization. Agricultural importers, for example, push for eliminating subsidies (governmental financial support) on developed countries' agricultural products in order to reduce the cost of imports. Members of the U.S. industrial sector seek to increase and harmonize regulatory health, safety, and environmental standards, in part so that competitive industries in the developing world cannot inexpensively create the same products. The pharmaceutical industry would like heightened protection for intellectual property (i.e., drug patents) so that it receives due compensation for the costs of research and development and is not immediately undersold by generics producers who reverse engineer the drugs.

Just as the interested economic actors prioritize certain items on the liberalization agenda, they remain wary of the priorities of others. Developing countries would like trade liberalization to eventually lead to more sustainable economic and social development, but they resist environmental commitments. The developed world, meanwhile, pushes for environmental protection but hesitates to allow flexibility for lesser developed countries, fearing the developed nations would be unable to compete with countries conforming to lower environmental standards.

Impacts on Sustainability

Economists accept that free trade generally has a positive impact on trade flows. One study shows that trade volumes were up 120 percent in 2000 alone, largely due to the WTO's trade liberalization. The same study indicates that, in manufacturing, where trade barriers came down, trade volumes increased, and where barriers remained high, trade volumes were little or even negatively affected. (Trade volume is measured by the number of goods and services traded in a given time period.) For example, trade in clothing, footwear, and agriculture has changed little in recent years because the developed world has maintained protection over those sectors (Subramanian and Wei 2007).

Although trade liberalization has led to increased trade volumes and economic growth in a few cases, the sustainability of that growth and its impact on the environment are unclear. After the signing of NAFTA, incomes and employment rose significantly in the northern part of Mexico. Likewise, exports in manufacturing increased quickly. But much of this improvement can be attributed to the *maquiladora* industry, which is largely disconnected from the rest of the Mexican economy (Salas 2001). Such economic gains may not last unless the free trade policies encourage the transfer of valuable technology and help build local economies through forward and backward economic linkages. (Forward linkages are distribution chains between the producer and its customers, and backward linkages are distribution chains between the producer and its suppliers.)

Economic sustainability is not the only concern. As trade flows increase so does the need to transport goods and services, depleting fossil fuels that are not sustainable over time. Thus environmental concerns have begun to play a more central role in international trade negotiations. In addition to the CTE's work, the WTO is engaged in the issues that concern environmental interest groups. The WTO maintains that its role is to continue to liberalize trade, while ensuring that environmental protection does not interfere with trade and that trade rules do not interfere with domestic environmental provisions (WTO 2006, 6).

In addition to the WTO, bilateral and regional agreements have addressed the role of environmental protection in trade liberalization. NAFTA was the first "significant trade agreement" to include environmental provisions—in a side letter to the agreement. Other agreements that have more enforceable provisions followed (Gallagher 2009).

Balancing Economic and Environmental Sustainability

The principle of sustainable development has become a priority in global trade negotiations. Differences of opinion remain, however, over the specific methods of promoting such development and which pillar of sustainability should take precedence. The primary controversy concerns the capabilities of developing nations to conform to the environmental commitments demanded by the developed world.

Many argue that while the developing world needs market access to enter the world economy, it also needs specific policies that build up domestic industries and institutions in order to be globally competitive. These policies could provide developing countries with the flexibility to control the movement of capital, encourage technology transfer, and "generate the resources they need to protect the environment" (WTO 2006, 7). For low-income nations, reducing poverty is the main priority. But the developed world, responding to the pressures of environmental interest groups, maintains that environmental protection must accompany poverty reduction and economic development. Some WTO members recognize that environmental commitments must consider developing countries' capacity to embrace and enforce those commitments. Outside multilateral trade negotiations, however, developing countries often must acquiesce to the demands of their developed trade partners in order to acquire market access.

Growth and Change

The theory behind trade liberalization, when combined with environmental awareness, shows promise despite the antagonistic relationship between free trade and sustainability. As countries continue to remove trade barriers, global competition in all sectors should increase. The result should be more-efficient markets and more opportunities for technological and economic development in the developing world. Efficient markets could allow environmentally friendly technology to transfer across borders. Since poverty has been identified as a primary cause of environmental destruction, true economic development from free trade could have a positive effect on the environment in the future.

A main critique of trade liberalization methods such as the WTO and regional or bilateral agreements is that the developed world demands liberalization from lesser developed countries without removing its own trade-distorting barriers. For example, the developing world must reduce tariffs on textiles and sensitive agricultural products, but the United States and the European Union maintain substantial subsidies on agriculture (World Bank 2007, 40). Thus, many argue that we will not achieve global sustainability until we remove such barriers and approach fully implemented free trade.

Many people doubt the fundamental principles of free trade. The financial crisis that began in late 2007 has highlighted market flaws, leading people to question whether markets should remain free of government intervention. Countries have reintroduced protectionist measures to guard their economies from a deeper recession. The DDA has been stalled almost since its inception, and many countries' negotiators no longer anticipate achieving multilateral trade liberalization via the WTO. Meanwhile, small-scale trade agreements proliferate as countries form bilateral and regional trading blocs to gain market access.

As applied, free trade has not had a definitive positive impact on sustainable development. Growing trade volumes have increased global transportation, worsening air and water pollution and depleting natural resources. Rapid industrialization in places such as Mexico and China has taken its toll on the environment. Economically, trade liberalization has lifted some out of poverty but overall has not been able to shrink the gap between rich and poor.

Still, sustainability concerns have gained importance significantly since the U.N.'s Earth Summit in 1992. Trade agreements, bilateral or multilateral, can no longer ignore issues of sustainable economic and environmental development. If the growing network of bilateral and regional agreements acts as a set of building blocks toward global free trade, and those agreements contain flexible provisions for environmental protection and economic development, then free trade in the future may prove sustainable after all.

Rachel Denae THRASHER
*Pardee Center for the Study of the
Longer-Range Future, Boston University*

See also in the *Berkshire Encyclopedia of Sustainability*: **Agriculture; Base of the Pyramid (BOP); Consumer Behavior; Development, Sustainable; Equator Principles; Financial Services Industry; Global Reporting Initiative (GRI); Information and Communication Technologies (ICT); Poverty; True Cost Economics; United Nations Global Compact**

FURTHER READING

Ackerman, Frank, & Gallagher, Kevin P. (2008). The shrinking gains from global trade liberalization in computable general equilibrium models: A critical assessment. *International Journal of Political Economy, 37*(1), 50–77.

Adler, Matthew; Brunel, Claire; Hufbauer, Gary Clyde; & Schott, Jeffrey J. (2009). *What's on the table? The Doha Round as of August 2009* (Working Paper Series 09-6). Retrieved October 13, 2009, from http://www.iie.com/publications/wp/wp09-6.pdf

Baker, Dean. (2008). Trade and inequality: The role of economists. *Real-World Economics Review, 45,* 23–32. Retrieved September 22, 2009, from http://www.paecon.net/PAEReview/issue45/whole45.pdf

Baldwin, Richard, & Low, Patrick. (Eds.). (2009). *Multilateralizing regionalism: Challenges for the global trading system.* New York: Cambridge University Press.

Bhagwati, Jagdish. (2008). *Termites in the trading system: How preferential agreements undermine free trade.* New York: Oxford University Press.

Folsom, Ralph H. (2008). *Bilateral free trade agreements: A critical assessment and WTO regulatory reform proposal* (Legal Studies Research Paper No. 08-070). Retrieved September 22, 2009, from http://papers.ssrn.com/sol3/papers.cfm?abstract_id=1262872

Gallagher, Kevin P. (2009, November). NAFTA and the environment: Lessons from Mexico and beyond. In Kevin P. Gallagher, Timothy A. Wise, & Enrique Dussel Peters (Eds.), *The future of North American trade policy: Lessons from NAFTA* (pp. 61–69). Retrieved December 11, 2009, from http://www.bu.edu/pardee/files/2009/11/Pardee-Report-NAFTA.pdf

Mol, Arthur P. J., & van Buuren, Joost C. L. (Eds.). (2003). *Greening industrialization in Asian transitional economies: China and Vietnam.* Lanham, MD: Lexington Books.

Salas, Carlos. (2001). The impact of NAFTA on wages and incomes in Mexico. In Bruce Campbell, Carlos Salas, & Robert Scott, *NAFTA at seven: Its impact on workers in all three nations* (pp. 12–20). Washington, DC: Economic Policy Institute.

Smith, Adam. (1904). *An inquiry into the nature and causes of the wealth of nations* (Edwin Cannan, Ed.) (Vols. 1–2). London: Methuen.

Stenzel, Paulette L. (2002). Why and how the World Trade Organization must promote environmental protection. *Duke Environmental Law and Policy Forum, 13*(1), 1–54. Retrieved October 13, 2009, from http://www.law.duke.edu/shell/cite.pl?13+Duke+Envtl.+L.+&+Pol%27y+F.+1

Subramanian, Arvind, & Wei, Shang-Jin. (2007). The WTO promotes trade, strongly but unevenly. *Journal of International Economics, 72*(1), 151–175.

Thrasher, Rachel Denae, & Gallagher, Kevin. (2008). *21st century trade agreements: Implications for long-run development policy* (Pardee Paper No. 2). Retrieved October 13, 2009, from http://www.bu.edu/pardee/files/documents/PP-002-Trade.pdf

World Bank. (2007). *World development report 2008: Agriculture for development.* Retrieved September 22, 2009, from http://siteresources.worldbank.org/INTWDR2008/Resources/WDR_00_book.pdf

World Trade Organization (WTO). (1994). Relevant WTO provisions: Text of 1994 decision [Decision on trade and environment]. Retrieved October 13, 2009, from http://www.wto.org/english/tratop_e/envir_e/issu5_e.htm

World Trade Organization (WTO). (2001). Doha WTO ministerial 2001: Ministerial declaration. Retrieved October 23, 2009, from http://www.wto.org/english/thewto_e/minist_e/min01_e/mindecl_e.htm

World Trade Organization (WTO). (2006). Trade and environment at the WTO. Retrieved September 18, 2009, from http://www.wto.org/english/tratop_e/envir_e/envir_e.htm World Trade Organization (WTO). (2009). Trade and environment. Retrieved September 21, 2009, from http://www.wto.org/english/tratop_e/envir_e/envir_e.htm

Fair Trade

The fair trade movement began in the mid-twentieth century when nonprofit organizations bought textiles and crafts from poor regions and sold them to developed regions. By 2000, agricultural products made up the majority of products. The fair trade model, recently adopted by multinational corporations, includes direct trade with producers, long-term trading relationships, standardized labeling and pricing, environmental sustainability, and sustainable production.

The term *fair trade*, coined to contrast with the "unfair" practices of the global trading system, historically referred to a wide range of initiatives involving government intervention in the market. The fair trade movement, as it is understood in the twenty-first century, is a network of producer-consumer partnerships that aim to promote development for small-scale producers. The hallmarks of these fair trade partnerships are fair prices and wages.

The fair trade network developed from a prototype launched in the middle of the twentieth century by the Oxford Committee for Famine Relief (now Oxfam) in the United Kingdom and the Mennonite Central Committee in Canada. Both organizations independently bought goods from poor regions of the world for sale in industrialized regions and countries. Initially their efforts to provide a living wage and fair prices for producers in the developing world were largely charitable.

The fair trade movement became more market oriented in the 1980s due to the widespread acceptance of neoliberal economic ideas. The movement, described by Fairtrade Labelling Organizations International (FLO) as an effort to reform the trading system from within, is made up of labeling organizations, retailers, importers, and organized groups of fair trade producers that have established a goal to inform consumers about (and create a market niche

for) ethically traded goods. The key international fair trade organizations are the FLO, the World Fair Trade Organization (formerly the International Fair Trade Association), the Network of European World Shops, and the European Fair Trade Association (all based in Europe); and the U.S.-based Fair Trade Federation. Each provides resources, research and development, and networking for fair trade producers, importers, and retailers.

Fair Trade, Economics, and the Environment

Four principles shape the fair trade model: direct trade between importers and producers, the establishment of long-term trading relationships, minimum pricing, and a price premium added to the goods (Nicholls and Opal 2005, 33). These principles underlie the basic standards required for fair trade certification. Direct trade increases the producers' market access, in part by providing information and credit to improve their businesses. Long-term trading relationships ensure that both producers and importers have an interest in sustainable production practices. The minimum price, or price floor, plays the most direct role in establishing fair prices and wages. It incorporates the costs of production, the cost of living, and any additional costs incurred by complying with fair trade standards, potentially encouraging poor producers to remain in their trade rather than leave it in favor of subsistence farming and unemployment. Importers must pay producers a social premium that is added to the base price of every fair trade product. The premium is earmarked for social development projects in the community and for business development. In some cases, farms have used fair trade premiums to become certified for organic production, a step toward environmental sustainability.

Environmental sustainability and sustainable production are defining characteristics of the fair trade movement. Every set of fair trade standards contains a section on environmental development that requires resource management systems, awareness of environmental impacts, and compliance with all local laws and regulations. The movement also promotes the use of nonsynthetic fertilizers and biological pest controls and even encourages organic farming where practical. Finally, proponents of the fair trade model advocate for including the environmental and social costs of production into the product price.

Impacts and Corporate Responses

The fair trade market is concentrated in two sectors: agriculture and textiles/crafts. Although crafts and textiles originally made up the majority of fair trade goods, food makes up about 80 percent. Key crops include coffee, tea, cocoa, sugar, and bananas. Since 1988, when the first Fairtrade organization established in Holland adopted the name Max Havelaar for use on its label—this character from a popular nineteenth-century Dutch novel was a government official who struggled for economic reform in the Dutch colonies—global sales in fair trade products have exploded. During the 1990s, the value of these products in Europe grew more than 400 percent, and it increased by 3,000 percent in the United Kingdom between 1994 and 2003 (Fridell 2007, 64; Nicholls and Opal 2005, 192–193). But studies since 2003 have shown slowed growth and even a decline in countries such as Switzerland, Germany, and the Netherlands, where fair trade products have been available since the beginning of the movement (Fridell 2007, 64).

Although fair trade grew substantially since its inception in the late 1980s, it made up only 0.01 percent of all global trade in 2001. Nevertheless, the fair trade movement's value cannot be measured in dollars and cents alone. The movement traditionally involved small producers selling to relatively marginalized alternative trading organizations. Now, some twenty years later, large multinational corporations (MNCs) have begun to invest in fair trade goods. Companies such as Dole (bananas) and Starbucks (coffee) entered the fair trade market, devoting a small percentage of their overall sales to fair trade. The "mainstreaming" of the fair trade movement has shifted the focus to consumer demand, leading to renewed profitability for firms in the fair trade market (Nicholls and Opal 2005, 100).

Consumer demand has driven many companies to promote market-based ethical consumption. Perhaps the best-known example is Starbucks' commitment to buying coffee that is "responsibly grown, ethically traded" (Starbucks Coffee Company 2009), and whose partnership with TransFair USA and FLO, beginning in fiscal year 2009, will help small-scale coffee growers develop sustainable practices of production. The U.S.-based Whole Planet Foundation, likewise, has committed to ethically traded goods by establishing economic partnerships with Whole Foods Market suppliers in the developing world. Anecdotally, the evidence shows that, whether or not fair trade is effective, it has spawned a larger movement of consumer awareness that is changing the face of agricultural trade (House of Commons International Development Committee 2007, 9).

Challenges and Controversies for the Future

The fair trade movement has not been without critics. Despite many anecdotes of success and empowerment, some have argued that fair trade is, at best, ineffective, and at worst, economically stunting. As mentioned in the discussion above regarding the impact of fair trade and corporate responses to it, fair trade goods make up only a tiny fraction of the global market. At most, fair trade coffee amounts to 5 percent of coffee sales in any consumer economy (Sidwell 2008). Furthermore, fair trade production is concentrated in the richer developing countries. Fifty-one of the world's fair-trade certified producer organizations are located in Mexico, where the average annual income is US$9,000. In Ethiopia, where the average citizen earns US$700 per year, there are only four (Sidwell 2008, 10–11). Fair traders point out, however, that compared with the conventional global markets, the fair trade movement is relatively new. Every movement begins at the bottom, and fair trade growth patterns indicate that, even if growth slows, the addition of new markets could allow the movement to continue to expand in years to come (Fridell 2007, 65).

Another critique of the movement points out that the price floor may keep people working in economically unsustainable agriculture rather than increasing production efficiency or improving the quality of their products (Sidwell 2008). Fair trade proponents argue instead that the minimum price actually increases market efficiency by allowing people to continue farming when they would otherwise be engaged in only subsistence agriculture or nothing at all (Nicholls and Opal 2005). As of 2009, no research has proved or disproved either viewpoint. The best conclusion is that fair trade policies may not have the same effect in every location and that positive effects may be counteracted by negative ones elsewhere.

Despite potential weaknesses in the fair trade model, the past twenty years have shown that consumer awareness and ethical consumption programs are here to stay. The fair trade movement and its products will likely continue to grow, albeit at a diminished rate, and companies will continue to seek new ways to promote goods that are both grown sustainably and responsibly and traded ethically.

Rachel Denae THRASHER
*Pardee Center for the Study of the
Longer-Range Future, Boston University*

See also in the *Berkshire Encyclopedia of Sustainability*: **Agriculture; Consumer Behavior; Corporate Citizenship; CSR and CSR 2.0; Ecolabeling; Equator Principles; Global Reporting Initiative (GRI); Human Rights; Investment, Socially Responsible (SRI); Sustainable Value Creation**

FURTHER READING

Brown, Michael Barratt. (1993). *Fair trade: Reform and realities in the international trading system*. London: Zed Books.

Fairtrade Labelling Organisations International. (2009a). Generic Fairtrade standards for small producers' organizations. Retrieved September 30, 2009, from http://www.fairtrade.net/fileadmin/user_upload/content/2009/standards/documents/Aug09_EN_SPO_Standards.pdf

Fairtrade Labelling Organisations International. (2009b). Our vision. Retrieved September 30, 2009, from http://www.fairtrade.net/our_vision.html

Fridell, Gavin. (2007). *Fair trade coffee: The prospects and pitfalls of market-driven social justice*. Toronto: University of Toronto Press.

House of Commons International Development Committee. (2007). *Fair trade and development: Seventh report of session 2006–07*. London: Parliamentary House of Commons.

Nicholls, Alex, & Opal, Charlotte. (2005). *Fair trade: Market-driven ethical consumption*. London: Sage Publications.

Sidwell, Marc. (2008). *Unfair trade*. Retrieved September 29, 2009, from http://www.adamsmith.org/images/pdf/unfair_trade.pdf

Starbucks Coffee Company. (2009). Ethical sourcing: Sustainable prices for quality coffee. Retrieved October 1, 2009, from http://www.starbucks.com/SHAREDPLANET/ethicalInternal.aspx?story=pricesAndQuality

Stiglitz, Joseph E., & Charlton, Andrew. (2005). *Fair trade for all: How trade can promote development*. New York: Oxford University Press.

Governance

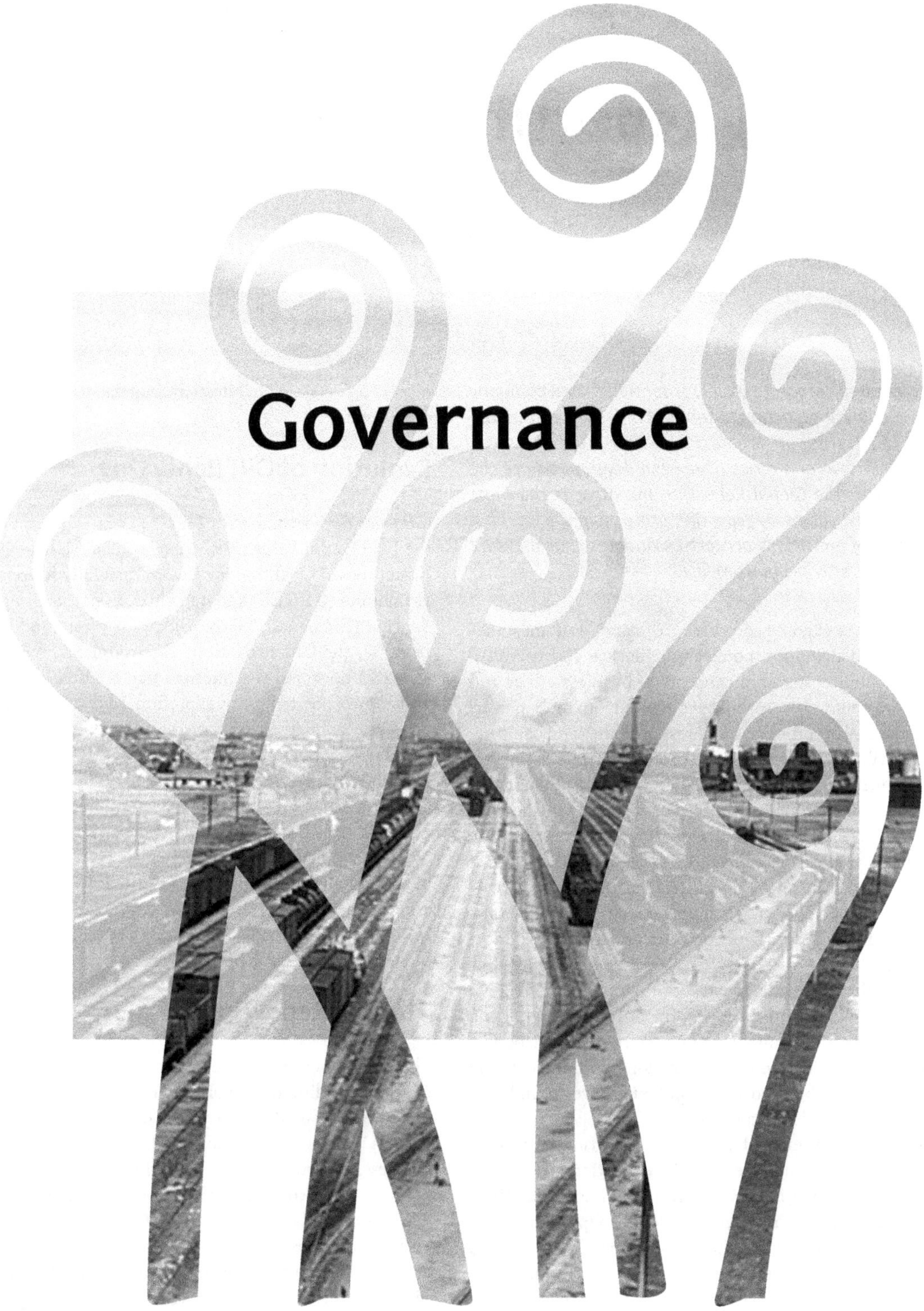

Global Reporting Initiative (GRI)

Attention to corporate social responsibility and company sustainability reporting requires a means of evaluating and monitoring an organization's business activities. Although several metrics have been developed since the late 1990s, the Global Reporting Initiative is the most widely used voluntary reporting protocol in the world. It consists of universally accepted standards that measure a business's "triple bottom line."

In an era of exposed corporate greed and resultant stakeholder demand for more comprehensive and pervasive accountability, standard concepts of business ethics and environmental stewardship have evolved into more powerful markers of corporate social responsibility and company sustainability reporting (both known as CSR). Universal guidelines have been developed and periodically updated and refined to promote increased operational transparency and to level informational reporting asymmetries. The demands and expectations of investors and other entities affected by a business's operations have served as a catalyst for the development and implementation of universally accepted standards to benchmark an organization's performance. These monitoring systems are used to measure ethical, social, and environmental performance—better known as the "triple bottom line," a form of business reporting that accounts not only for return on investment (the traditional reporting model) but also for environmental and social values. They also aid the potential investor in his or her investment decision making.

One such example of a voluntary reporting protocol—and the one most widely used internationally—is the Global Reporting Initiative (GRI) G3 Guidelines. These guidelines consist of an independent group of standards that offer a universal method of sustainability reporting. Businesses that present themselves to such scrutiny integrate their financial, environmental, and social performance

reports into a single publication available to the public for open review.

Evolution of GRI Reporting

GRI was first developed in 1997—partially in response to the 1989 Exxon Valdez offshore oil spill in Alaska—by the Boston-based Coalition for Environmentally Responsible Economies (CERES) and quickly evolved into a separate division (Buchanan, Herremans, and Westwood 2008). In 2002, the United Nations Environment Programme (UNEP) bolstered the international credibility of GRI, which incorporated as a nonprofit organization and relocated its headquarters to Amsterdam. Precipitated by multistakeholder input, numerous changes to GRI measurement standards resulted in the third version of the guidelines, or G3, launched in October 2006. Currently, GRI is regarded as one of the most adopted and well-recognized methods of sustainability reporting, and it has been implemented by more than 60 percent of the Global 1000 corporations; a plethora of nongovernmental organizations (NGOs), including the United Nations; and thousands of small and medium enterprises (SMEs).

The GRI Reporting System

The GRI reporting framework consists of guidelines or queries regarding the reporting entity's operations. These measurement standards have been developed through continuous interaction with individuals representing academe, business, industry, civic organizations, labor unions, and public and governmental offices emanating from over sixty countries.

The guidelines provide core content for organizations of all sizes, geographical locations, and types. They include several terms: *indicators* measures performance; *protocols* explain the methodologies of indicators; and *sector supplements* augment the guidelines by adding content unique to certain segments of a particular industry. More specifically, the indicators contain queries pertaining to how a company's operations affect economic, environmental, human rights, labor, product responsibility, and societal issues. The protocols support each indicator by providing definitions for key terms used by each indicator and explaining the indicator's intended scope. As the "recipe" for the indicators, the protocols reflect the way in which reporting should be addressed. Sector supplements basically provide a customized version of the reporting guidelines. Several examples of industries addressed by specific sector supplements include automotive, construction and real estate, electric utilities, logistics and media, NGOs, oil and gas, and telecommunications.

G3 reporting elements are grouped into categories of economic (EC), environmental (EN), and social responsibility (SR) factors. Each of these categories is then further subdivided into individual metrics identified as "Core," or essential components, and "Additional," or supplemental components. The designation of a letter rating from A to C depends upon the number of metrics addressed and the quality and correctness of the material provided. Essentially, the measurement metrics could be identified as *how* the report is presented (for example, its clarity, level of assurances, and timeliness); *what* the report should contain as outlined by GRI's economic, environmental, and social indicators; and *whom* the submitted material affects (a designation of that entity's stakeholders). Therefore, the desired reporting outcome is to relay the extent by which company practices have impacted the Earth, people, and economies. Comprehensive, transparent reporting allows the company to reassess its strategies, provide information affecting market relations, benchmark and/or demonstrate sustainable practices, and compare its performance with other reporting companies over time. The reporting organization may self-declare its report without further assessment, elect to be audited by internal GRI personnel, or employ the assurances services of a private third-party auditor.

In addition to letter ratings, GRI offers "pluses," with $A+$ ostensibly representing the ultimate rating of integrated performance. Juxtaposed to comprehensive CSR (qualitative reporting), it is less difficult to audit financial records since numbers (quantitative reporting) are less subject to multiple interpretations. These independent audits, also known as assurance reports, must be specifically requested by the reporting company when it determines its application level. If the company indicates in its report that a third party audit was conducted, that assurance report will typically accompany the company's submission. GRI will not examine the veracity of a third-party audit. Alternatively, the reporting entity may specifically request GRI (through its network of Directors, Secretariat team, and Technical Advisory Committee) to perform this assurance process. While GRI's assessment ensures that sample research on the company's standard disclosures has been conducted and that the guidelines were used appropriately, its conclusions do not measure the quality or value of the report's content. If an independent auditor is used, GRI only checks for the presence of an external assurance statement.

Shareholder vs. Stakeholder

At a time when businesses and governments are facing conflicts that far exceed acts of internal fraud or malfeasance, and as the domestic market continues to morph internationally, there has been a transfer of focus from the individual "shareholder" to the varied and multifaceted "stakeholder." GRI has recognized this transition: the identification of a company's stakeholders is critical in achieving the highest level of transparency in reporting. In current literature, the stakeholder has been defined to include "any individual or group who can affect or is affected by the actions, decisions, policies, practices, or goals of the organization" (Carroll and Bucholtz 2006, 67). Therefore, under this broadened term, the stakeholder would represent a company's other critical constituents, including its employee pool, union representatives, the media, political units, geographic areas affected by the presence of the product manufactured or service rendered, related markets, underdeveloped and developing countries, the larger ecosystem, and ostensibly the consumer. GRI has addressed each of these stakeholders in formulating its guidelines.

Shareholders, by common definition and historical development, have encompassed persons who invest in companies, acquiring tangible evidence of their respective investments—usually in the form of stock certificates—and who expect quick, favorable financial returns. With worldwide market symbiosis, the individual concern has had to defer to more defined collective consequences. With the realities of carbon dioxide emissions threatening the ecological balance and dangerously placing all life forms in serious peril, transparent reporting and comprehensive accountability have risen to the forefront in the search for remedial answers. Therefore, the manufacture of products and creation of services must now be measured against the effects and impact upon the

"stakeholder." GRI, through its G3 Guidelines, provides a comprehensive method of measuring such impact.

International Reporting Guidelines

The GRI sustainability guidelines are recognized as the most integrated framework for disclosure of a business's social and environmental performance, incorporating a broad range of performance metrics. Other social reporting systems include the ISO 14000 series (International Organization for Standardization), an internationally recognized environmental certification process regarded as more inclusive of all societal and environmental stakeholders that moves beyond mere compliance to developing policies of continuous improvement; ISEA Standard AA1000 (Institute of Social and Ethical Accountability), which focuses primarily on social and ethical accounting; the Copenhagen Charter, an international standard involving stakeholder communications and the commitment of key management figures to open dialogue with certain identifiable stakeholders; SAI 8000 (Social Accountability International), a system of accounting that concentrates primarily on the organization's labor practices; and EMAS (European Management Audit System), measurement indicators primarily targeted to European Union–based companies espousing environmental policies.

Inherent Deficiencies in Voluntary Reporting

Ostensibly, there will always be deficiencies in any type of reporting that involves any degree of subjectivity. And without mandatory reporting, how truly effective is reporting on a voluntary basis? Without a universal mandate for CSR, certain queries are inevitable. For instance, how truly comprehensive is a company's voluntary effort to reveal its strengths and deficiencies as well as define the overall ramifications of its business operations on its stakeholders? What are the organization's checks and balances and are they implemented on a temporary or permanent basis? What safeguards are in place to separate rhetoric from reality?

One would naturally expect there to be a certain amount of "greenwashing" and sugarcoating of facts within the report in order to lure the would-be investor and repel the investigating consumer advocate or inquiring politician. If the stakeholder is being given an increased role in dialoging with the reporting company, should not the stakeholder then participate in that business's development of its organizational scheme, its growth and business goals, and its particular mission? Reporting *to* or *about* nontraditional stakeholders would logically presuppose that

these interested parties are in continual discourse with the reporting entity.

Self-reporting assumes that the reporter is speaking the truth, and it is not always possible to confirm the substance of the information disseminated. It is usually a chief officer who selects the information to be released, material that might be technically correct but present a distorted image of the business's operations. Trade secrets—encompassing everything from a product recipe to a customer list—are given special exemption protection, but such absence of information may undercut the goal of comprehensive transparent and sustainability reporting.

While GRI identifies detailed reporting standards, it is still the prerogative of the reporting entity to define its particular stakeholders.

The Future of GRI

GRI is a dynamic organization, continuously responding to rapidly developing technologies and feedback for additional, modified, or deleted guideline queries to respond to the needs of business and its many stakeholders. Assurance reporting, guideline categorization, and digitalizing its reporting "language" are key examples of GRI's commitment to providing the best methods of comprehensive, transparent reporting.

Sector Supplements

As all industries cannot be adequately evaluated by a "one size fits all" set of metrics, GRI has created individual categories for certain types of businesses as mentioned previously, formulating indicators unique to such industries. GRI has determined that these sectors require specialized guidance to complement, not substitute for, the Guidelines.

Matchmaker Program

The GRI organization inaugurated a "matchmaker" program with the launching of the G3 protocol to offer institutions of higher learning an opportunity to become part of a three-tiered process of reporting, verification, and critique.

Business entities voluntarily submit information concerning their operations, nature, and composition of products produced, scope of business influence and dealings, and details of labor and management interaction (the reporting element). The information disseminated is then audited by an independent entity that is allowed access to the company for verification, follow-up, and substantiation of information provided (the audit/verification element). Finally, as an affirmation of the auditing process, an institution of higher learning is invited to review and assess the reports prepared by both entities (the critique element). The findings of all three organizations are then summarized and the company is then rated. This rating and the G3 Protocol conclusions are stored online with GRI, offering the public additional details regarding stakeholder effect.

Universal Labeling

In an attempt to uniformly segregate and identify the components, characteristics, and effects of a business's operations as well as to facilitate the electronic communication of business and financial reporting, GRI is participating in the development of "eXtensible (sic) Business Reporting Language" (XBRL) and moving toward global uniform reporting and the configuration of data in a digital format compatible with financial reporting requirements. This method of organization is accomplished by placing a "tag" on certain numbers and qualitative material that can be recognized by computers and downloaded, analyzed, and stored. This process essentially filters variables and labels, helping both investors to base decisions upon sustainability information and researchers to import desired information into their data systems. For example, "GHG" would represent greenhouse gases and alert the researcher or potential investor to that particular data. In this manner, a comprehensive taxonomy list may be developed for worldwide usage.

National Annexes

As specific regions and countries pose unique features, GRI is attempting to modify its guidelines to reflect how these differences might impact the reporting process. Cultural distinctions endemic to specific countries and regions often produce a different perspective as to how the reporting entity's operations impact their respective communities. In this manner, GRI faces the challenge of identifying and labeling these indicators of community impact and assessing compliance with suggested practices.

GRI has undoubtedly pioneered the world's most extensive and widely used sustainability reporting protocol. As the framework continues to respond to changing global dynamics, GRI strives to respond accordingly through its consensus-seeking process that draws in contributors globally, representing industry, governance, labor, and professional institutions. Acknowledging the flaws of trade secret protection and potentially inaccurate self-assessment, GRI remains committed to continuous improvement to effect the highest level of transparency in sustainability reporting.

Elizabeth F. R. GINGERICH
Valparaiso University College of Business Administration

See also in the *Berkshire Encyclopedia of Sustainability*: **Accounting; CSR and CSR 2.0; Ecolabeling; Equator Principles; Performance Metrics; Stakeholder Theory; Transparency; Triple Bottom Line**

FURTHER READING

Bartiromo, Maria. (2008, May 8). Bill Joy on going green, Google, Apple, and Microsoft. *BusinessWeek*, pp. 19–20. Retrieved September 29, 2009, from http://www.businessweek.com/magazine/content/08_20/b4084019471312.htm

Buchanan, Mark; Herremans, Irene; & Westwood, Joanne. (2008). Student engagement and sustainability reporting: The Global Reporting Initiative Matchmaker Program. Retrieved September 29, 2009, from http://www.globalreporting.org/NR/rdonlyres/C6864151-9DAC-4EC1-B8F9-96B7F8B7824C/0/GRIMatchmakerProgram_MarkBuchanan2008.pdf

Carroll, Archie B., & Bucholtz, Ann K. (2006). *Business and society: Ethics and stakeholder management* (6th ed.). Mason, OH: Thompson Southwestern Publishing.

Global Reporting Initiative. (2009). Retrieved September 29, 2009, from http://www.globalreporting.org

Habermas, Jürgen. (1990). *Moral consciousness and communicative action* (Christian Lenhardt & Shierry Weber Nicholsen, Trans.). Cambridge, MA: MIT Press. (Original work published 1983)

Ord, Gavan (2008). Major changes in the air. *Intheblack, 78*(2), 13.

Pulver, Simone. (2007). Making sense of corporate environmentalism. *Organization & Environment, 20*(1), 21–25.

Reynolds, MaryAnn, & Yuthas, Kristi. (2007). Moral discourse and corporate social responsibility reporting. *Journal of Business Ethics, 78*(1–2), 47–64.

Stern, Nicholas, (2007). *The economics of climate change: The Stern Review.* Cambridge, U.K.: Cambridge University Press.

XBRL could push sustainability reporting into the realm of the CFO. (2007, December 21). *The Environmental Leader.* Retrieved September 29, 2009, from http://www.environmentalleader.com/2007/12/21/xbrl-could-push-sustainability-reporting-into-the-realm-of-the-cfo/

Climate Change Disclosure

Publicly traded companies in the United States are required to disclose to the Securities and Exchange Commission any material information about how climate change and its consequences may affect their operations and financial results. Assessing the materiality of climate change and its consequences to a company is complicated because governmental policies and regulations (including proposed ones), court decisions, public expectations, and marketplace competition have all been evolving, with the pace accelerating in 2009.

As public attention to climate change continues to build and more climate change initiatives are proposed, businesses face a variety of challenges. One challenge faced by public companies is the need to assess how climate change and its consequences affect disclosures to investors. In the United States (the focus of this article), the rules of the Securities and Exchange Commission (SEC), the agency in charge of regulating the securities industry, govern a public company's disclosure obligations. (Private companies generally have no such disclosure obligations.) The SEC rules provide, among other disclosure requirements, that a public company divulge material risks and "known trends or uncertainties" that may be material to the company. Accordingly, a company must consider making disclosures about future matters even though their timing and impact may be uncertain. A company's consideration of climate change and its consequences is particularly complicated because this is a rapidly evolving and dynamic area. On 27 January 2010, the SEC approved an interpretive release confirming that the consequences of climate change, if material, are to be described in SEC filings and setting forth disclosure guidance to provide clarity and to enhance consistency of reporting.

The number of U.S. public companies including some level of climate change disclosure in their SEC reports has been increasing every year. As a result of the SEC's recent interpretive release and several 2009 developments, more companies will need to consider whether to begin including climate change disclosures in their SEC reports. Even those companies already making climate change disclosures will need to consider revising, and in some cases expanding, their disclosures. Some of the most notable developments in 2009 included:

- The U.S. House of Representatives passed the American Clean Energy and Security Act (also know as the Waxman-Markey bill), the first climate change legislation adopted by either house of Congress. Several climate change legislative alternatives are being discussed by various members of the Senate. President Obama's pledge of a provisional target to reduce greenhouse gas emissions by 2020 in the range of 17 percent below 2005 levels—made in advance of the December 2009 Copenhagen conference on climate change and confirmed pursuant to the Copenhagen Accord—should help to assure Senate attention to such legislation in 2010.
- The U.S. Environmental Protection Agency (EPA) initiated a number of significant actions in 2009. Three of the more significant were finalizing rules to require greenhouse gas reporting by large emitters beginning in 2010; proposing rules that would require permits for new facilities (or existing facilities undergoing major modifications) that emit over 25,000 tons of greenhouse gases annually; and the "endangerment finding" on 7 December 2009 under the Clean Air Act that greenhouse gas emissions endanger public health and welfare, which could possibly portend even broader greenhouse gas regulation by the EPA.

- On 27 October 2009, the SEC staff, in a reversal of its prior position, issued a bulletin that is expected to facilitate and encourage shareholder proposals to require that a company provide greater disclosure about its climate change risks. The timing of the staff's bulletin was intended to permit the inclusion of more of these shareholder proposals in proxy statements for the upcoming proxy season.
- Consumer-oriented companies continued their "green" announcements and publicity in 2009. Perhaps the most noteworthy was Walmart's announcement in July 2009 that it was requiring sustainability reports by its suppliers (over 100,000 globally) so that Walmart can begin developing sustainability ratings for its products.
- Significant court decisions were handed down in 2009 regarding greenhouse gas emissions, with the decision of the U.S. Court of Appeals for the Second Circuit in *State of Connecticut v. American Electric Power* receiving the most attention. The Second Circuit's decision, on 21 September 2009, was the first to find that the federal common law of public nuisance applied to claims to abate global warming. The court reinstated common law nuisance claims alleging that the emissions by the five power companies named as defendants had contributed to global warming, thereby injuring the defendants' infrastructure and low-lying properties. Shortly after the Second Circuit's decision was announced, the U.S. Court of Appeals for the Fifth Circuit arrived at a similar result in *Comer v. Murphy Oil USA*. The U.S. District Court for the Northern District of California, however, came to a different result in *Native Village of Kivalina & City of Kivalina v. ExxonMobil Corp. et al*. The District Court's decision was issued after *Connecticut* but before *Comer* and was expected to be appealed to the U.S. Court of Appeals for the Ninth Circuit.

As a result of these developments and in light of the SEC's recent interpretive release, public companies will need to consider how the evolving climate change landscape affects disclosure in their SEC filings. They will need to assess whether climate change and its consequences represent a risk, trend, or uncertainty that may be material to their finances and operations. Given the dynamic nature of this issue, this assessment will likely need to be conducted on a continuing basis. Companies will also need to consider whether they are making other public (but non-SEC) climate change disclosures, as many public companies increasingly are, and ensure that they are not selectively disclosing material climate change information in these other public venues without including such material information in SEC reports.

SEC Disclosure Requirements

The touchstone for determining whether disclosure is required under the SEC rules is materiality: whether or not there is a substantial likelihood that a reasonable investor would consider the information important in making his or her investment or voting decision (*TSC Industries v. Northway* 1976). The materiality of contingent or speculative events, such as proposed climate change legislation, is to be assessed by balancing the probability of an event occurring with its anticipated magnitude to the company (*Basic Inc. v. Levinson* 1988).

Key among the SEC's specific disclosure rules is the requirement that companies describe in their annual reports any known trends, uncertainties, or other factors that are reasonably likely to have a material effect on their business, earnings, or financial condition. This is intended to enable investors to view businesses through the eyes of management and thus increase the overall transparency of their reporting. SEC rules also require companies to disclose, if material, what effect compliance with environmental laws may have on their earnings, capital expenditures, and competitive position. According to SEC rules, companies must also disclose any material pending administrative or judicial proceeding to which they are, or may become, a party. In addition, any such proceeding arising under any federal, state, or local provisions regulating the discharge of materials into the environment must be described if it falls within certain parameters specified in the SEC rules.

Several groups (most prominently Ceres, an investor network) had petitioned the SEC in 2009 and earlier to provide more definitive guidelines regarding climate change disclosure. As noted before, the SEC approved an interpretive release on 27 January 2010 providing such disclosure guidance. In its interpretive release, the SEC highlighted the following areas as examples of where climate change and its consequences, if material to a company's business, may trigger disclosure requirements: the impact of existing and potential laws and regulations; the risks or effects of international accords and treaties relating to climate change; the indirect consequences of legal, technological, political and scientific developments regarding climate change that may create new opportunities or risks (e.g., increased or decreased demand for a company's product due to the greenhouse gas emissions associated with the product); and the actual and potential physical impacts of climate change on the company's business.

Disclosure Considerations

A corporation evaluating whether climate change disclosures are advisable will need to consider several general factors applicable to a broad range of companies, as well as factors more specific to the corporation's particular circumstances. Perhaps foremost among such factors is the increasing call for greater governmental action to counter climate change. This would include international actions that may result from negotiations for a successor to the Kyoto Protocol, as well as actions by individual countries or regions acting independently or in anticipation of, or pursuant to, any international agreements including the Copenhagen Accord.

For public companies that have their operations and sales based primarily in the United States, the prospect of federal legislation and its potential consequences will be a critical consideration in evaluating whether climate change disclosures are necessary. These potential consequences could include the regulation of greenhouse gas emissions; for energy-intensive companies that could mean higher fossil fuel costs. Similarly, such legislation could affect the availability and costs of raw materials. In addition, proposed legislation contains a number of mandates that go well beyond merely regulating greenhouse gas emissions at their sources. Pending legislation provides for building codes and appliance standards and contemplates a "renewable portfolio standard" that requires electric utilities to obtain a percentage of their electricity through renewable sources of energy, such as wind, solar, or biomass. The legislation is expected to have substantial implications for the agriculture sector due to its carbon offset and sequestration entitlements for agriculture and its effects on grain prices and energy and fertilizer costs.

In addition to prospective legislation, companies must consider various regulatory actions, such as those by the EPA. As noted, the EPA has adopted rules mandating the reporting of greenhouse gas emissions by certain companies and has proposed rules that would require construction and operating permits for new facilities (or facilities undergoing major modifications) that emit over 25,000 tons (approximately 22,680 metric tons) of greenhouse gases annually. These permits would require the use of the best available control technologies. Also, the EPA, together with the U.S. Transportation Department and the Obama administration's active involvement, finalized an accelerated increase in the corporate average fuel economy (CAFE) standards and imposed the first-ever greenhouse gas standard on cars and light-duty trucks in 2009.

Companies also will need to consider statutes and regulations in the states in which they operate. Before the aforementioned federal actions on climate change, a number of states (e.g., California, which has been particularly active) had adopted their own climate change measures. For example, six states and one region have adopted enforceable caps on greenhouse gases, twenty-nine states have renewable portfolio standards, and twenty-three states have adopted energy efficiency resource standards requiring that specific levels of energy savings be met by energy efficiency programs. The extent to which state measures may be eclipsed, preempted, or largely unaffected by federal action remains to be determined.

Companies will also need to consider climatic changes predicted for areas in which they operate. This might include the potential for more droughts in the southwestern United States, which would be particularly relevant to companies that rely heavily on water supplies. The threat of rising sea levels in coastal areas may be material depending on where a company's facilities are located and could include higher insurance premiums from areas deemed at high risk from hurricanes.

The nature of a company's industry, of course, is another key factor to be considered. For example, climate change is obviously an issue of critical importance to electric utilities and energy producers and to the insurance industry. Companies in retail industries have also highlighted their concerns about climate change. Recognizing the importance that many consumers give the issue, many companies have increasingly been promoting their "green" efforts. These companies include Walmart, Coca-Cola, Pepsi, Nike, Wells Fargo, HP, Dell, Yahoo, IBM, and Google. In September 2009, Apple announced the carbon footprints for its devices based on their full lifecycle impact, including during their use. Apple's approach was favorably contrasted by some with the more limited method of calculating carbon footprints by many of Apple's competitors, including HP and Dell, which were ranked number one and two, respectively, in *Newsweek*'s inaugural "Green Score" rankings of the 500 largest U.S. companies (McGinn 2009).

Many companies have begun to review the sustainability performance of their supply chains. Walmart announced in July 2009 that each of its more than 100,000 suppliers must provide reports regarding the sustainability of the supplier's products and its supply chain. Walmart plans to use this information to develop sustainability ratings for the products it sells. Their efforts are a continuation of efforts it began in 2007 to monitor the sustainability of its supply chain. Walmart's earlier effort led to the creation by the Carbon Disclosure Project (CDP) of the Supply Chain Leadership Collaboration (SCLC), currently comprised of twenty-eight "blue chip" companies such as Cadbury, Dell, HP, Imperial Tobacco, L'Oréal, Nestle, and PepsiCo.

The survey questions asked by Walmart suggest some of the areas to which its many suppliers, including those that are public companies, will need to give attention (Walmart 2009a). The first four of the fifteen questions are:

1. Have you measured your corporate greenhouse gas emissions?
2. Have you opted to report your greenhouse gas emissions to the Carbon Disclosure Project (CDP)?

3. What is your total annual greenhouse gas emissions reported in the most recent year measured?
4. Have you set publicly available greenhouse gas reduction targets? If yes, what are those targets?

Reporting to the CDP may have important implications for companies that begin such reporting and may also bear on their SEC reporting obligations. The CDP requests detailed information about greenhouse gas emissions and related matters. The CDP's questionnaire asks specific questions about the risks and opportunities to the reporting company that climate change presents. It requests a breakdown of, and the methodology for calculating, a company's Scope 1 emissions (direct emissions), Scope 2 emissions (indirect emissions from the consumption of purchased electricity, heat, or steam), and Scope 3 emissions (other indirect emissions, including those due to employee business travel). The questionnaire asks for greenhouse gas and energy reduction plans and targets and also inquires about greenhouse gas emissions avoided, emission intensity, energy use, and carbon trading. If the company is a supplier it must also provide additional specified information intended to assist its customers in estimating the extent to which the supplier's Scope 1 and 2 emissions are linked with the services and goods it provides to its customers.

In addition, the CDP questionnaire asks that a company describe its "governance practices" for sustainability. Specifically the CDP's questionnaire asks what board or executive committee has overall responsibility for the company's decision making on climate change; whether individual employee efforts are assessed or incented; and how the company communicates its climate change risks/opportunities and sustainability efforts.

In addition, a company reporting to the CDP should be aware of how such reports may potentially reflect on its competitive position. On 24 September 2009, the CDP announced that reporting would be available online and that upgraded reporting software would facilitate comparisons between competitors on sustainability performance. Such comparisons could be relevant in several ways. Exelon, the gas and electric utility, is quoted in CDP's 2009 Supply Chain Report, for example, as stating: "All other things being equal, a greener supplier would be given preference" (CDP 2009d, 4).

Any company reporting to the CDP will have to make sure it is not selectively disclosing material information about climate change and its consequences without disclosing the same information in its SEC reports. This same concern about "selective disclosure" can arise from information on a company's website, in its marketing or press materials, reports to investors and analysts, or participation in surveys. If such public disclosures in non-SEC venues are considered to be material, their omission in the company's SEC filings would highlight defects in these filings and possibly violate regulations prohibiting selective disclosure.

In evaluating disclosure obligations, companies need to consider a number of factors, such as whether climate change and its consequences present opportunities. This would be true for companies involved in "cleantech" ("green" technology), energy efficiency, energy transmission, and sustainable construction. In some instances, superior sustainability performance may provide a competitive advantage.

Outlook

The legislative and regulatory landscape related to climate change is changing and has begun to accelerate at a rapid pace. In addition, an increasing number of climate change initiatives are being undertaken by many organizations and corporations. Public companies in the United States will need to assess climate change disclosures against this backdrop while being mindful of the following:

- remaining compliant with federal and state disclosure laws and regulations
- managing current, and in many cases adopting new, disclosure controls and procedures to ensure they remain well positioned to comply with future disclosure obligations
- addressing the climate change interests and expectations of investors
- managing customer and supplier relationships in regard to climate change matters
- maintaining a corporate image consistent with their business strategies and core values
- ensuring that business opportunities arising from climate change are identified, appropriately communicated, and, to the extent required, adequately disclosed

Steve RHYNE
K&L Gates LLP

This article is adapted from an e-alert entitled "Climate Change Disclosure for U.S. Public Companies" (December 2009) and a white paper entitled "Climate Change: A Mounting Disclosure Risk?" (February 2009), each commissioned by the law firm K&L Gates. The firm wishes to make it known that "this publication is for informational purposes only and does not contain or convey legal advice. The information herein should not be used or relied upon in regard to any particular facts or circumstances without first consulting with a lawyer."

See also in the *Berkshire Encyclopedia of Sustainability*: **Accounting; Cap-and-Trade Legislation; Ecosystem Services; Financial Services Industry; Transparency**

FURTHER READING

American Clean Energy and Security Act of 2009 (Engrossed as Agreed to or Passed by House), H.R. 2454 [EH], 111th Cong. (2009). Retrieved November 3, 2009, from http://thomas.loc.gov/cgi-bin/query?z?c111:H.R.2454:

Apple Inc. (2009). Apple and the environment. Retrieved November 3, 2009, from http://www.apple.com/environment/

California Public Employees' Retirement System, et al. (2009, November 23). Supplemental petition for interpretive guidance on climate risk disclosure [Petition to the U.S. Securities and Exchange Commission]. Retrieved December 15, 2009, from http://www.sec.gov/rules/petitions/2009/petn4-547-supp.pdf

Carbon Disclosure Project (CDP). (2009a). Retrieved November 3, 2009, from https://www.cdproject.net/

Carbon Disclosure Project. (2009b). CDP 2009 (CDP7) information request. Retrieved November 3, 2009, from https://www.cdproject.net/CDP%20Questionaire%20Documents/CDP7_2009_Questionnaire.pdf

Carbon Disclosure Project (2009c). CDP 2009 information request (with supplier module). Retrieved November 3, 2009, from https://www.cdproject.net/CDP%20Questionaire%20Documents/CDP_2009_Supplier.pdf

Carbon Disclosure Project (2009d). Supply chain report 2009. Retrieved November 3, 2009, from https://www.cdproject.net/CDPResults/65_329_201_CDP-Supply-Chain-Report_2009.pdf

Clean Energy Jobs and American Power Act (introduced in Senate), S.1733 [IS], 111th Cong. (2009). Retrieved November 3, 2009, from http://thomas.loc.gov/cgi-bin/query?z?c111:S.1733:

Dutzik, Tony, et al. (2009). *America on the move: State leadership in the fight against global warming, and what it means for the world*. Retrieved December 14, 2009, from http://cdn.publicinterestnetwork.org/assets/6a1e91dbfae141e88e1cacd49bb6a1fe/America-on-the-Move.pdf

Greenhouse Gas Protocol Initiative. (2009). FAQ. Retrieved November 3, 2009, from http://www.ghgprotocol.org/calculation-tools/faq#high_6

Investor Network on Climate Risk. (2009, June 12). [Letter to the U.S. Securities and Exchange Commission]. Retrieved December 15, 2009, from http://www.ceres.org/Document.Doc?id=478

K&L Gates LLP. (2009a). Climate change disclosure for U.S. public companies. Retrieved December 15, 2009, from http://www.climatelawreport.com/2009/12/articles/topic-alerts/climate-change-disclosure-for-us-public-companies/

K&L Gates LLP. (2009b). Emissions of greenhouse gases & global warming—regulation through litigation? Who is liable for damages arising from global warming? Retrieved November 3, 2009, from http://www.klgates.com/newsstand/Detail.aspx?publication=5991

K&L Gates LLP. (2009c). Greenhouse gas emission control: BACT to the future. Retrieved December 14, 2009, from http://www.climatelawreport.com/2009/12/articles/topic-alerts/greenhouse-gas-emission-control-bact-to-the-future/

K&L Gates LLP. (2009d). Mandatory reporting scheme for U.S. Retrieved November 3, 2009, from http://www.klgates.com/newsstand/Detail.aspx?publication=5971

McGinn, Daniel. (2009, September 21). The greenest big companies in America. *Newsweek*. Retrieved November 3, 2009, from http://www.newsweek.com/id/215577

Regional Greenhouse Gas Initiative. (2009). Retrieved September 8, 2009, from http://www.rggi.org/home

Regulation FD, 17 C.F.R. § 243. (2009). Regulation for fair disclosure. Retrieved November 3, 2009, from http://www.law.uc.edu/CCL/regFD/index.html

Regulation S-K—Description of Business, 17 C.F.R. § 229.101. (2009). Standard instructions for filing forms under the Securities Act of 1933, Securities Exchange Act of 1934, and Energy Policy Act of 1975. Retrieved November 3, 2009, from http://www.law.uc.edu/CCL/regS-K/SK101.html

Regulation S-K—Legal Proceedings, 17 C.F.R. § 229.103. (2009). Standard instructions for filing forms under the Securities Act of 1933, Securities Exchange Act of 1934, and Energy Policy Act of 1975. Retrieved November 3, 2009, from http://www.law.uc.edu/CCL/regS-K/SK103.html

Regulation S-K— Management's Discussion and Analysis of Financial Condition and Results of Operations, 17 C.F.R. § 229.303. (2009). Standard instructions for filing forms under the Securities Act of 1933, Securities Exchange Act of 1934, and Energy Policy Act of 1975. Retrieved November 3, 2009, from http://www.law.uc.edu/CCL/regS-K/SK303.html

Rhyne, Stephen K.; Jones, Sean M.; Wyche, James R.; Rhue, Julia R. (2009). Climate change: A mounting disclosure risk?. Retrieved October 16, 2009, from http://www.klgates.com/files/Publication/23667169-8000-4e22-b350-0317d2b3b9b1/Presentation/PublicationAttachment/a1b94ed4-d8ec-40b4-9860-11664359c5fa/Climate_Change_White_Paper.pdf

United States Environmental Protection Agency. (2009). Climate change—state and local governments: State planning and measurement. Retrieved September 8, 2009, from http://epa.gov/climatechange/wycd/stateandlocalgov/state_planning.html#four

U.S. Securities and Exchange Commission. (2005). Shareholder proposals: Staff legal bulletin no. 14C (CF). Retrieved November 3, 2009, from http://www.sec.gov/interps/legal/cfslb14c.htm

U.S. Securities and Exchange Commission (2010). Commission Guidance Regarding Disclosure Related to Climate Change (CF). Retrieved February 2, 2010 from http://www.sec.gov/rules/interp/2010/33-9106.pdf

U.S. Securities and Exchange Commission. (2009). Shareholder proposals: Staff legal bulletin no. 14E (CF). Retrieved November 3, 2009, from http://www.sec.gov/interps/legal/cfslb14e.htm

Walmart. (2009a). Sustainability product index: 15 questions for suppliers. Retrieved November 3, 2009, from http://walmartstores.com/download/3863.pdf

Walmart. (2009b). Walmart announces sustainable product index. Retrieved November 3, 2009, from http://walmartstores.com/FactsNews/NewsRoom/9277.aspx

Walter, Elisse B. (2009). SEC Rulemaking—"Advancing the Law" to protect investors [Speech by SEC commissioner October 2, 2009]. Retrieved November 3, 2009, from http://www.sec.gov/news/speech/2009/spch100209ebw.htm

Basic Inc. v. Levinson, 485 U.S. 224, 238. (1988). Retrieved November 3, 2009, from http://openjurist.org/485/us/224/basic-incorporated-v-l-levinson

Chiarella v. United States, 445 U.S. 222, 235. (1980). Retrieved November 3, 2009, from http://openjurist.org/445/us/222

Comer v. Murphy Oil USA, No. 07–60756, 2009 WL 3321493 (2009). Retrieved November 3, 2009, from http://www.ca5.uscourts.gov/opinions/pub/07/07-60756-CV0.wpd.pdf

Native Village of Kivalina & City of Kivalina v. ExxonMobil Corp. et al., No. C08-1138, 2009 WL 3326113 (2009).

State of Connecticut v. American Elec. Power Co., Inc. and *Open Space Inst., Inc. v. American Elec. Power Co., Inc.*, Nos. 05-5104-CV and 05-5119-CV, 2009 WL 2996729 (2009). Retrieved November 3, 2009, from http://www.ca2.uscourts.gov/decisions/isysquery/c666f8c7-e550-4739-95b0-2cd8b3172172/1/doc/05-5104-cv_opn.pdf#xml=http://www.ca2.uscourts.gov/decisions/isysquery/c666f8c7-e550-4739-95b0-2cd8b3172172/1/hilite/

TSC Industries v. Northway, 426 U.S. 438, 439. (1976). Retrieved November 3, 2009, from http://openjurist.org/426/us/438

Energy Subsidies

Government-funded energy subsidies are used around the world to help expand access to energy sources and increase energy production. Almost all energy sources have received subsidies at some point. Energy subsidies play, and will continue to play, a major role in global energy policies for both sustainable and traditional resources.

Energy subsidies have long been used to help promote, support, and expand access to energy sources. The producers and consumers of virtually every type of energy source, from fossil fuels to renewable and sustainable resources, have received subsidies. This is true for more traditional sources, such as hydropower, coal, oil, and gas, as well as for newer or emerging sources, such as nuclear, biomass, wind, and solar energy.

Subsidy programs have been a part of most government energy policies used to expand access to energy, and such subsidies are likely to play a significant role in expanding access to sustainable energy sources as well. These subsidies vary depending on location, motivation, and political ideology.

Types of Energy Subsidies

There are four primary types of energy subsidies. These government-funded programs can take many forms, but typically take one of the following forms: (1) direct spending, (2) tax reduction, (3) support for research and development (R&D), and (4) government-run programs facilitating access.

Direct Spending

Direct spending programs are programs through which the government provides payments directly to either consumers or producers of energy. These payments can be payments for the production of a certain amount of the supported resource or payments directly to consumers.

One example of a direct subsidy is a targeted program such as the Low Income Home Energy Assistance Program (LIHEAP). LIHEAP is a federal program in the United States designed to help low-income households with their energy bills, primarily by supporting immediate energy needs.

Direct subsidies could also be part of regulatory programs or taxes designed to improve the environment or combat climate change. As some recent legislative proposals have suggested, proceeds from a cap-and-trade program or a carbon tax could be used to fund subsidies for renewable and sustainable energy projects.

Tax Reductions

Tax reduction programs can take the forms of tax deductions (reducing taxable income upon which taxes are calculated) and tax credits (reducing an overall tax obligation). The reductions can be linked to energy production or investment in energy infrastructure.

Production Tax Credits

One common energy subsidy takes the form of a production tax credit (PTC). This credit is calculated by multiplying the credit amount (e.g., 2.1 cents per kilowatt hour) by the amount of power generated (e.g., 80 kilowatt hours). The PTC is paid each year for the duration of the specified credit period, which varies by law and often by the type of energy produced. A PTC usually has restrictions on who can receive the generated power, such as a requirement that the generated power be sold to an unaffiliated purchaser. Finally, because the PTC is used to support developing or (relatively) costly energy sources, most PTCs will have a price cap that gradually phases out the credit as the price of the generated power increases.

Investment Tax Credit

Another often used renewable and sustainable energy subsidy is the investment tax credit (ITC). Rather than basing the credit on energy production, an ITC is based on the cost of the renewable or sustainable energy facility or the property costs for such a facility. Eligible facilities are determined by statute, and often include projects with high start-up costs, such as geothermal technologies, solar projects, and nonutility-scale wind projects. ITCs provide a credit for a certain percentage of the project costs; the credit is typically vested over a certain time frame (e.g., an ITC of 30 percent of the project could be captured by the developer at 20 percent of the credit per year).

Consumer Energy Credits and Tax-Free Grants

Consumer-side grants and credits can also be used to promote sustainable energy practices. These subsidies can take the form of tax credits, which reduce the amount of tax owed dollar for dollar, or tax deductions, which provide for a certain percentage reduction of the tax owed. Examples of consumer-side tax credits or deductions include home energy efficiency credits (e.g., replacing windows), residential renewable energy credits (e.g., solar water heaters), and credits for renewable or alternative fuel vehicles. Finally, some governments use tax-free grants to promote energy efficiency and sustainable energy practices. Canada, for example, provides up to $5,000 in tax-free grants for residents who undergo an energy efficiency audit before renovating.

Research and Development

Research and development (R&D) subsidies are often used to increase energy supplies and to improve energy production efficiencies and technologies. Such subsidies are not expenditures that necessarily impact energy production or prices, but when the subsidies lead to useful technologies and processes they can impact future prices and rates of production.

R&D subsidies often take the form of government-sponsored grants that are used to help reduce or otherwise offset the initial risks related to developing or installing new technologies. In addition, R&D subsidies can be used to fund test projects for promising, but unproven, technologies or sites. Such grants are often part of a public–private partnership, where the governmental subsidy is matched with funds from other interested parties. As an example,

a recent program funded through the U.S. Department of Energy offered $338 million in government grant money for geothermal research and development, and private and other nonfederal sources provided additional funds exceeding that amount.

Government-Run Programs Facilitating Access

Government programs increasing access to energy are often programs targeted at specific regions. Such subsidy programs may provide government-funded programs that bring large amounts of electricity to market in the targeted region. These subsidy programs may also indirectly subsidize portions of the electricity industry through loans and loan guarantees to facilitate the construction of infrastructure necessary to make energy accessible.

Virtually all governments are providing subsidies to increase access to and the availability of energy. A good example of an early program is the success of the United States' Rural Electrification Act (REA), which provided the long-term financing and technical expertise needed to expand the availability of electricity to rural customers. In 1963, President John F. Kennedy explained that, since the passage of the REA in 1936, more than nine hundred cooperative rural electrification systems were built with the assistance offered by government-subsidized financing.

The REA's financial undertaking and related risk were enormous, thus necessitating subsidization. The program provided more than $5 billion to approximately 1,000 borrowers, facilitating construction of more than 1.5 million miles of power lines that, in the 1960s, served 20 million American people. In the end, the investment was remarkably sound. As of 1963, there was only one reported delinquent payment of those approximately 1,000 borrowers. The total expected losses on the $5 billion of financial assistance provided were less than $50,000. This low level of default is particularly striking in today's global financial environment.

Few investors were willing to invest in the rural electrification project without federal subsidization in the form of financing; the success of the project, however, was overwhelming. As an example, in 1963, North Dakota–based REA-funded cooperatives served an average of about one metered farm per mile of line, compared to the average urban-area utility system of thirty-three electric meters per mile of line, thus serving an amazing 97 percent of the state's population.

Regardless of the financing concerns, the subsidies were justified because it was believed that the REA raised the standard of living, strengthened the U.S. economy, and improved national security by providing the power necessary to increase industrial activity. President Kennedy

(1964) explained the effects of the government subsidy to electrify rural America: "What was 30 years ago a life of affluence, in a sense today is a life of poverty."

The current need for energy and infrastructure subsidies in emerging markets is similarly essential to the need found in prior years in the United States. Subsidies in these emerging markets—including China, India, and major parts of Africa—are expected to be substantial, as access to basic energy sources becomes a reality for millions of people currently lacking significant, if any, access to electricity. These subsidies could potentially promote sustainable energy sources, but that is by no means a foregone conclusion. In the United States, the REA subsidies promoted increased access to energy of all sources, but especially fossil fuel sources. In fact, today more than 90 percent of North Dakota's power still comes from coal-fired electricity generators.

That same infrastructure, however, can be used to move renewable-sourced electricity, if desired. As such, all over the United States the infrastructure subsidized to promote access electricity could be used to help promote access to renewable and sustainable energy sources.

The Role of Subsidies in Energy Policy

Although the type and extensiveness of government intervention varies widely, most governments use energy subsidies as some portion of their overall energy policy. These subsidies were traditionally used to support energy production and development, increase access to energy, and improve economic output. Many developed countries still provide subsidies for coal and natural gas extraction, and petroleum consumption is still subsidized in some of the major oil-exporting nations.

Today's subsidies often target the same goals, but the use of subsidies has evolved to include environmental goals and provide incentives for sustainable energy development. In pursuit of sustainable energy markets, many governments use subsidies and mandates to promote the use of sustainable energy sources. These subsidies have led to criticisms that renewable-sourced energy is being unfairly subsidized and promoted, even though more traditional forms of energy are less expensive (Ralls 2006, 452). Such criticisms ignore the fact that many traditional energy sources have costs that are not fully internalized, thus making them appear cheap, when, in fact, such sources are quite costly. That is, some costs of traditional sources, such as air pollution or carbon dioxide emissions that could cause global warming, are not part of the cost of consumption. These costs are often not added to—or internalized—the overall costs by consumers of fossil fuels.

Many who complain about renewable or sustainable energy subsidies argue that a "freer" market would provide more efficient markets and facilitate proper incentives for renewable and sustainable sources that are viable (Boaz 2005, 446). Removing renewable incentives in the name of free markets, however, means that all incentives related to energy sources should be eliminated. Only then can one really appreciate what "the market" actually wants. Arguing to reduce or eliminate subsidies for renewable energy sources is essentially a market-based argument cloaked in a source-based argument (e.g., a preference for fossil fuels over renewable sources). A true free-market argument recognizes that subsidies for traditional fuels are rampant as well, and would ask for a repeal of all such subsidies.

The incentives for traditional, nonrenewable fuel energy still outweigh renewable industry incentives in many places. Some argue that the idea that subsidies for conventional energy far outweigh those for renewable energy is somewhat misleading. That is, they argue

that the amount of subsidies received per megawatt hour to support fossil fuels is significantly less than the subsidies received to support renewable energy (Lieberman 2010, 3). These subsidies can indicate different things, however, depending upon how one looks at the issue.

Most calculations of subsidies per source do not consider the full range of energy subsidies and their impact on markets, for example, ignoring the negative externalities flowing from some of the fossil fuel energy sources receiving subsidies. More specifically, using a per-unit comparison—considering a strict per-megawatt-hour amount of subsidies—does not look at the total market impact. As an example, a government loan to a small car company might amount to $5,000 per auto produced, while a similar loan to a major automaker might amount to only $2,000 per auto produced. The loan to the small automaker could be millions of dollars, while the loan to the large automaker would be a bailout worth billions of dollars. Thus, the per-auto number would not accurately reflect the actual market impact of the subsidies.

Recent U.S. energy subsidies provide another good example. According to an Energy Information Administration (EIA) report, federal energy-specific subsidies and support to all forms of energy were estimated at $16.6 billion for fiscal year (FY) 2007. These EIA numbers for energy subsidies per megawatt hour (MWH) of energy break down as follows:

- Coal: $0.44/MWH
- Natural gas: $0.25/MWH
- Nuclear: $1.59/MWH
- Hydroelectric: $0.67/MWH
- Solar: $24.34/MWH
- Wind: $23.37/MWH

There is no doubt that changes in the distribution of subsidies by fuel type between 1999 and 2007 indicate a U.S. governmental redirection of priorities and a greater support for renewable energy subsidies, a redirection paralleled in many parts of the world. In the United States, subsidies for renewables increased to 29 percent of total subsidies and support in 2007, up from 17 percent in 1999. In total dollars, this means that renewables accounted for $4.875 billion of the $16.581 billion in total 2007 energy subsidies. This means that $11.706 billion went to energy projects not related to renewable energy (EIA 2008, xii).

As such, it can be argued that the total dollars spent on traditional energy resources provide a greater market distortion than dollars spent on renewables. Thus the overall impact of dollars spent on traditional U.S. fuel subsidies is greater than—more than twice—that spent on renewables. Providing subsidies for traditional fuel sources continues, even though companies that provide such sources

are often well-established businesses that have (or should have) sound business models and methods. When such subsidies are used, the expectation is that more of whatever is being subsidized will result. Thus, subsidies for renewables should lead to more renewables, and subsidies for fossil fuels, however small, will also lead to more fossil fuels than would occur without the subsidies. This subsidization of fossil fuels serves to limit the effectiveness and slows the development of subsidies for sustainable energy sources, because the full benefit for sustainable sources is being offset by the support of more traditional energy sources.

Renewable energy sources account for a small percentage of total energy globally, as well as in the United States (7 percent in the United States for 2008), but that number is growing rapidly (EIA 2008, xii). If the stated goal is to produce more renewable energy, one option is to subsidize the cost. As a comparison, in the United States, the federal government subsidized nuclear power, and the investments (at least arguably) paid off. Those subsidy dollars spent in the 1950s are not reflected in today's subsidy costs, so nuclear power may appear significantly cheaper now than it is from a total cost perspective. Again, the nonsubsidy-related cleanup costs in places like Hanford, Washington—where nuclear waste has required billions of dollars of remediation efforts—have caused significant financial costs not usually added into today's costs.

The Future

Energy subsidies play, and will continue to play, a major role in global energy policies. There are significant tensions between the competing goals of current subsidies. Continuing subsidies for traditional fossil fuel sources serves to impede the progress of sustainable development, yet it may be essential for providing near-term access to energy for developing nations. Subsidies for renewable and sustainable sources provide incentives and opportunities for more environmentally friendly resources, yet misplaced incentives may improperly support resources that are not, and never will be, economically viable, thus impeding progress for other more promising sustainable energy sources.

There are some indications that the goals of sustainable development and economic development are becoming more possible. Countries, such as China, that have been reluctant to commit to sustainable practices and emissions reductions because of the potential negative impact on economic growth have nonetheless provided massive government subsidies to promote renewable energy manufacturing. Subsidies for renewable and sustainable energy will likely continue to increase as sustainable development becomes more obviously linked to economic development.

Energy subsidies for all energy sources are likely to be the norm for the foreseeable future.

Joshua P. FERSHEE
University of North Dakota School of Law

See also in the *Berkshire Encyclopedia of Sustainability*: **Climate Change Disclosure—Legal Framework; Climate Change Mitigation; Development, Sustainable—Overview of Laws and Commissions; Energy Conservation Incentives; Energy Security; Free Trade; Green Taxes; Investment Law, Energy; Utilities Regulation**

FURTHER READING

Boaz, David. (Ed.). (2005). *Cato handbook on policy*. Washington, DC: Cato Institute.

Cooper, Christopher, & Sovacool, Benjamin K. (2007). Renewing America: The case for federal leadership on a national renewable portfolio standard (RPS). Retrieved September 2, 2010, from http://www.newenergychoices.org/dev/uploads/RPS%20Report_Cooper_Sovacool_FINAL_HILL.pdf

Energy Information Administration (EIA). (2008). Federal financial interventions and subsidies in energy markets 2007. Retrieved September 2, 2010, from http://www.eia.doe.gov/oiaf/servicerpt/subsidy2/index.html

Fershee, Joshua P. (2008). Changing resources, changing market: The impact of a national renewable portfolio standard on the U.S. energy industry. *Energy Law Journal, 29*, 49–77.

Fershee, Joshua P. (2009). Atomic power, fossil fuels, and the environment: Lessons learned and the lasting impact of the Kennedy energy policies. *Texas Environmental Law Journal, 39*, 131–146.

Fershee, Joshua P. (2009). The geothermal bonus: Sustainable energy as a by-product of drilling for oil. *North Dakota Law Review, 85*(4), 893–905.

Kennedy, John F. (1964). Address at the University of North Dakota, 25 September 1963. In *Public papers of the presidents of the United States:*
John F. Kennedy, 1963 (pp. 715–719). Washington, DC: United States Government Printing Office.

Koplow, Douglas. (1996). Energy subsidies and the environment. In *Subsidies and environment: Exploring the linkages* (pp. 201–18). Paris: Organisation for Economic Co-operation and Development (OECD).

Kosmo, Mark. (1987). Money to burn? The high costs of energy subsidies. *World Resources Institute*. Retrieved October 6, 2010, from http://pdf.wri.org/moneytoburn_bw.pdf

Lieberman, Ben. (2010). Is wind the next ethanol? Retrieved November 5, 2010, from http://cei.org/sites/default/files/Ben%20Lieberman%20-%20Is%20Wind%20the%20Next%20Ethanol_0.pdf

Mann, Roberta F. (2009). Back to the future: Recommendations and predictions for greener tax policy. *Oregon Law Review, 88*(2), 355–404.

Mann, Roberta F., & Rowe, Meg. (forthcoming 2010). Taxation. In Michael B. Gerrard (Ed.), *The law of clean energy: Efficiency and renewables*. Chicago: ABA Publishing.

Ralls, Mary Ann. (2006). Congress got it right: There's no need to mandate renewable portfolio standards. *Energy Law Journal, 27*, 451–472.

Rural Electrification Act of 1936. (1936, May 20). Chap. 432, Title I, § 1, 49 Stat. 1363. (Current version at 7 U.S.C. § 901 [2006].)

Spence, David B. (2010). The political barriers to a national RPS. *Connecticut Law Review, 42*(5), 1451–1473.

Union of Concerned Scientists. (2009). Production tax credit for renewable energy. Retrieved September 19, 2010, from http://www.ucsusa.org/clean_energy/solutions/big_picture_solutions/production-tax-credit-for.html

Vandenbergh, Michael P.; Ackerly, Brooke A.; & Forster, Fred E. (2009). Micro-offsets and macro-transformation: An inconvenient view of climate change justice. *Harvard Environmental Law Review, 33*(2), 303–348.

von Moltke, Anja; McKee, Colin; & Morgan, Trevor (Eds.). (2004). *Energy subsidies: Lessons learned in assessing their impact and designing policy reforms*. Sheffield, U.K.: United Nations Environment Programme (UNEP) & Greenleaf Publishing.

Green Taxes

Green taxes increase the financial burden associated with activities that cause harm to the environment, providing incentive to reduce pollution. A government levies green taxes on products that create pollution, using the revenue either to address the environmental problem or for other purposes. Another way governments can continue to green the tax code is by offering tax benefits for activities that protect the environment.

People usually think about government regulations when they consider how society can protect the environment. Regulations, such as preventing the use of ozone-depleting chemicals or limiting discharges into water bodies, can help to reduce pollution by preventing businesses and people from engaging in polluting activities.

Green taxes provide a different approach to reducing pollution. They increase the price of environmentally damaging activities by imposing a tax on the harmful activity or product. This price signal should cause people to take damage to the environment into account as they make their economic decisions. Like other taxes, green taxes generate revenue for the government, but they are different from other taxes because their linkage to an environmental problem makes them "green."

Which taxes qualify as green taxes has been a question of some debate. How "green" must a tax be to qualify as a green tax? The Organisation for Economic Co-operation and Development (OECD), the International Energy Agency, and the European Commission use the term *environmentally related taxes*. They look at whether the commodity being taxed (the tax base) is related to an environmental problem. Their useful definition describes environmentally related taxes as

> any compulsory, unrequited payment to general government levied on tax-bases deemed to be of particular

environmental relevance. The relevant tax-bases include energy products, motor vehicles, waste, measured or estimated emissions, natural resources, etc. Taxes are unrequited in the sense that benefits provided by government to taxpayers are not normally in proportion to their payments. (OECD 2006, 26)

The concept of an unrequited payment distinguishes taxes from fees. A person paying a tax does not expect to receive any particular service in return. By contrast, a person paying a fee for waste removal, for example, does expect the government to provide a service in return. Consequently, a green tax is a payment linked just to the fact that the activity will have some impact on the environment. People occasionally will use the term *green fees* to describe these payments, even though the measure is technically a tax.

Other names have also been used to describe green taxes, such as environmental taxes, ecotaxes, Pigouvian taxes, and environmental levies. One name may be more politically attractive than another depending on the point in time, geographic area, or audience, and they may have different nuances in meaning. They all, however, share the fact that the tax is imposed on something that is related to a particular environmental problem. Carbon taxes are one type of green tax. This article uses *green taxes* as a general term referring to environmentally related taxes as defined above.

Green-Tax Theory

The theory of green taxes dates back to the publication (in 1920) of *The Economics of Welfare*, by the British economist Alfred C. Pigou (1877–1959). In his book Pigou suggested that society's economic welfare would be enhanced if industries had to look beyond their private-sector profit and make business decisions based on the effects (and the costs) of their activities on the public sector. Taxes on industry, he proposed, would be a way to build those costs right in to the private sector's decision-making process.

Pigou was not thinking exclusively about the costs of environmental damage, but his concept laid the foundation for green taxes when the environmental movement in the United States and Europe gained momentum in the 1960s and 1970s. Economists started thinking about "environmental externalities," the environmental costs imposed on society by our daily activities, and ways to "internalize" those costs, including through taxes. Pigou's theory assumed a new life, and academic literature now often refers to green taxes as Pigouvian taxes.

Green taxes are also associated with the polluter pays principle, first adopted by the OECD in the early 1970s and included in the international Rio Declaration on Environment and Development in 1992. The polluter pays principle places the cost of pollution or pollution prevention on the polluter, rather than society.

As green-tax theory developed, another economic principle came into play as well—the idea that using taxes rather than regulation could achieve environmental protection at a lower cost to society. Under this "least cost abatement" theory, economists compared command-and-control regulations with green taxes. They reasoned that regulations requiring all parties to engage in the same degree of pollution reduction were less economically efficient than taxes that allowed people to decide whether it was more economically efficient to lower the level of pollution (and avoid paying the tax) or to pay the tax. For example, a factory that could easily reduce or eliminate its emissions would do so, while a factory that would have to buy expensive pollution-control equipment would not. If the tax was set at the right level, overall pollution levels would fall at less cost than if all factories were required to install the same equipment.

Thus green taxes are conceptually based in large part on the idea of economic efficiency. By building environmental costs into decision making, the private sector can decide how to most efficiently reduce pollution. As a result, green taxes are often referred to as market-based instruments. Unlike regulations, which impose specific requirements, they send a price signal that affects decision making in the marketplace. Green taxes are not the only market-based instruments. As discussed in the section on carbon taxes, permit-trading systems are also market-based instruments.

Green-Tax Design

The mere mention of taxes often inspires images of the accountant with the green eyeshade and causes readers to quickly close the book. In their essence, however, green taxes are quite simple. They involve a very straightforward formula:

$$\text{Tax Base} \times \text{Tax Rate} = \text{Tax Revenue}$$

First, one must identify a commodity related to the environmental problem (the tax base). Then one decides how much to tax each unit of that commodity (the tax rate). Applying the tax to each unit will generate money for the government (tax revenue), and government will decide how to use that revenue. It may use the money to try to solve the environmental problem or use it for unrelated purposes.

The design of green taxes can involve interesting twists that adjust this basic formula, such as whether to allow exemptions for certain types of activities or whether to increase the tax rate over time, augmenting the incentive to avoid pollution and adapting to inflation. Stripped down to its essentials, however, the basic formula is intriguingly simple and can be applied to a wide variety of situations.

Green Taxes in Practice

Because each country has the freedom to decide whether to use green taxes and determine the extent of their reach, it is challenging to present a global view of green taxes. The OECD and European Environment Agency (EEA) have compiled an electronic database of the environmentally related taxes used in fifty-nine countries, which offers a very useful source of information about the level of activity in different governments (OECD and EEA 2010). This section briefly summarizes the extent to which countries are using green taxes and highlights several green taxes as examples, but readers will find more information on environmentally related taxes, fees, and charges in the OECD/EEA database.

In the thirty-one countries that are members of the OECD, revenue from environmentally related taxes in 2008 ranged from 2.92 percent of total tax revenue in the United States to 9.44 percent in Denmark. The weighted average for all thirty-one countries was 5.25 percent (OECD and EEA 2010). The taxes address a range of types of environmental problems—air and water pollution, climate change, waste management, natural-resource management, noise, and more. The following examples offer an indication of how they operate.

Gasoline Taxes

Taxes on motor fuels, most notably gasoline, are significant environmentally related taxes in many countries. Using gasoline to power vehicles results in a number of environmental problems: for example, it generates carbon dioxide that contributes to climate change, and nitrogen oxide and volatile organic compounds that add to smog.

Countries tax unleaded gasoline at different rates. The OECD/EEA database analyzed tax rates in the OECD countries in 2009, calculating the cost of the tax (measured in euro cents) imposed on one liter of fuel in each country. The federal and state taxes in the United States and Canada were 7.9 euro cents and 15.2 euro cents per liter, respectively, while taxes in European countries were much higher. Iceland had the lowest tax of any European country at 36.4 euro cents and Turkey the highest at 88 euro cents. In other examples, France taxed at a rate of 60.7 euro cents, Germany at 65.5 euro cents, and the United Kingdom at 63.1 euro cents. Thus, the taxes in Europe are roughly five to ten times higher than taxes in the United States. In the Pacific region, Australia taxed fuels at 21.4 euro cents, while Japan used the higher rate of 41.4 euro cents (OECD and EEA 2010).

Most taxes on motor fuels did not start as green taxes but rather served as a useful source of revenue for the government to maintain the highway system and for other general purposes. Nevertheless, today they are environmentally related taxes because the tax base—the motor fuels—is relevant to the environment. The increase in the price of gasoline can encourage less driving, the use of mass transit, and the purchase of more fuel-efficient vehicles.

Countries may use some of the revenue from gas taxes to help address environmental problems. For example, in the United States, federal taxes on gasoline are dedicated to the Highway Trust Fund, which funds the national highway system but also helps finance mass transportation and other measures that reduce environmental problems associated with driving. In addition, the federal government imposes a tax of 8 cents (in U.S. dollars) on each barrel of oil produced in or imported into the United States to help the government respond to oil spills (U.S. IRC 1986, section 4611).

There also are other ways in which green taxes can address the problems of transportation. For example, taxes at the time of purchase can take into account the fuel efficiency of a vehicle, as can annual registration fees. The United States has placed a tax on the purchase of "gas-guzzler" cars since 1978, but the tax predates the era of sport-utility vehicles (SUVs) and has never been updated to apply to SUVs. London and other cities are using congestion fees to discourage people from driving their cars into urban areas and to encourage the use of public transportation and bicycles.

Sulfur Taxes

The problems associated with fossil fuels are not limited to the transportation sector. When fossil fuels containing sulfur are burned to generate electricity or for other purposes, they may produce sulfur dioxide that is harmful to air quality. Some countries impose a tax on the sulfur content of the fuel. Since 1996, Denmark has placed a tax on fossil fuels at a rate of 2.7 euros per kilogram of sulfur (Speck 2008, 44). Although President Nixon proposed a tax on sulfur dioxide in 1972, the United States has instead approached the problem of sulfur dioxide emissions from power plants and transportation by regulating the levels of sulfur dioxide emissions and the sulfur content in diesel fuels.

Pesticide Taxes

Some countries have taxed pesticides to reduce their use. For example, in 1986 Denmark adopted a tax designed to reduce the use of pesticides by 50 percent over the next ten years, a goal that it realized with a 47 percent reduction by 1997. It subsequently increased the amount of tax and used the extra revenue for measures that could further reduce pesticide use and encourage organic farming (Andersen, Dengsoee, and Pederson 2001, 71–73).

Plastic Bag Taxes

In 2002, Ireland fueled an international trend when it imposed a tax of 15 euro cents on plastic shopping bags, which increased to 22 cents in 2007. Customers at retail stores must pay the tax if they leave the store with new plastic bags; this encourages them to bring their own bags (Revenue Ireland 2010). The use of plastic bags dropped by 95 percent (Cadman, Evans, Holland, and Boyd 2005, 7).

Hazardous Waste Taxes

Realizing that industrial activities were contaminating land with hazardous waste, the U.S. government passed a law in 1980—the Comprehensive Environmental Response, Compensation, and Liability Act, or CERCLA—that held the polluters liable for cleaning up the land. As part of the law, it also imposed a tax on certain hazardous chemicals and a tax on corporate income, helping to finance the so-called Superfund, a fund the government could use to clean the site if the parties responsible for the pollution could not be located. In this case, the green taxes were not high enough to actively discourage pollution, but the revenue helped the government address the environmental problem.

Water-Withdrawal Taxes

Green taxes can not only put a price on pollution, but also recognize the value of limited natural resources, such as water. In 1964, France adopted a system of water fees that charged for pollution and imposed a charge for abstracting water (Tuddenham 1995, 204). Some states in Germany have imposed a tax on the withdrawal of water from groundwater and surface water bodies, starting with a tax adopted by Baden-Württemberg in 1988 (Kraemer 1995, 231).

Climate Change and Carbon Taxes

A major environmental issue facing the world in the twenty-first century is climate change. Climate change is caused by the emission of greenhouse gases into the atmosphere. The gases create a "greenhouse effect" that captures heat in the Earth's atmosphere, causing disruptions in climatic patterns. Carbon dioxide released from the combustion of fossil fuels, which have significant carbon content, accounts for 57 percent of global greenhouse gas emissions (Stern 2006, 195). Consequently, societies need to determine how to reduce their reliance on fossil fuels. Attaching a price to fossil fuels' carbon dioxide emissions is one key way to reduce greenhouse gas emissions in the long term. Carbon taxes can achieve this result.

What Is a Carbon Tax?

A carbon tax is a tax on the carbon content of fossil fuels, which include coal, oil, gasoline, and natural gas. The ideal tax base would be the actual carbon dioxide emissions that result from burning the fuel, but that tax base would be hard to administer. How would one count the emissions coming from the tailpipe of each car running on gasoline? The carbon in fossil fuels, however, usually is released into the atmosphere when it is burned. Gasoline going into a car or coal feeding a power plant will each generate a predictable level of emissions, based on the carbon content of the fuel. Consequently, the actual carbon content of the fuel before combustion can predict the carbon dioxide emissions and serve as a sound and convenient way to calculate emissions.

A carbon tax, therefore, is usually based on each ton of carbon content in fossil fuels or the presumed carbon dioxide emissions attributable to that content. For example, it might impose a tax of thirty dollars per ton of carbon dioxide attributable to carbon in coal that was sold to a coal-fired power plant, or thirty dollars per ton of carbon dioxide attributable to carbon in gasoline that will be distributed to gas stations and used by cars.

A carbon tax will fall heaviest on coal, which is the most carbon-intensive fossil fuel, and lightest on natural gas, which is the least carbon intensive. As a result, it will tend to discourage the use of coal and encourage shifts to lower-carbon fossil fuels and alternatives to fossil fuels, such as renewable energy. The effectiveness of the tax will depend on how high the tax rate is—how much the tax increases the price. A higher tax rate will encourage a stronger behavioral response. A carbon tax could be expanded to include other greenhouse gases.

A carbon tax is different from a gas tax even though they both apply to fossil fuels. A carbon tax applies to each ton of carbon content in a fuel, tying the tax directly to the environmental problem of carbon dioxide emissions. A traditional gas tax is based on the volume of gasoline, such as a gallon in the United States or a liter in Europe, so drivers in the United States, as of mid-summer 2010, pay a federal tax of 18.4 cents per gallon (U.S. IRC 1986, section 4081). Taxing the volume of the fuel can increase the price and cause people to think about energy conservation. The linkage to environmental problems exists, making the gas tax an "environmentally related tax," but for climate change purposes, the linkage is a bit less direct than a carbon tax.

Increasing the cost of fossil fuels may also affect a country's competitive position. For example, if oil manufacturers or producers in other countries do not have to pay a similar carbon tax, they can produce goods more cheaply and potentially undercut their competition. To avoid this problem, a carbon tax can be imposed on fossil fuels, and products made with fossil fuels, entering the country. This "border-tax adjustment" will put imported products on an equal footing with domestic products after they cross the border and come into the country.

A significant tax increase on fossil fuels, which currently are often essential to everyday life, can also pose hardships for lower-income people. They will have to pay more for basics, such as home-heating oil and driving to work, until society finds new sources of energy and affordable alternative technologies. As a result, special measures may be needed to avoid hardships, such as special tax relief and government programs that help low-income homeowners improve the energy efficiency of their homes. As a new tax, a carbon tax will generate new revenue that the government might use for these purposes.

Carbon Taxes in Practice

Several examples of existing carbon taxes illustrate their features. The Canadian province of British Columbia adopted a carbon tax in 2008. The tax is quite simple and straightforward. It applies to fossil fuels burned within the province, which account for almost 70 percent of the province's greenhouse gas emissions. The tax started at a rate of ten Canadian dollars per ton of carbon dioxide emissions and increases by five dollars per year until it reaches thirty dollars in 2012. Revenue from the tax allowed the government to provide tax relief to individuals and businesses, including low-income households (Duff 2008, 95–97).

Denmark has had a carbon tax in place since 1992, which works side-by-side with its energy tax and sulfur tax on fossil fuels. It now applies to fossil fuels used in the household, service, and industrial sectors, but not in the transportation sector, which is covered by other energy taxes. The carbon-tax component of the Danish system is currently set at a rate of twelve euros per ton of carbon dioxide. Industries, however, may pay varying lower levels of tax depending on how they are using the fossil fuels and whether they have entered into voluntary agreements to increase their energy efficiency. Denmark has used the revenue to reduce taxes on labor and to invest in energy saving (Speck 2008, 44–47).

Sweden also has a long history of using carbon taxes. As part of a tax-reform effort to reduce income taxes, it adopted a carbon tax in 1991. The carbon tax started at forty-three euros per ton of carbon dioxide. Indexed for inflation since 1995, the tax rate rose 106 euros per ton of carbon dioxide in 2008. This tax on nontransportation fossil fuels works in combination with a longstanding energy tax, a sulfur tax enacted in 1991, and a nitrogen oxide charge enacted in 1992 that apply to the same fuels. The design details of the carbon tax provide some relief for industry (Speck 2008, 50–52).

These European examples illustrate the relationship between carbon taxes and other taxes that may apply to the same fuels. Traditional taxes on energy, such as the gas tax, were designed primarily to generate revenue. While carbon taxes also generate revenue, they focus on the specific environmental problem of climate change. Sulfur taxes target the environmental problems caused by sulfur emissions. They serve different purposes, but policy makers will think about their relative and combined tax burdens.

A recent study of carbon and energy taxes, combined with other tax reforms, in the Nordic countries and Germany found that greenhouse gas emissions fell 4–6 percent between the mid-1990s and 2004. Sweden and Finland experienced the largest reductions, and Sweden is projected to achieve up to a 7 percent reduction in the years leading to 2012 (Andersen and Ekins 2009, 262–263).

Double-Dividend Theory

One of the theories used to support carbon taxes is that they can generate a "double dividend." A carbon tax of any significance can provide an environmental dividend by reducing greenhouse gas emissions. A carbon tax also will generate substantial revenue for the government, given the pervasiveness of fossil fuels. Using that revenue to reduce taxes that may be hindering the economy, such as income taxes or social security taxes, may provide a second dividend—a stronger economy with higher employment or gross domestic product. The result is a revenue-neutral shifting of tax burdens rather than a net increase in taxes. This is sometimes described quite simply as a way of "taxing bads, not goods."

The idea of a revenue-neutral tax shift, often called "environmental tax reform," fueled European countries' interest in carbon and energy taxes in the 1990s. While imposing carbon taxes alone could have had a detrimental effect to the economy, the combination of taxes and fossil fuels with tax relief for income and social security taxes in six European countries generally is having a positive effect on gross national product and employment (Barker, Junankar, Pollitt, and Summerton 2009, 183–184).

Carbon Tax versus Cap-and-Trade

Carbon taxes are not the only way to attach a price to carbon emissions. "Cap-and-trade" is another market-based approach that has become popular, and national and international debates are occurring about which approach, or combination of approaches, is best.

Under cap-and-trade, the government sets a regulatory limit on the total level of permissible carbon dioxide (or other greenhouse gas) emissions. It does not regulate individual polluters, but it requires polluters to obtain an allowance or permit for each unit of emissions, such as one allowance for each ton of carbon dioxide emitted during the year. The government issues only the number of allowances that will permit emissions up to the regulatory limit (the cap) for the country as a whole. Polluters have the choice of reducing their pollution or finding an allowance that will allow them to continue their emissions. Hence, the government sets a cap, and allowances are traded to companies that generate pollution, generating the term *cap-and-trade*.

The cap-and-trade approach is not limited to greenhouse gas emissions. It has been used in the United States to control other pollutants, such as sulfur dioxide from coal-fired power plants that contributed to acid rain.

Both carbon taxes and cap-and-trade systems attach a price to carbon dioxide emissions, but in different ways. Under a carbon tax, the tax rate sets the price for carbon dioxide emissions. Under cap-and-trade, the trading price on the market sets the price for allowances for carbon dioxide emissions. As a result, a carbon tax provides a fixed price but cannot precisely predict the level of carbon dioxide emissions, while cap-and-trade sets a fixed level of emissions but does not offer a stable price.

The debate about whether to use carbon taxes or cap-and-trade has focused in large part on the trade-offs of having a fixed price versus having a fixed quantity of emissions. A number of economists have argued in favor of a fixed price. People also argue that carbon taxes are simpler to administer and avoid the risks and costs of creating new trading markets. Political and institutional considerations, however, can enter the picture as well. For example, the European Union cannot adopt a continent-wide tax, such as a carbon tax, without unanimous consent of its member countries. It instead has adopted a trading system for industrial carbon dioxide emissions called the European Union Emissions Trading Scheme, which will be expanded to cover aviation emissions. The federal government in the United States has debated cap-and-trade proposals, but has not taken any action. China reportedly is considering a carbon tax.

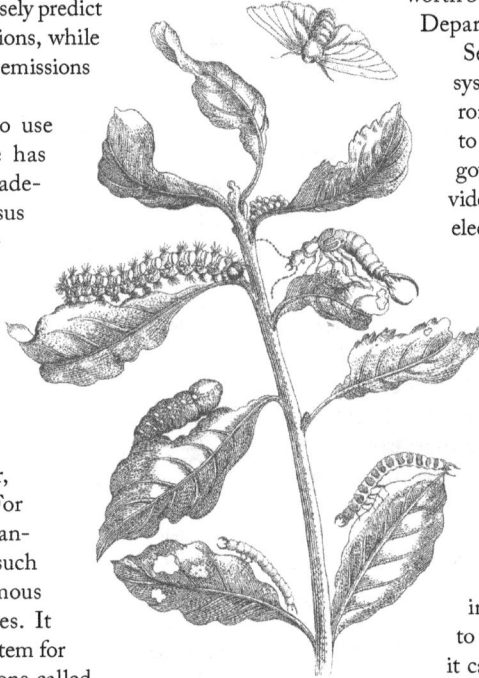

Greening the Tax Code

Green taxes are based on the idea that the price of products and activities should include some or all of the cost of the environmental damage they cause. There are two other ways in which the tax system can adjust prices in ways that will help the environment.

First, government can repeal existing tax benefits that encourage polluting activities and products. Taking away these benefits in effect will increase the price of pollution and prevent the government from being in a position where it aids the activities it wants to prevent. At a summit of the G20 in September 2009, world leaders agreed

to phase out and rationalize over the medium term inefficient fossil fuel subsidies. . . . Inefficient fossil fuel subsidies encourage wasteful consumption, reduce our energy security, impede investment in clean energy sources and undermine efforts to deal with the threat of climate change. (Pittsburgh Summit 2009, 3)

Consistent with that call, U.S. President Barack Obama's proposed budget for fiscal year 2011 proposed repealing tax subsidies for fossil-fuel production worth 39 billion dollars over ten years (U.S. Department of Treasury 2010, 151).

Second, government can use the tax system to deliver tax benefits for environmentally positive activities it wants to encourage. For example, the federal government in the United States provides tax benefits for the production of electricity from renewable sources, such as wind, and landowners' donations of conservation easements that permanently protect land—just two of numerous environmentally oriented tax benefits.

In sum, the tax system can serve as a price-delivery mechanism. Through green taxes, it can raise the price of environmentally damaging activities. By repealing subsidies for harmful activities, it can help level the playing field. By providing tax benefits to environmentally positive activities, it can lower their price and encourage their use.

Green Taxes in the Long Term

Since the 1970s, interest in greening the tax code has increased significantly. Market-based approaches are now part of the common parlance as people think about how to protect the environment. Market-based approaches, including taxes, rarely stand alone as the only solution to an environmental problem. Government may also use regulations, public education, spending programs, labeling programs, and other measures to address different facets of the problem. People are increasingly aware, nevertheless, of the potential to use price-based mechanisms to try to influence behavior.

Increased use of green taxes will mean that the traditional governmental taxing agencies, such as the U.S. Internal Revenue Service, will become more involved in environmental protection, and the traditional environmental agencies, such as the U.S. Environmental Protection Agency, will become more familiar with tax measures. Similarly, environmental advocates need to understand tax principles. As a hybrid environmental-tax approach, green taxes and green-tax incentives cross the traditional boundaries of power and thinking. Government officials and scholars thus need to study the actual effectiveness of green taxes to ensure that they are achieving their goal of environmental protection. Measuring the real-world effectiveness is not easy, but it is essential.

A key question for the future of green taxes is whether countries will adopt carbon taxes or trading programs to address climate change, some combination of the two, or look for other means to reduce reliance on fossil fuels. Widespread use of carbon taxes would represent a significant development in the history of green taxes, but even without that step, many opportunities will remain to use green taxes to reduce pollution and the overuse of resources.

Janet E. MILNE
Vermont Law School

See also in the *Berkshire Encyclopedia of Sustainability*: **Climate Change Disclosure—Legal Framework; Climate Change Mitigation; Copenhagen Climate Change Conference 2009; Energy Conservation Incentives; Energy Subsidies; Environmental Law—Europe; Environmental Law—United States and Canada; Natural Resources Law; Polluter Pays Principle; Utilities Regulation**

FURTHER READING

Andersen, Mikael S. (1994). *Governance by green taxes: Making pollution prevention pay*. Manchester, U.K.: Manchester University Press.

Andersen, Mikael S.; Dengsoee, Niels; & Pedersen, Anders B. (2001). *An evaluation of the impact of green taxes in the Nordic countries*. Copenhagen: Nordic Council of Ministers.

Andersen, Mikael S., & Ekins, Paul. (2009). *Carbon energy taxation: Lessons from Europe*. Oxford, U.K.: Oxford University Press.

Andersen, Mikael S., & Sprenger, Rolf-Ulrich. (2000). *Market-based instruments for environmental management: Politics and institutions*. Cheltenham, U.K.: Edward Elgar Publishing.

Barker, Terry; Junankar, Sudhir; Pollitt, Hector; & Summerton, Philip. (2009). The effects of environmental tax reform on international competitiveness in the European Union: Modelling with E3ME. In Mikael S. Andersen & Paul Ekins (Eds.), *Carbon energy taxation: Lessons from Europe* (pp. 147–214). Oxford, U.K.: Oxford University Press.

Baumol, William J., & Oates, Wallace E. (1988). *The theory of environmental policy* (2nd ed.). Cambridge, U.K.: Cambridge University Press.

Cadman, James; Evans, Suzanne; Holland, Mike; & Boyd, Richard. (2005). *Proposed plastic bag levy—Extended impact assessment* (Environment Group Research Report 2005/06). Edinburgh, U.K.: Scottish Executive.

Duff, David. (2008). Carbon taxation in British Columbia. *Vermont Law Review, 10*, 85–105.

Durning, Alan T., & Bauman, Yoram. (1998). *Tax shift*. Seattle, WA: Northwest Environment Watch.

European Environment Agency (EEA). (2006). *Using the market for cost-effective environmental policy: Market-based instruments in Europe*. Copenhagen: Author.

Gale, Robert; Barg, Stephen; & Gillies, Alexander. (Eds.). (1995). *Green budget reform: An international casebook of leading practices*. London: Earthscan.

Kraemer, R. Andreas. (1995). Water resource taxes in Germany. In Robert Gale, Stephen Barg & Alexander Gillies (Eds.), *Green budget reform: An international casebook of leading practices* (pp. 231–241). London: Earthscan.

Määttä, Kalle. (2006). *Environmental taxes: An introductory analysis*. Cheltenham, U.K.: Edward Elgar Publishing.

Milne, Janet E. (2003). Environmental taxation: Why theory matters. In Janet E. Milne, Kurt Deketelaere, Larry Kreiser & Hope Ashiabor (Eds.), *Critical issues in environmental taxation: International and comparative perspectives* (Vol. I, pp. 3–26). Richmond, U.K.: Richmond Law & Tax.

Milne, Janet E. & Andersen, Mikael S. (forthcoming). *Handbook of research on environmental taxation*. Cheltenham, U.K.: Edward Elgar Publishing.

Milne, Janet; Ashiabor, Hope; Kreiser, Larry; & Deketelaere, Kurt. (Eds.). (2006–2010). *Critical issues in environmental taxation* (Vols. I–VIII). Oxford, U.K.: Oxford University Press.

Muller, Adrian, & Sterner, Thomas. (Eds.). (2006). *Environmental taxation in practice*. Aldershot, U.K.: Ashgate.

Organisation for Economic Co-operation and Development (OECD). (1995). *Environmental taxes in the OECD Countries*. Paris: OECD.

Organisation for Economic Co-operation and Development (OECD). (1996). *Implementation strategies for environmental taxes*. Paris: OECD.

Organisation for Economic Co-operation and Development (OECD). (2001). *Environmentally related taxes in OECD countries: Issues and strategies*. Paris: OECD.

Organisation for Economic Co-operation and Development (OECD). (2006). *The political economy of environmentally related taxes*. Paris: OECD.

Organisation for Economic Co-operation and Development (OECD) & European Environment Agency (EEA). (2010). Database on instruments used for environmental policy and natural resources management. Retrieved June 10, 2010, from http://www2.oecd.org/ecoinst/queries/index.htm

Pigou, Arthur C. (1920). *The economics of welfare*. London: Macmillan.

The Pittsburgh Summit. (2009). Leader's statement: The Pittsburgh Summit. Retrieved November 15, 2009, from http://www.pittsburghsummit.gov/mediacenter/129639.htm

Revenue Ireland. (2010). Environmental levy on plastic bags. Retrieved June 8, 2010, from www.revenue.ie/en/tax/env-levy/environmental-levy-plastic-bags.html

Snape, John, & de Souza, Jeremy. (2006). *Environmental taxation law: Policy, contexts and practice*. Aldershot, U.K.: Ashgate.

Speck, Stefan. (2008). The design of carbon and broad-based energy taxes in European countries. *Vermont Law Review, 10*, 31–59.

Stern, Nicholas. (2006). *The economics of climate change: The Stern review*. Cambridge, U.K.: Cambridge University Press.

Surrey, Stanley. (1973). *Pathways to tax reform*. Cambridge, MA: Harvard University Press.

Tuddenham, Mark. (1995). The system of water charges in France. In Robert Gale, Stephen Barg & Alexander Gillies (Eds.), *Green budget reform: An international casebook of leading practices* (pp. 200–219). London: Earthscan.

U.S. Department of Treasury. (2010, February). General explanations of the administration's fiscal year 2011 revenue proposals. Washington, DC: Department of the Treasury.

U.S. Internal Revenue Code of 1986 (IRC), 26 U.S.C. Title 26.

Weizsäcker, Ernst U. von, & Jesinghaus, Jochen. (1992). *Ecological tax reform: A policy proposal for sustainable development*. London: Zed Books.

Investment Law, Energy

Countries worldwide have sovereignty over their natural resources and may develop them according to their own environmental laws and regulations. International law recognizes the need for modern investment treaties—such as the North American Free Trade Agreement and the Energy Charter Treaty—that include provisions affecting the energy industry and its sustainability. Assessing how such treaties will impact the foreign investment climate in participating states remains a challenge for the future.

It is widely accepted that foreign investment is critical for sustainable development, and more so with respect to the oil and gas industry, a capital-intensive industry with a long gestation period (Elder 1991; Ginther, Denters, and de Waart 1995; Vale Columbia Centre and WAIPA 2010). Although international law recognizes national sovereignty over natural resources, international law places limitations on the exercise of such sovereign rights in a situation where it causes harm to other states or when it is pursued in an unsustainable manner (Cameron 2010). Consequently, the emergence of sustainability laws has had an impact on worldwide energy investments (Sands 1995).

The development and use of oil, gas, and nuclear energy are subject to specific international regulation. Other sources of energy—coal and renewable sources such as wind, solar, and geothermal—are scarcely regulated by international instruments. Because the effects of their operations are thought to be confined within national borders, they constitute an insignificant percentage of the global energy mix, and/or they cause relatively less damage to the environment as to attract much international attention. The development and use of oil, gas, and nuclear energy pose more serious environmental, health, social, and cultural consequences; they may result in oil spills, pollution and degradation of the environment, displacement of local communities, or accidents (Smith and RMMLF 2010; Park 2002; Gao 1998; Horbach 1999).

The North American Free Trade Agreement (NAFTA) and the Energy Charter Treaty (ECT), two multilateral trade and investment treaties, have direct relevance to the energy sector and how it might be developed in a sustainable manner. Other relevant international instruments include the Law of the Sea Convention 1982, Climate Change Convention 1992, the Convention on Biodiversity 1992, the United Nations Framework Convention on Climate Change (UNFCC) 1997, the Kyoto Protocol 1997, and the increasing network of bilateral investment treaties (Cameron 2010; Vandevelde 2010). This article focuses only on NAFTA and the Energy Charter Treaty because, generally speaking, the key provisions on investment in both treaties are similar to those contained in most other investment treaties, and, more specifically, both contain explicit provisions on sustainability. Additionally, the ECT deals exclusively with the energy sector, and NAFTA contains a chapter on energy.

Historical Background and Objectives

After fourteen months of negotiations, the leaders of the United States, Canada, and Mexico signed NAFTA on 7 October 1992, and the treaty came into effect on 1 January 1994. NAFTA was built upon the Canada-United States Free Trade Agreement of 1989. Before NAFTA came into effect, however, a Supplementary Agreement was reached in August 1993, upon the insistence of President Clinton, to address concerns over protection of the environment and workers' rights, neither of which were sufficiently addressed in the original NAFTA. The

Supplemental Agreement is a comprehensive trade and investment agreement that affects all aspects of doing business in Canada, Mexico, and the United States. It seeks to eliminate barriers (such as tariffs) to the free flow of goods and services, removes restrictions to investment, and strengthens intellectual property rights among the three countries. It was envisaged by the contracting states as an effort toward establishing a free trade area in the North American continent (similar to the European Union and the European Free Trade area) so as to enhance the competitiveness of the region in global trade and investment (Smith and Cluchey 1994). For the Canadian government, the main objectives for signing NAFTA were to get Canadian goods, services, and capital access to Mexico on an equal footing with the United States, and to make Canada attractive to foreign investors wishing to invest in the North American market (Saunders 1994). From the United States' perspective, NAFTA would help provide closer and more stable sources of energy supplies from Canada and Mexico and reduce its over reliance on the more unstable Middle Eastern oil (Smith and Cluchey 1994).

The ECT is the result of a political initiative in Europe in the early 1990s following the end of the Cold War and the disintegration of the Soviet Union. The then Dutch prime minister initiated the process by suggesting the creation of a European energy community and urged the development of the European Energy Charter, a nonbinding political declaration signed in The Hague in 1991 by fifty-six states, including the European Community and Australia, where ratification is still in progress. The Charter "represents a political commitment to cooperate in the energy sector, based on the principles of development of open and efficient energy markets" (Corell 2005). The participants to the Charter did acknowledge the need for a binding international legal framework for effective cooperation in the sector, and so negotiations for the ECT started in late 1991.

The ECT and the Protocol on Energy Efficiency and Related Environmental Aspects (PEEREA) were signed in Lisbon on 17 December 1994 and came into force on 16 April 1998. Although the United States and Canada participated in the negotiations, they did not sign the treaty. As the name suggests, the ECT is a sectoral agreement; it deals solely with the energy industry and covers issues of trade, investment, transit, and environment.

The main goals of the initial negotiation parties were to help the Eastern European countries transition to market economies by injecting Western investment into their energy sector, which would help in ensuring security of energy supplies to western Europe. In this regard, the ECT "plays an important role as part of an international effort to build a legal foundation for energy security, based on the principles of open, competitive markets and sustainable development" (Energy Charter Secretariat n.d.). For the Eastern European and resource countries, "the main attraction of the treaty was to appear attractive, to be seen to play the rules of the global economy, reduce their political risk perception and not to be left out of possibly significant energy policy dialogue" (Wälde 2004). Overall, the "fundamental aim of the ECT is to strengthen the rule of law on energy issues by creating a level playing field of rules to be observed by all participating governments, thereby mitigating risks associated with energy-related investment and trade" (Energy Charter Secretariat n.d.). To date, the ECT has been signed by fifty-four members while twenty-four countries act as observers.

Energy Investment

With regard to energy, NAFTA Article 602 states that the agreement "applies to measures relating to energy and basic

petrochemical goods originating in the territories of the Parties and to measures relating to investment and to the cross-border trade in services associated with such goods." With respect to the Mexican energy sector, NAFTA falls short of achieving the objective of creating a common energy market and the liberalization of the sector. Due to historical and constitutional reasons, limitations are placed on foreign involvement in Mexico's energy sector, and these policies are reflected in NAFTA. Chapter 6, Annex 602.3, reserves to the Mexican state or its state entities all activities relating to exploration and exploitation of oil and gas, ownership and operation of pipelines, all foreign trade, transportation, storage, and distribution of Mexican crude oil and natural gas. Thus, NAFTA may have less impact on energy trade and investment in Mexico than it does in the United States and Canada, which "are bound to permit the free flow of energy goods and investments and of services throughout the energy sector" in accordance with the agreement (Herman 1997). This has the effect of constraining the ability of future Canadian governments from reverting to the old nationalistic and protectionist energy policy of the 1980s as reflected in the National Energy Programme of 1980 (Saunders 1994). Even with regard to Mexico, there are possibilities for foreign investment in the nonbasic petrochemicals and certain aspects of electricity generation sectors, which are not subject to the constitutional restriction on investment (Saunders 1994). Energy investment under NAFTA chapter 6 is reinforced by chapter 11, which is the most important chapter because it defines the rights and obligations of investors and the state parties. Similar to other investment treaties, including the ECT (Part III, Articles 10–17), NAFTA chapter 11 provides for a definition of protected "investment" and "investors," and the standard of treatment to be accorded such investments and investors from other member states. The standards of treatment include national and most-favored-nation treatment, fair and equitable treatment, full protection, and security. Other provisions that address more specific situations include conditions on expropriation of covered investment, guarantees on rights of free transfer of payments related to an investment, prohibition on performance requirements, and provisions intended to promote transparency or access to courts. These substantive provisions are backed by investor-state or state-state dispute resolution provisions. The first provision vests in the foreign investor a direct action (through international arbitration) against the host state for alleged violation of the investor's substantive rights, and the second includes a dispute settlement mechanism between the two state parties concerning the interpretation or application of the treaty (Vandevelde 2010; Konoplyanik and Wälde 2006). Over the years, several cases have been brought by foreign investors seeking to challenge measures adopted by host states that were alleged to not conform to their international investment treaty obligations under the applicable treaty (Vandevelde 2010; Salacuse 2010).

Sustainable Development

Both NAFTA and the ECT contain provisions on sustainability. In its preamble, the NAFTA state parties signal their support to promote sustainable development. In order to achieve this objective, the treaty permits each contracting state to take appropriate measures to ensure that investment activity in its territories is implemented in a manner consistent with environmental protection, provided such measures are consistent with the overall objectives of NAFTA. Furthermore, as specified by Article 1114(2), "it is inappropriate to encourage investment by relaxing domestic health, safety, or environmental measures."

In addition, the NAFTA Side Agreement on Environmental Cooperation provides for sanctions for lax enforcement of domestic environmental laws and standards. The provisions are to ensure that trade and investment activities in the member states' territories are conducted in a sustainable manner by preventing a "race to the bottom" approach by member states. Thus the Side Agreement (Article 1) expresses the willingness of the parties to promote certain conditions:

- sustainable development based on cooperation and mutually supportive environmental and economic policies
- enhanced compliance with and enforcement of environmental requirements
- transparency and public participation in developing environmental norms
- economically effective environmental measures

Under the Side Agreement, members of the public, including nongovernmental organizations (NGOs), are allowed to challenge a state party if it fails to effectively enforce its environmental laws or regulations. The Side Agreement establishes the Commission for Environmental Cooperation (CEC), the institutional framework to receive petitions from members of the public and, if necessary, investigate the claims and prepare a factual record, which might be published by the Council. (The Council is the CEC's governing body, composed of high-level environmental authorities from Canada, Mexico, and the United States.) The process has been utilized by many individuals and organizations with varying degrees of success. Hence, it has been described as a "'spotlighting' instrument intended to enhance governmental accountability and transparency" (Markell 2010; Knox 2010).

Similarly, Article 19 of the ECT enjoins member states to "strive to take precautionary measures to prevent or minimize environmental degradation" and to "take account of environmental considerations throughout the formulation and implementation of their energy policies." The treaty also requires that the member states take specific actions relating to the following:

- the promotion of market-based price reform and fuller reflection of environmental costs and benefits
- the encouragement of international cooperation
- information sharing on environmentally sound and economically efficient energy policies
- the promotion of environmental impact assessment activities and monitoring
- the promotion of public awareness on relevant environmental programs
- the research and development of energy efficient and environmentally sound technologies, including the transfer of technology

Although these are soft law and not legally binding obligations, they may have indirect legal implications, such as "justifying regulatory measures subject to the scrutiny of the investment protection regime" (Wälde 2001). Furthermore, the Protocol on Energy Efficiency and Related Environmental Aspects (PEEREA) requires member states to formulate policy principles aimed at improving energy efficiency, reducing negative environmental impact, and fostering international cooperation between member states. The implementation of the PEEREA would provide transition economies with good practices and an opportunity to share experiences and policy advice on energy efficiency issues with their Western counterparts.

Impact and Current Challenges

According to the United States government, NAFTA has achieved its core goals of expanding trade and investment between the three countries. It asserts that "from 1993 to 2007, trade among the NAFTA nations more than tripled, from $297 billion to $930 billion" and that "business investment in the United States has risen by 117 percent since 1993, compared to 45 percent increase between 1979 and 1993" (Office of the United States Trade Representative 2008). With respect to the energy sector, the business and legal climate in Canada and Mexico have become more hospitable to foreign energy-related investment as a result of NAFTA (Smith and Cluchey 1994). Concerning sustainable development, it has been noted that the NAFTA regime "has had its greatest success as a regional effort to promote sustainable development. It has contributed to stronger environmental protections, especially in Mexico," and it has formed a basis for subsequent United States Free Trade Agreements to include environmental protection provisions (Knox 2010). But concerns over the

fairness or neutrality of the process, the slow pace of the procedure, and the apparently "toothless" character of the mechanisms have marred the success of the Side Agreement on Environment (Markell 2010; Knox 2010). Furthermore, one of the strongest challenges facing NAFTA, the ECT, and other investment treaties relates to how to reconcile the obligations of the state parties toward foreign investors and the needs for regulatory autonomy in the areas of environmental protection and human rights. The absence of clear guidelines in the investment treaties on how to resolve such potential conflicts poses a serious legal and policy challenge to state parties and foreign investors who have to rely on the interpretative decisions of arbitral tribunals (Kingsbury and Schill 2010; Vandevelde 2009).

Some general conclusions can be drawn from this overview of energy investment law. First, although every country has sovereignty over its natural resources and the right to develop them in accordance with its environmental laws and regulations, modern investment treaties such as NAFTA and the ECT may constrain a member-state's discretion. Second, modern investment treaties vest substantive and procedural rights in foreign investors to challenge egregious host-state measures before international tribunals in a manner never before known under general international law. Third, it is not yet settled how to strike a proper balance between energy investment and sustainable development, hence the uncertainty in the legal relationship between foreign investors and host states. Finally, it is difficult to assess the extent to which modern investment treaties, such as NAFTA and the ECT, have contributed to improving the investment climate in the energy sector of the state parties.

Peter CAMERON and Abba KOLO
University of Dundee

See also in the *Berkshire Encyclopedia of Sustainability*: **Climate Change Disclosure—Legal Framework; Climate Change Mitigation; Development, Sustainable—Overview of Laws and Commissions; Energy Conservation Initiatives; Environmental Law—United States and Canada; Environmental Law, Soft vs. Hard; Free Trade; Investment Law, Foreign; Green Taxes; Utilities Regulation**

FURTHER READING

Cameron, Peter. (2010). *International energy investment law: The pursuit of stability*. Oxford, U.K.: Oxford University Press.
Corell, Hans. (2006). Introduction to the Energy Charter Treaty. In Clarisse Ribeiro (Ed.), *Investment arbitration and the Energy Charter Treaty* (pp. 1-3). Huntington, NY: JurisNet.
Elder, P. S. (1991). Sustainability. *McGill Law Journal, 36*, 831–834.
Energy Charter Secretariat. (n.d.) About the charter. Retrieved November 23, 2010, from http://www.encharter.org/index.php?id=7
Gao, Zhiguo. (1998). Environmental regulation of oil and gas in the twentieth century and beyond: An introduction and overview. In Zhiguo Gao (Ed.), *Environmental regulation of oil and gas* (pp. 3–58). London: Kluwer Law International.

Ginther, Konrad; Denters, Erik; & de Waart, P. J. I. M. (1995). *Sustainable development and good governance.* Dordrecht, The Netherlands: M. Nijhoff.

Herman, Lawrence L. (1997). NAFTA and the ECT: Divergent approaches with a core of harmony. *Journal of Energy and Natural Resources Law, 15*, 129–133.

Horbach, Nathalie. (1999). Lacunae of international nuclear liability agreements. In Nathalie Horbach (Ed.), *Contemporary developments in nuclear energy law* (p. 43). London: Kluwer Law International.

Kingsbury, Benedict, & Schill, Stephan. (2010). Public law concepts to balance investors' rights with state regulatory actions in the public interest – the concept of proportionality. In Stephan Schill (Ed.), *International investment law and comparative public law* (pp. 75–104). Oxford, U.K.: Oxford University Press.

Knox, John H. (2010). The neglected lessons of the NAFTA environmental regime. *Wake Forest Law Review, 45*, 391–424.

Konoplyanik, Andrei, & Wälde, Thomas. (2006). Energy Charter Treaty and its role in international energy. *Journal of Energy and Natural Resources Law, 24*(4), 523–558.

Markell, David. (2010). The role of spotlighting procedures in promoting citizen participation, transparency, and accountability. *Wake Forest Law Review, 45*, 425–467.

Office of the United States Trade Representative. (2008). NAFTA facts. Retrieved November 23, 2010, from http://www.ustr.gov

Park, Patricia. (2002). *Energy law and the environment.* London: Taylor & Francis.

Salacuse, Jeswald W. (2010). *The law of investment treaties.* Oxford, U.K.: Oxford University Press.

Sands, Philippe. (1995). International law in the field of sustainable development: Emerging legal principles. In Winfried Lang (Ed.), *Sustainable development and international law* (pp. 53–66). London: Graham & Trotman / M. Nijhoff.

Saunders, J. Owen. (1994). GATT, NAFTA and the North American energy trade: A Canadian perspective. *Journal of Energy and Natural Resources Law, 12*, 4–9.

Smith, Ernest E. & Cluchey, David P. (1994). GATT, NAFTA and the trade in energy: A US perspective. *Journal of Energy and Natural Resources Law, 12*, 27–58.

Smith, Ernest E., & Rocky Mountain Mineral Law Foundation (RMMLF). (2010). *International petroleum transactions* (3rd ed.). Denver, CO: Rocky Mountain Mineral Law Foundation.

Vale Columbia Centre & World Association of Investment Promotion Agencies (WAIPA). (2010). Investment promotion agencies and sustainable FDI: Moving towards the fourth generation of investment promotion. Retrieved November 23, 2010, from http://www.vcc.columbia.edu/files/vale/content/IPASurvey.pdf

Vandevelde, Kenneth. (2009). A comparison of the 2004 and 1994 U.S. model BITs. In Karl Sauvant (Ed.), *Yearbook on international investment law & policy 2008–2009* (pp. 283–315). Oxford, U.K.: Oxford University Press.

Vandevelde, Kenneth. (2010). *Bilateral investment treaties.* Oxford, U.K.: Oxford University Press.

Wälde, Thomas. (2001). International disciplines on national environmental regulation: With particular focus on multilateral investment treaties. In Permanent Court of Arbitration (Ed.), *International investments and protection of the environment* (pp. 29-47). The Hague, The Netherlands: Kluwer Law International.

Wälde, Thomas. (2004). The Energy Charter Treaty: Expanding the liberalization of energy industries. Unpublished paper on file with the authors.

Investment Law, Foreign

As multinational corporations seek to reduce costs, they increasingly turn to developing countries in order to conduct business. The way in which that business is conducted can have substantial impacts on the environment and human rights of communities within host states. The proper legal management of foreign investment can help to promote sustainable development by setting standards that protect the environment and human health.

Foreign investment law, policies, and practices impact a diverse range of areas well beyond the field of investment, reaching into issues such as environmental protection, human rights, and economic development. For this reason, foreign investment inflows, and the international legal framework regulating their protection, can have both positive and negative consequences for the states in which foreign investors operate, termed *host states*. In particular, foreign investment and international investment law can have profound implications for sustainable development policies.

Foreign Investment and Sustainable Development

The relationship between foreign investment activities and the sustainability objectives of host states is complex, involving the potential for substantial economic benefits and increased standards of living, but also the risk of detrimental social and environmental effects.

Foreign Direct Investment Inflows

The term *foreign investment* encompasses both foreign direct investment and foreign portfolio investment. Foreign direct investment is defined by the U.N. Conference on Trade and Development (UNCTAD) as

> investment involving a long-term relationship and reflecting a lasting interest and control by a resident entity in one economy (foreign direct investor or parent enterprise) in an enterprise resident in an economy other than that of the foreign direct investor (FDI enterprise or affiliate enterprise or foreign affiliate). FDI implies that the investor exerts a significant degree of influence on the management of the enterprise resident in the other economy. Such investment involves both the initial transaction between the two entities and all subsequent transactions between them and among foreign affiliates, both incorporated and unincorporated. (UNCTAD 2008)

Foreign portfolio investment is described as including:

> a variety of instruments which are traded (or tradeable) in organized and other financial markets: bonds, equities and money market instruments. The International Monetary Fund even includes derivatives or secondary instruments, such as options, in the category of FPI. The channels of cross-border investments are also varied: securities are acquired and sold by retail investors, commercial banks, investment trusts (mutual funds, country and regional funds, pension funds and hedge funds). (UNCTAD 1999)

Global flows of foreign capital continued to increase at exponential rates from 2000 until the global financial crisis that engulfed financial markets in 2008–2009 and slowed growth (UNCTAD 2009). UNCTAD reports indicate that global foreign direct investment reached an estimated $897 billion in 2005, a 29 percent increase on 2004 figures. The upward trend continued, with 2006 experiencing a 38 percent increase overall on 2005, reaching $1,306 billion in global foreign direct investment inflows, followed by the high point of $1,979 billion in 2007 (UNCTAD 2008). Despite the global impact of the financial crisis, however, all regional groupings of developing economies—namely Africa, Latin America, and Asia—have continued to record increases in foreign direct investment inflows (UNCTAD 2008; UNCTAD 2009). Global levels of foreign capital inflows are expected to resume their upward trend in 2011 (UNCTAD 2009).

These figures do not mean that foreign direct investment distribution among states is equal; many developing countries do not have the necessary funds to promote the desired levels of development. Addressing inequalities in the funding of development is a key component of the Millennium Development Goals as set out in the U.N. Millennium Declaration (2000). This was also a key issue for the International Conference on Financing for Development in Monterrey, Mexico, in March 2002, which produced the Monterrey Consensus, a document that sought to address financing for development through a comprehensive, cross-institutional, and partnership-emphasizing approach.

Foreign investment inflows can potentially involve substantial benefits for host states. Increased levels of capital in the economy; the initiation of new infrastructure projects; increased employment levels; increased economic growth rates; and the introduction of new, safer, and more efficient technologies can generate wealth and increase standards of living in host states (Hunter, Salzman, and Zaelke 2002, 1268–1274). There are also many reasons for multinational corporations to engage in foreign direct investment. Generally, decisions to expand into foreign investment are made to lower costs or to generate further profits through expansion into new markets. The reduction of costs might be achieved through low-cost production processes, cheaper labor, an abundance of inexpensive raw materials, tax incentives, or the avoidance of import/export tariffs (Hunter, Salzman, and Zaelke 2002, 1269).

Foreign Investment Practices: Controversies

There is a more controversial side, however, to foreign investment inflows. Significant causes of concern include the means by which such costs-savings are made and the consequences of these activities for host states, particularly for local communities. The concern surrounds whether these lower costs, and the consequential increase in the level of foreign investment, are achieved at the expense of the social fabric or environmental conditions of the local community (Zarsky 1999; Neumayer 2001). Are the production processes cheaper because the environmental standards are lower or because the true environmental costs are not reflected in the prices? Is the actual cost of repairing environmental damage from corporate activities an externality imposed on the local community? Is the cost of labor cheaper because there are no worker protection measures in place? In the midst of fierce competition to attract foreign investment, will states lower their domestic environmental and health standards, effectively engaging in what is called a regulatory "race to the bottom," so as to further reduce the costs of doing business and thus become more attractive to potential foreign investors? (Hunter, Salzman, and Zaelke 2002, 1269–1274; Zarsky 1999; Neumayer 2001, 41–67). In summary, what are the environmental politico-legal consequences of interstate competition for foreign investment? (Esty and Geradin 1998).

These questions raise the specter of "pollution havens" and "regulatory chill." The pollution haven theory is based on the premise that in order to remain competitive in the market for foreign investment, states will set unacceptably low environmental standards, or set adequate standards but not enforce them, essentially causing the unraveling of environmental restrictions—hence the description "race to the bottom" (Zarsky 1999; Neumayer 2001). The hypothesis is that multinational corporations that cannot continue environmentally damaging practices in developed states as a result of increasingly restrictive environmental protection standards will be able to export those practices to developing states with low environmental protection measures, producing so-called pollution havens.

The regulatory chill, or "political drag," argument puts forward the idea that the fear of a loss of competitiveness in international markets, as well as capital flight from states with high environmental standards, has led policy makers to refrain from raising environmental standards and tightening regulations. The theory does not require there to be any actual movement of investment dollars to states offering pollution havens, only the existence of the fear that there might be capital flight (Neumayer 2001; Esty and Geradin 1998). A version of the regulatory chill theory also affects international investment disputes. The argument is that the threat of investor claims against the host state may preclude the strengthening of environmental regulation. It has been suggested that the fear of facing investor claims not only encompasses the potential for large damages awards, but is also driven by the substantial costs involved in defending arbitral proceedings (Tienhaara 2009). Indeed, commentators have pointed to a number of incidents as examples of investment dispute–related regulatory chill, including the withdrawal of Canadian legislation banning a fuel additive on environmental and health grounds following the commencement of investor-state arbitration; the abandonment of highly restrictive tobacco legislation following threatened investor claims; and the non-implementation of new forestry legislation in Indonesia prohibiting the operation of open-cast mining in designated areas following discussions with foreign-owned mining corporations (Tienhaara 2009).

International Investment Agreements

Foreign investment is governed by different legal instruments at individual, national, and international levels. At the individual level, an investor may enter into contracts with the host state that governs the operation of the investment. Nationally, states often implement domestic legislation regulating the conditions under which foreign investment is permitted. Internationally, foreign investment is protected by a network of bilateral investment treaties and investment provisions within free trade agreements, such as chapter 11 of the North American Free Trade Agreement (NAFTA). These international investment protection agreements now number approximately three thousand (Newcombe and Paradell 2009) and are the dominant mechanism through which investment protection is pursued at the international level. Such treaties also contain the central tenets of international investment law.

Background of International Investment Agreements

Prior to the development of bilateral investment treaties, foreign investment disputes fell within an area of customary international law known as the diplomatic protection of aliens. In the wake of a wave of postcolonial nationalizations and the advent of the so-called New International Economic Order in the mid-twentieth century, capital-exporting states developed bilateral investment treaties as a more effective mechanism to protect foreign investment. The first bilateral investment treaty was entered into in 1959 between Germany and Pakistan.

The particular scope of foreign investment protection contained within each bilateral investment treaty varies, yet they all possess core protection guarantees, such as adherence to the national treatment standard, most-favored-nation treatment requirements, fair and equitable treatment, and guarantees against uncompensated expropriation of the investment. The national treatment standard provides that foreign investors and their investments are to be "accorded treatment no less favorable than that which the host state accords to its own investors" (Dolzer and Schreuer 2008). Guarantees of most-favored-nation status entail extending to investors of signatory states any privilege or benefit that has been granted to a third state (Newcombe and Paradell 2009). Key components of the fair and equitable treatment standard are the legitimate expectations of the investor regarding the regulatory framework of the host state, the maintenance of a stable legal and business environment, and following due process (Newcombe and Paradell 2009; McLachlan, Shore, and Weiniger 2007).

International law also permits expropriation of foreign-owned property, but only if the expropriation is for a public purpose, if it is nondiscriminatory and is not of an arbitrary nature, and if compensation is paid. Direct expropriation of an investment is not difficult to identify as it involves the seizure of physical assets. More subtle forms, however, are inherently less identifiable as compensable action. The various manifestations are characterized by a diminution

in property rights or interference with property interests without a formal transfer of ownership. This category of indirect expropriation, together with other claims such as alleged breaches of the fair and equitable treatment standard, is increasingly forming the basis for challenges by the investor to public welfare regulation in the host state, such as environmental protection measures, health and safety requirements, and social policy initiatives. This trend has significant implications for the implementation of domestic sustainability programs within host states, as such challenges have the potential to limit policy options and preclude the introduction of new regulatory approaches.

Legal Challenges

Over the last decade, there has been an increasing number of disputes between investors and host states concerning the treatment given to investments by government bodies. These disputes have often involved allegations of breaches of bilateral investment treaties or investment provisions within free trade agreements. The majority of such treaties contain dispute-settlement clauses permitting an investor to require that the host state resolve the dispute before an international arbitral tribunal, a system known as investor–state arbitration. This system is a decentralized dispute-settlement mechanism comprising ad hoc arbitral panels. There is no permanent dispute-settlement body and no appellate facility. Most investment treaties, however, specify a particular set of procedural rules to govern the establishment and operation of individual tribunals, such as the rules for the International Centre for the Settlement of Investment Disputes (ICSID) and the U.N. Commission on International Trade Law (UNCITRAL). These rules can have significant implications for the management of hearings as they determine procedures on the appointment of arbitrators, the ability of third parties to submit amicus curiae briefs, and whether there is public access to the documents and hearings. These restrictions have drawn criticism, largely on the basis that the lack of transparency surrounding the proceedings and the commercial model adopted are inappropriate for investor–state arbitration given that public interest issues are necessarily implicated in disputes involving the state (Tienhaara 2009; Van Harten 2007).

Considerable controversy has also surrounded the potential impact that international investment law and the system of investor–state arbitration can have on the domestic sustainability programs of host states. This concern has been generated by recent investor challenges to the introduction of new regulation designed to meet the environmental, health, social, economic, or human rights needs of host states. For example, investors have brought claims against states that have established affirmative

action employment policies, created regulations protecting groundwater from contamination with harmful chemicals, restricted mining on lands of indigenous cultural significance, taken emergency financial measures, prohibited the use of potent pesticides, and banned fuel additives to protect human health and the environment (*Methanex Corporation v. United States*, 2005; *Glamis Gold v. United States*, 2009; *Sempra Energy International v. Argentina*, 2007; *Dow Agro Sciences LLC v. Canada*, filed 2009; *Ethyl Corporation v. Canada*, 1999; *Foresti v. South Africa*, filed 2007). Investors in these cases claimed that the new regulatory measures detrimentally affected the value of their investments and therefore breached the applicable investment treaty. When such claims are successful, host states can be required to pay large compensation awards to investors. For these reasons, it has been argued that international investment law and investor–state arbitration can impinge on host state policy creation, including on domestic sustainable development programs.

Sustainable Finance

In contrast to the circumstances surrounding investor–state arbitration, there is a more positive form of interaction between foreign investment practices, law, and sustainability objectives. New trends in corporate behavior have emerged over the last decade that may influence foreign investment practices and the substantive development of international investment law. The adoption of voluntary codes setting standards for environmental corporate conduct, the integration of corporate social responsibility programs, the establishment of ethical investment funds, and the emergence of the sustainable finance movement all reflect an increasing shift in emphasis toward accommodating public concerns about the role of multinational corporations in socially and environmentally harmful practices (Assadourian 2006; McBarnet 2007; Jeucken 2004). *Sustainable finance* is the term coined to describe the process of integrating environmental and social criteria into investment and financial decision making. As attention has turned to the wider effects of corporate practices, companies needed to respond to pressure from consumers, nongovernmental organizations, shareholders, and other stakeholders to improve their social and environmental performance.

This shift in the expectations of corporate conduct has also had an impact within the investment sector, leading to a different emphasis in more recent bilateral investment treaties, termed *new generation BITs* (Newcombe 2007). Traditionally, bilateral investment treaties have not referred to public interest issues or the policy needs of the host state, focusing solely on investment protection and promotion. In contrast, several recent international investment agreements, such as the U.S.-Uruguay Bilateral Investment Treaty, contain express references to sustainable development, protection of the environment, and the health and safety of the public in the host state (Newcombe 2007). These initiatives perhaps point to a future in which an enhanced level of awareness of sustainability issues can be developed within international investment law and investor–state arbitration.

Kate MILES
University of Sydney

See also in the *Berkshire Encyclopedia of Sustainability*: **Development, Sustainable—Overview of Laws and Commissions; Fair Trade; Free Trade; International Law; Investment Law, Energy**

FURTHER READING

Assadourian, Erik. (2006). Transforming corporations. In the Worldwatch Institute (Ed.), *State of the world 2006* (p. 171). New York: W. W. Norton & Company.

Cordonier Segger, Marie-Claire; Gehring, Markus; & Newcombe, Andrew. (Eds.). (forthcoming). *Sustainable development in international investment law.* Montreal: Centre for International Sustainable Development Law.

Dolzer, Rudolf, & Schreuer, Christoph. (2008). *Principles of international investment law.* New York: Oxford University Press.

Esty, Daniel C., & Geradin, Damien. (1998). Environmental protection and international competitiveness: A conceptual framework. *Journal of World Trade, 32*(3), 5–46.

Hunter, David; Salzman, James; & Zaelke, Durwood. (2002). *International environmental law and policy* (2nd ed.). New York: Foundation Press.

Jeucken, Marcel. (2004). *Sustainability in finance: Banking on the planet.* Delft, The Netherlands: Eburon Academic Publishers.

McBarnet, Doreen. (2007). Corporate social responsibility beyond law, through law, for law: The new corporate accountability. In Doreen McBarnet, Aurora Voiculescu & Tom Campbell (Eds.), *The new corporate accountability: Corporate social responsibility and the law* (p. 9). Cambridge, U.K.: Cambridge University Press.

McLachlan, Campbell; Shore, Laurence; & Weiniger, Matthew. (2007). *International investment arbitration: Substantive principles.* Oxford, U.K.: Oxford International Arbitration Series.

Neumayer, Eric. (2001). *Greening trade and investment: Environmental protection without protectionism.* London: Earthscan Publications Ltd.

Newcombe, Andrew. (2007). Sustainable development and investment treaty law. *The Journal of World Investment & Trade, 8*, 357–408.

Newcombe, Andrew, & Paradell, Lluís. (2009). *Law and practice of investment treaties: Standards of treatment.* Alphen aan den Rijn, The Netherlands: Wolters Kluwer.

Tienhaara, Kyla. (2009). *The expropriation of environmental governance: Protecting foreign investors at the expense of public policy.* New York: Cambridge University Press.

United Nations Conference on Trade and Development (UNCTAD). (1999). Foreign portfolio investment (FPI) and foreign direct investment (FDI): Characteristics, similarities, complementarities and differences, policy implications and development impact. Retrieved January 16, 2008, from http://www.unctad.org/en/docs/c2em6d2&c1.en.pdf

United Nations Conference on Trade and Development (UNCTAD). (2007). *World investment report 2007: Transnational corporations, extractive industries and development.* Retrieved March 2, 2008, from http://www.unctad.org/en/docs/wir2007_en.pdf

United Nations Conference on Trade and Development (UNCTAD). (2008). Foreign direct investment: Statistics. Retrieved January 16, 2008, from http://unctadstat.unctad.org/ReportFolders/reportFolders.aspx?sRF_ActivePath=P,5,27&sRF_Expanded=,P,5,27&sCS_ChosenLang=en

United Nations Conference on Trade and Development (UNCTAD). (2009). *World investment report 2009: Transnational corporations, agricultural production and development.* Retrieved January 20, 2010, from http://www.unctad.org/en/docs/wir2009_en.pdf

United Nations Millenium Declaration. (2000). United Nations General Assembly Res. 55/2, Doc. A/55/L.2.

Van Harten, Gus. (2007). *Investment treaty arbitration and public law.* Oxford, U.K.: Oxford University Press.

Zarsky, Lyuba. (1999). Havens, halos and spaghetti: Untangling the evidence about foreign direct investment and the environment. In *Foreign Direct Investment and the Environment* (pp. 47–73). Paris: Organisation for Economic Co-operation and Development.

COURT CASES

Dow Agro Sciences LLC v. Government of Canada, Notice of Arbitration (31 March 2009).

Ethyl Corporation v. Canada, Jurisdiction Phase, 38 ILM 708 (1999).

Glamis Gold Ltd v. United States of America, Award (June 2009).

Methanex Corporation v. United States of America, 44 ILM 1345 (2005).

Piero Foresti and others v. Republic of South Africa, ICSID Case No. ARB(AF)/07/1

S. D. Myers, Inc. v. Canada, Partial Award (Decision on the Merits) (November 2000).

Sempra Energy International v. Argentina, Award, ICSID Case No. ARB/02/16 (2007).

Financial Services

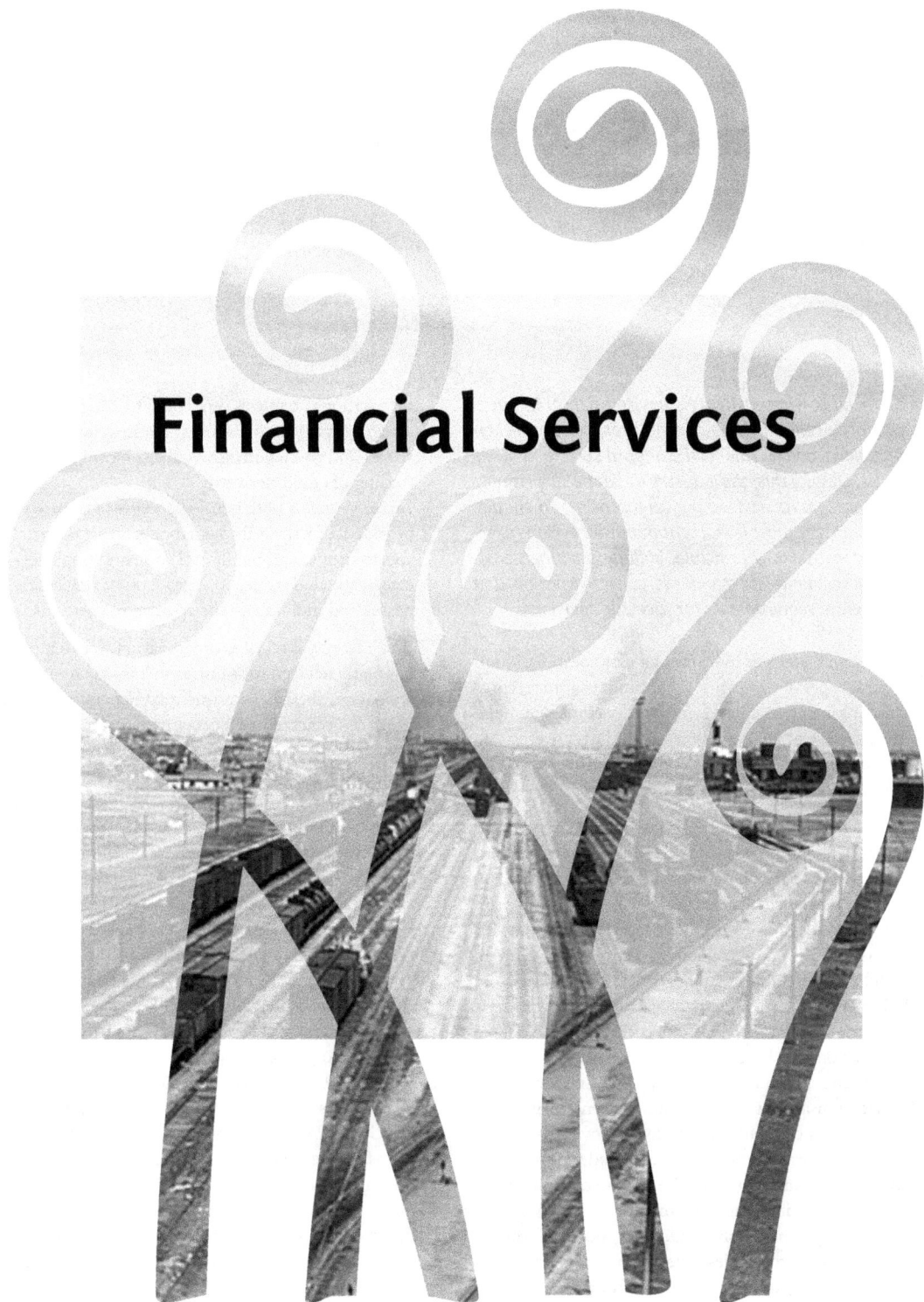

Financial Services Industry

The financial services industry's environmental impacts are primarily related to its carbon footprint, its reach through loans, and its financial standard setting in other industries. Despite this, the industry has done surprisingly little to decrease its environmental footprint. To change this situation, the most important potential actions exercise the precautionary principle, including defined environmental sustainability standards, collective action, and environmental requirements for investor decisions.

The financial services industry is a vast combination of various types of companies, spanning insurance, commercial banking, investment firms, and asset management. For the purpose of an analysis of the industry's approach to sustainability, the Global Reporting Initiative (2009) divides the industry into four segments:

- *Retail banking* includes the provision of private and commercial banking services to individuals. This category includes banking for more affluent clients, such as wealth management and portfolio management services. Also, retail banking covers other services to individuals such as transaction management, payroll management, small loans, foreign exchange services, derivatives, and similar types of instruments.
- *Commercial and corporate banking* covers transactions for organizations and businesses of all sizes, including commercial and corporate banking, project and structured finance, transactions with medium-size enterprises, and the provision of financial services to government and government departments. Services include advisory services, mergers and acquisitions, equity/debt capital market services, and leveraged finance.
- *Asset management* involves handling pools of capital on behalf of third parties invested in a wide range of asset classes, including equities, bonds, cash, property,

international equities, and private hedge funds. This category includes investment banking with trading in shares and share derivatives, fixed income trading, and trading of credit derivatives.
- *Insurance* covers both pension and life insurance services provided directly or through independent financial advisors to the general public and company employees. This category includes insurance products or services for businesses and individuals and reinsurance services.

Some financial services organizations try to be full service, usually referred to as universal banks. Others attempt to specialize, such as investment banks and hedge funds. Regulations enacted in every country control what organizations can and cannot do in terms of providing financial services. Yet regardless of the restrictions, this vast industry has a major impact on economies. For example, 2008 U.S. commercial banking revenues, as one sector of financial services, were estimated to be $695 billion (IBIS World Industry Reports 2008).

Due to the worldwide economic situation, from September 2008 to early 2010 the world has witnessed massive subsidies given to financial services organizations, including mandated provision of funds to U.S. banks under the Troubled Asset Relief Program (TARP). Any commentary on financial services cannot ignore the tremendous power these organizations have on the world economies, as witnessed by their primary role in the various government bailouts during the economic recession (United States Government Accountability Office 2009). This early twenty-first-century crisis is clearly a collective failure of financial markets as well as of government policies and financial sector regulation and supervision.

The financial services industry has a tremendous impact on organizations by influencing personal wealth, access to education through loans, community viability, and even the ability of governments to implement policies. Given its size and its tremendous leverage on world economies, this industry must take a major role to improve the environment. These influences are magnified when loans are not available to fund innovations for decreasing a business's environmental footprint. This article addresses what is being done in the financial services industry related to environmental sustainability and the challenges the industry sector will face going forward.

Sustainable Practices and Innovations

Many different discourses occur around sustainability, making definition of the term difficult and the identification of relevant corporate practices equally difficult (Dryzek 2005; Gray 2006). The scholar Arieh Ullmann (1985), one of the first to analyze sustainability in financial services, concludes that social reporting, in general, is a confused state of varied theories, concepts, and inconsistent functional terms. More recent data and improved theory show a weak relationship between environmental performance and corporate disclosure sustainable practices (McCammon 1995). The relationship between market performance and social disclosure is far from conclusive, however (see Gray 2006 for a review of this literature).

Thus when we discuss the financial services industry performance as related to environmental sustainability, we should keep in mind the confused state of definitions and of relationships and the lack of incentives to invest in socially responsible activities. We cannot conclude that the industry is not interested or unwilling. We can conclude that the investment targets are far from clear. We can conclude that the more data that point to the industry's actual or perceived environmental impacts, the more corporate action will change. The demonstrable impacts will influence organizational reputation, perceived management competence, and risk management (Orlitsky and Benjamin 2001). In light of this confusion around theory and measurement, we can point to some directions that the industry is taking.

One way to phrase these discourses is to compare and contrast definitions of sustainability as the politics of constraint versus the politics of the possible:

> Environmentalism offered something profoundly important to America and the world. It inspired an appreciation for, and an awe of the beauty and majesty of, the nonhuman world. It focused our attention . . . but environmentalism has also saddled us with the albatross we call the politics of limits, which seeks to constrain human ambition, aspiration, and power rather than unleash and direct them. (Nordhaus and Shellenberger 2007, 16–17)

The politics of constraint expect certain actions to be taken that limit our use of resources and focus our attention on humans as the main cause of environmental degradation. Preservation, conservation, and a more radical "limits to growth" approach refer to a massive need to survive (Meadows, Randers, and Meadows 2004). Environmental groups combat the impacts of business organizations on our society, such as those in the financial services, and create an adversarial atmosphere among the various societal stakeholders. This type of discourse defines *sustainability* as preserving at least what we have today without further deterioration in our economy, our environment, and our society, a classic reference to the Brundtland Commission's commentary on sustainable development (United Nations World Commission on Environment and Development 1987).

This discourse contrasts with the rhetoric of ecological modernization and the green parties across the world. These other approaches emphasize positive actions that balance a triple bottom line approach, that is, a balance of outcomes in light of the inevitable growth our world faces. It approaches the issues of sustainability as the cooperative efforts that support human growth with innovation and new approaches to intractable problems. Extreme aspects of this discourse have been advocated by ecofeminists or ecospiritualists (Dryzek 2005).

These two discourses (or views) on the financial services industry define most approaches that have been taken to address environmental sustainability. Regardless of the approach the industry takes on environmental sustainability, both lead one to conclude that the precautionary principle is the prudent course of action. This principle specifies that regardless of the state of knowledge about environmental sustainability, we should act as if we need dramatic actions to offset the ill effects of environmental degradation (Gollier, Jullien, and Treich 2000). This principle demands that financial services organizations take deliberate actions to offset carbon emissions and act in a manner that increases beneficial outcomes for our environment.

Before proceeding, however, we must note that the discourse around sustainability is matched by a discourse on risk and the financial services industry. Many commentators on the recent financial turmoil point to the way in which financial markets affect peoples psychologically, and how peoples' reactions impact the industry. These impacts stem from citizens' insecurity about investments, the lack of trust of corporate managers, and the desire to have

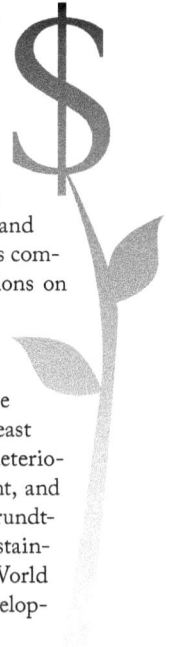

governments punish corporations for losing money, despite the fact that investing comes with risks and rewards. Thus the focus on sustainability, and whether or not the industry follows the politics of constraints or the politics of the possible, may be influenced by society's view of the financial services industry.

What Organizations Are Doing

The impact of the financial services sector on society and the environment derives mostly from the capital it employs—from financing infrastructure projects in developing nations to providing loans to businesses—with effects that can change the risk profiles of borrowers and lenders (PricewaterhouseCoopers 2009). The industry has a large built environment, as evidenced by branches of banks, large office towers, and a tremendous energy infrastructure to support trading and communication related to all sorts of markets and information exchange.

The industry faces, now as in the past, a myriad of challenges and opportunities to impact environmental sustainability. If one were to take a broad view of sustainability that includes environment and society, some of the major issues that financial services organizations face are brand and reputation management; environmental and social impacts of project financing; accessibility to services for underserved markets (Yunus 2003); environmental and social risk management in lending related to climate change (and the impact on borrowers, insurers, financial markets); socially responsible investment, lending, and marketing; compliance with regulatory requirements; and the environmental footprint of facilities.

Some authors state that financial services organizations—especially those in Europe—have a financial motivation to integrate sustainability into business (Russo and Fouts 1997). The scholar Olaf Weber (2005) maintains that integrating sustainability practices into the banking business is motivated by philosophical backgrounds, such as anthroposophy, or personal concerns, such as the agendas of public bank owners. These strategies lead to new sustainable products, such as venture capital funds and microcredit funds, or green mortgages, all of which are needed to foster sustainable development. Weber (2005) also found that financial institutions use five approaches (which he calls "models") to successfully integrate sustainability into the banking business: event related integration of sustainability, sustainability as a new banking strategy, sustainability as a value driver, sustainability as a public mission, and sustainability as a requirement of clients. Several of these challenges can be discussed under two headings: climate change initiatives, including those related to operations and the built environment, and environmental impact investing, including socially responsible investing and markets.

Climate Change Initiatives

The shift to a low-carbon economy is already under way, and businesses—especially energy, transport, and heavy manufacturers—are finding that they must get ready for it. Despite creating relatively low emissions as they conduct their work, financial services are not immune from a need to respond.

Changes in the global climate system during the twenty-first century are projected to have dramatic impacts on the world, including temperature increases, the rise in sea levels, dramatic precipitation and humidity changes, extreme wind and rain storms, and related events (Sussman and Freed 2008, 5).

If current climate science holds true and we take the average predictions, global greenhouse gas emission ideally should decrease by 90 percent from today's levels by 2050, containing global warming below 2°C (IPCC 2007). To reach this goal, the economy's carbon productivity would have to increase by 5 to 7 percent a year, compared to a historic rate of just 1 percent. Carbon productivity, which shows how emissions performance of an economy develops over time, is measured in gross domestic product (GDP) per unit of greenhouse gas emissions. This prescription decouples economic growth from emission growth (Enkvist, Nauclér, and Oppenheim 2008).

If humanity already possesses the fundamental scientific, technical, and industrial know-how to solve the carbon and climate problem for the next half century, then we would expect that the financial services industry has at its disposal a portfolio of technologies to meet the climate challenges we face. The financial services industry, unlike many industries, has shown surprisingly little evidence of activity in these areas. Some businesses take voluntary reductions in emissions, signing protocols such as the American College & University Presidents' Climate Commitment (2010). Buying carbon credits, investing in new technologies, and changing product designs are other carbon mitigation strategies. Few of these strategies are evident in the financial services industry (Hoffman 2006).

Many companies describe how climate change began as an endeavor within a functional area (such as environmental affairs) but diffused from the periphery to the core and, in the process, became an issue of strategic importance to the company. No such evidence exists in the financial services industry. In fact, by analogy, the finance and accounting functional areas were viewed as most resistant for climate-related strategies.

Swiss Re—the world's second largest reinsurer, providing insurance to insurance companies—was one of the first companies in the financial services industry to announce that it would eliminate or compensate for all of its greenhouse gas (GHG) emissions, with a goal of becoming carbon neutral by 2013. Swiss Re believes that reductions in global greenhouse gas emissions can be achieved through energy efficiency measures and by purchasing high-value emission certificates. It claimed to have reduced its own carbon dioxide emissions by more than 25 percent from 2003 to 2007 and offset the remaining emissions through certified emission reduction certificates, declaring to be a greenhouse gas neutral company since October 2003 (Swiss Re 2007).

Swiss Re is a classic example of using the precautionary principle. Swiss Re CEO Jacques Aigrain stated that "in the distribution of possible future outcomes of global warming, there is a significant tail representing very serious consequences. It is the prudent approach—a common practice in insurance and issues of financial stability—which requires us to take action today to mitigate global warming and to adapt to its consequences" (SEC 2007).

Industry views vary on whether or not climate change is significant. In a recent survey, Charles Schwab replied "N/A" to the question about physical risk of climate change, while Lehman Brothers stated that "physical risks pose a threat to the operations of all financial services firms and therefore the financial markets overall" (Sussman and Freed 2008, 10). Travelers, one of the largest providers of personal and commercial property and casualty insurance products in the United States, has taken several notable actions: using extensive risk modeling that includes climate change as a major risk factor, offering risk control services, and engaging in extensive community and government outreach to create greater awareness of this risk category.

Also in the United States, newresourcebank (2006) in the San Francisco Bay area offers extensive green resources. Some other efforts are made by Lloyd's Banking Group's sponsorship of the Corporate Leaders Group on Climate Change—part of the Prince of Wales's Business & the Environment Programme (2009), which is a collective business initiative to think about, challenge, and debate issues of corporate sustainability.

The financial services sector shows very little evidence of creating a positive impact on our environmental sustainability. This industry sector, unlike several others, does not have any coordinated effort to mitigate climate changes impacts, does not seem to have a systematic focus on climate change, and does not seem to put environmental sustainability at the forefront of its organizational strategies. Yet some progress has been made toward environmentally focused investing.

Environmentally Focused Investing

One place where the politics of possibility take concrete form is at the intersection of investment and innovation. Financial services organizations have modeled some of their investment strategies not on pollution control efforts but rather on past investments in infrastructure (such as railroads and highways) and innovative solutions for new businesses.

The financial sector began taking environmental risk into consideration by optimizing its own environmental performance (Weber 2005). There were two main reasons for this. First, banks wanted to decrease costs by reducing their use of energy, water, and materials (McCammon 1995). Second, they wanted to show their clients that "it pays to be green." As a next step, they introduced environmental risk management processes into credit management; some losses in the credit business caused by environmental risks justified such measures. At the same time, banks regarded the increase in environmental attitudes in society as a business opportunity. They subsequently created specialized credit products and mortgages as well as "green" or socially responsible funds, which invest in environmentally friendly or sustainable firms.

It has become increasingly difficult, however, to ascertain which kinds of measures or products labeled "green," "socially responsible," or "sustainable" have which kind of effect, both on banks and on sustainable development. Furthermore, it is difficult to determine which banks and financial institutions are the "sustainability leaders" in their sector.

One way the financial services industry has influenced sustainability efforts has been through the publication of information about companies' climate change efforts. These publications are aimed mainly at investors. Europeans had been the first to conduct this information exchange, such as Europe's utility sector sponsoring a publication with several new variables that made it possible to measure carbon emission against production and revenues. Goldman Sachs (2004) Energy Environmental and Social Index, a U.S. example of such a publication, is based on an analysis of thirty environmental and social metrics in eight categories.

The Carbon Disclosure Project (CDP) is a more ambitious effort. It is an independent not-for-profit organization that holds the largest database of corporate climate change information in the world. Based in the United Kingdom, it works with shareholders and corporations to disclose greenhouse gas emissions of major corporations. The CDP, which includes a group representing institutional investors that manages $10 trillion in assets, sent questionnaires to five hundred of the world's largest companies (mainly companies within the airline, automobile, retail, steel, power, insurance, and technology industries)

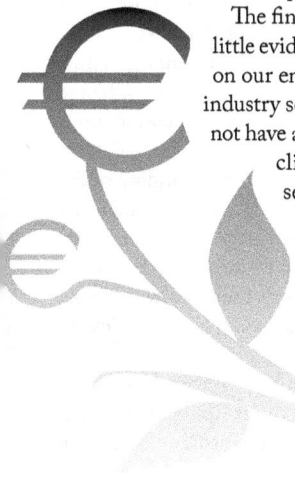

asking them to explain their emissions policies and strategies. The project published the results for investors to note in their future investment decisions (CDP n.d.).

Since its formation in 2000, CDP has become a major standard for carbon disclosure methodology and process, providing to the global marketplace primary climate change data obtained from responses to CDP's annual information requests, issued on behalf of institutional investors, purchasing organizations, and government bodies.

Institutional investors (such as banks, pension funds, and insurance companies) who signed CDP's information requests are known as signatory investors. CDP currently has 475 signatory investors, including global investment/finance houses such as Banco do Brasil, Barclays, HSBC, Goldman Sachs, Merrill Lynch, Mitsubishi UFJ, Morgan Stanley, National Australia Bank, Nedbank, and Sumitomo Mitsui Financial Group. Of the signatory investors interviewed for a CDP study, approximately 60 percent methodically identified which companies in their portfolio were either not responding to CDP or were providing poor or trivial answers (Riddell and Chamberlin 2007). The investors then used this information to further engage with these companies on the issue of climate risk. Twenty-six percent then went on to support shareholder resolutions for better disclosure on climate risk from some companies not complying with CDP disclosure.

Of the signatory investors interviewed, 13 percent encouraged their investment bankers to use CDP data when making new lending decisions. One pension fund identified their inclusion of climate risk evaluation criteria in their request for proposals to fund managers, citing that those fund managers who were able to demonstrate their signatory status to CDP were more likely to be awarded the contract. All of the investors interviewed agreed that the CDP data is a valuable resource and incorporated it into their decision-making process at some level (CDP n.d.).

As corporations create internal infrastructure to better understand GHG emissions accounting, the quality of data is expected to improve. Reviewing the CDP responses over the past five years alone is evidence that corporations are listening to their investors and responding to the threat of climate change.

Calvert, a socially responsible investment company, demonstrated particularly progressive use of CDP data conducting the following best practices:

- A qualitative analysis using CDP data evaluates companies on a sector-by-sector basis. The utility sector is the main target, but additional areas of focus are the oil and gas, auto, financial, insurance, and manufacturing sectors.
- Calvert specifically looks for a company's public policy outlook, mitigation strategies, trajectory information, management opportunities, and level of qualitative

information provided in a company's response to the CDP questionnaire.
- The information provided through CDP provides a platform for leaders and laggards, which is then incorporated into the decision-making process Calvert follows to invest in well-managed corporations.
- Calvert engages nonresponding corporations, which in some cases leads to shareholder resolutions and in others a change in response status to the CDP (n.d.).

Another effort that involved the financial services industries was the formation of the Equator Principles, a financial-industry benchmark for determining, assessing, and managing social and environmental risk in project financing (Equator Principles 2009).

Another comprehensive project has been the United Nations Environment Programme Finance Initiative (UNEP FI), a global network of signatories and partner organizations across the banking, insurance, and investment communities that focuses on the latest developments and emerging issues on finance and sustainability. UNEP FI works closely with over 170 financial institutions who are signatories to the UNEP FI Statements and a range of partner organizations to develop and promote linkages between the environment, sustainability, and financial performance. Through regional activities, a comprehensive work program, training programs, and research, UNEP FI carries out its mission to identify, promote, and realize the adoption of best environmental and sustainability practice at all levels of financial institution operations.

In the United States, the Coalition for Environmentally Responsible Economies (CERES, pronounced "series") is a national network of investors, environmental organizations, and other public interest groups working with companies and investors to address sustainability challenges such as global climate change. Its mission is to integrate sustainability into capital markets for the health of the planet and its people. CERES launched and directs the Investor Network on Climate Risk (INCR), a group of more than seventy leading institutional investors with collective assets of more than $7 trillion. Another effort is the Institutional Investors Group on Climate Change (IIGCC), a forum for collaboration between pension funds and other institutional investors on issues related to climate change. They seek to promote better understanding of the implications of climate change among members and other institutional investors; IIGCC also encourages companies and markets in which their members invest to address any material risks and opportunities to their businesses that are associated with climate change and to shift to a lower-carbon economy.

Swiss Re was ahead of the curve with its publication *Tackling Climate Change* in 1994. Swiss Re sought to bring climate change into policy and investment decisions, recognizing that it was more at risk from the physical impacts of climate change than many organizations. The insurance industry, in general, could experience dramatically increased costs due to growth of climate-related effects, including growth in natural disasters, disease, and mortality rates over the next ten years (UNEP FI 2002). In 2004, for example, the industry registered around $40 billion weather-related natural catastrophe losses, the largest amount in recorded history.

In 1996, Swiss Re started building up a sustainability portfolio of investments in companies supporting sustainable development, with particular emphasis on efficient resource utilization. Target investments focus primarily on alternative energy, water and waste management, and recycling. Investment clusters range from infrastructure / project finance–type investments to "CleanTech" venture capital. In 2006, the portfolio value grew substantially to CHF 376 million (CHF is the symbol for the Swiss franc). In April 2007, Swiss Re announced the successful close of the EUR 329 million European Clean Energy Fund, one of the largest funds of this type in Europe (Swiss Re 2007). The fund, a U.N.-accredited investment vehicle, provides capital to European clean energy projects that are environmentally beneficial and generate carbon credits or tradable renewable energy certificates. Swiss Re was the anchor investor in the fund and acts as carbon advisor for the selected projects (Swiss Re 2007). The fund was placed in Europe by Swiss Re's affiliate, Corning Research and Consulting. Other insurance companies have followed Swiss Re's lead, and many have been developing more accurate underwriting tools, such as catastrophe models, to establish appropriate exposure-based rates for insurance.

Some financial services companies have linked existing products to environmental sustainability, including complementary product offerings and emissions offsets (van Bellegem 2001). For example, GE's Money Earth Rewards Platinum MasterCard links purchases with offset products, similar to British Petroleum's Global Choice Program (Deutsch 2007). Barclay's offers the Barclaycard Breathe, from which .05 percent of what clients spend on the card goes to U.K.-based PURE, the Clean Planet Trust to fund government-approved environmental projects.

One small but interesting innovation occurred in Japan (Japan for Sustainability 2004). In 2003, three popular Japanese musicians—Takeshi Kobayashi, Kazutoshi, Sakurai, and Ryuichi Sakamoto—established a bank in Japan, known as the AP Bank Co. (AP stands for "Artists' Power" and "alternative power"). It was based on the Mirai Bank (Future Bank), which was launched and headed by environmental activist and writer Yu Tanaka. The Mirai Bank accepts funds invested by citizens and offers low-interest loans for environmental projects or citizen-based activities that the bank wants to encourage. Thus inspired by the Mirai Bank, Kobayashi, Sakamoto, and Sakurai decided to establish a bank of their own to provide low-interest financing for activities related to renewable energy, energy conservation, and environmental protection.

Merrill Lynch (2009) has taken bold moves despite its financial difficulties. As a provider of capital, the company facilitated financing for renewable and clean energy investments. Merrill Lynch claims that as a proprietary investor, it promoted investments in renewable and clean technologies, as a global wealth manager it provides solutions to integrate environmental investing into client portfolios, and through global research it publishes reports that highlight the risks and opportunities associated with the renewable and clean energy industry.

In the financing for Ulu Masen Ecosystem in Aceh, Indonesia, Merrill Lynch—in partnership with Carbon Conservation (working on behalf of the governor of Aceh)—came up with a deal that provides carbon financing for the world's first independently validated avoided deforestation project, which is compliant with Community, Climate, & Biodiversity Alliance (CCBA) standards (2008). CCBA is a partnership between leading companies, NGOs, and research institutes seeking to promote integrated solutions to land management around the world. The CCBA has developed voluntary standards to help design and identify land management projects that simultaneously minimize climate change, support sustainable development, and conserve biodiversity. It may not be the first avoided deforestation program, but it was one of the first to harness the power of an international investment bank and to link environmental benefits with companies' product offerings.

Merrill Lynch is using credits to create packaged products for institutional clients who want to offer ethical products to their retail customers. For example, a power company that wishes to offer a carbon-neutral electricity tariff, an airline offering carbon-neutral flights, or a car manufacturer who wants to carbon-neutralize its cars, would use Merrill's products.

Wells Fargo & Company (2008) announced that it has provided more than $3 billion in environmental financing—surpassing its goal to provide $1 billion in environmental finance commitments—two years ahead of schedule. Wells Fargo environmental financing included the provision of $2 billion in financing for building projects designed to meet U.S. Green Building Council's Leadership in Energy and Environmental Design (LEED) certification requirements; investing and committing more than $700 million to support solar and wind projects nationwide, enough to generate enough clean, renewable energy to power about 475,000 households; providing $500 million to support customers who have made environmental sustainability a key part of their missions; and providing $50 million to support nonprofit organizations that improve the environment in low- to moderate-income communities. Wells Fargo's $1 billion lending target was part of its ten-point environmental commitment aimed at helping to integrate environmental responsibility into its business practices (CSWire 2006).

Hewlett-Packard, PepsiCo, Procter & Gamble, and eight other global companies will measure their supply-chain emissions as part of their efforts to reduce greenhouse gases and to inform investors of their carbon footprint. The data will be fed to banks and funds, such as Goldman Sachs, Merrill Lynch, and HSBC Holdings, to help guide their lending and investment decisions (Morales 2008).

In 2007, Morgan Stanley partnered with Norwegian Det Norske Veritas (DNV), an independent risk-management and consulting foundation, to launch a Carbon Bank (Environmental Leader 2007). HSBC—the world's largest banking group—developed the Climate Confidence Index, which aimed to gauge public trends in attitudes about climate change and make them available to the public (HSBC 2007). The launch of the HSBC Climate Confidence Index is part of HSBC's broader strategy to contribute to tackling climate change. Other initiatives include the Global Environmental Efficiency Program, a $90 million commitment to reduce its own direct environmental impacts; the Carbon Finance Strategy to help clients respond to the challenges and opportunities of creating a low-carbon economy; and the HSBC Climate Partnership, a $100 million program involving four environmental groups and HSBC's employees to help reduce the impacts of climate change worldwide.

These projects provide a more hopeful look at what the industry is doing. Yet compared to other industries and the needs for environmental impact, the efforts are relatively meager. Unlike other sectors, the financial services industry has not focused on the challenges surrounding environmental sustainability and the need to play a major role in addressing these challenges. The next section addresses what the industry could do to address these challenges.

What Could the Industry Do?

If one were to consider only the short run, the outlook is bleak that the financial services industry will support and be part of environmental sustainability initiatives. The preoccupation with survival, the lack of evidence that their efforts have had any impact, and the lack of focus on environmental sustainability will contribute to a decrease in activity in this important area.

The financial services industry could have a major role to play, however. The industry could continue its development of investment metrics. A most important topic would be to verify the investment returns in those organizations that support and achieve climate reduction versus those that do not. For example, the efforts by HSBC, UNEP FI, Swiss Re, and others could have a major impact on the valuations of companies. If these financial services companies could produce data that investors trust, then substantial investments could be made to decrease the world's environmental footprint. In all likelihood, however, to produce these data the financial services organizations will need to partner with other organizations, such as the Global Reporting Initiative, or independent rating agencies, such as the Institute of Chartered Accountants in England and Wales or the Financial Accounting Standards Board in the United States (Gray 2006).

Banks should collectively adopt a set of principles in a code for responsible and sustainable banking that should be drafted in close consultation with national governments. According to Herman Mulder (2009), an independent advisor, the head of Group Risk Management at ABN AMRO from 1998 to 2006, and the initiator of the Equator Principles, such a code may include the following public commitments:

- incorporate and actively foster corporate social responsibility (CSR) and sustainable development (SD) in mainstream banking operations "in its own sphere of influence"; invest an explicit percentage of capital on an annual basis in SD business; set an explicit target for generating revenue from SD business; incorporate SD targets in business targets and performance appraisals; raise staff awareness and create active staff engagement by special programs;
- publish business principles, policies, analytics, risk management procedures, toolkits, performances in operations; define clear and consistent no-go interventions; offer an independent "grievance" procedure, allowing stakeholders to challenge the performance of an individual institution;
- incorporate SD issues in research, advisory, and lending operations with respect to its public and private sector clients; require similar, sector-specific disciplines from major clients, including the material contributors to the supply and distribution chains; emphasize the importance of verification and certification of products and services;

- require CSR and SD to be an explicit responsibility of a member of the European Managing Board or the United State's Boards of Directors; appoint a member in the European Supervisory Board or Boards of Directors in the United States with strong CSR and SD credentials; create an independent Advisory Council to the Board with focus on CSR and SD.

Another move the industry could make is to clean up its "own house" by enforcing high environmental standards for its buildings and workforce activities. Wachovia's major project in Charlotte, North Carolina, is exemplary (Charlotte Observer 2009). It plans to build its office tower according to Gold LEED certification standards and share space with Wake Forest University in an attempt to create a cultural campus that is both sustainable and efficient. Bank of America applied for Platinum certification for its New York office building in Bryant Park, yet another U.S. example of notable performance.

Bank of America, HSBC, Citigroup, and Swiss Re were once the sustainability leaders in the financial services sector, but their recent difficulties, especially Citigroup's, will curtail much of their efforts. Smaller, more versatile and less encumbered financial services organizations will likely lead the way for financing sustainability efforts. For example, in the United States, regional banks such as North Carolina-based BB&T could be leaders in financing renewable energy projects.

Banks manage and lend money. Most financial services organizations have capital requirements and offer incentives for people and companies to do business with them. Yet few have incorporated ways to monitor how clients implement and comply with environmental and social requirements built into agreements or transactions.

Further analyses will be necessary to measure the impact of integrating sustainable practices into the business strategies of the financial sector; initial approaches that can fulfill this necessity already exist. One example of such an approach is the sustainability balanced scorecard, which indicates the relation between the economic, environmental, and social performance of a firm (Figge et al. 2002).

Outlook

The financial services industry can help implement sustainable business practices by providing a market for climate exchange. This would involve facilitating markets that trade carbon credits, helping firms participate in the markets, and developing instruments that would provide financial security in such transactions. The aim of financial organizations such as the Chicago Climate Exchange, European Climate Exchange, Insurance Future Exchange, Montréal Climate Exchange, and Tianjin Climate Exchange is to

apply financial innovation and incentives to advance social, environmental, and economic goals through cap and trade systems with global affiliates and projects worldwide; derivatives exchanges that offer standardized and cleared futures and options contracts on emission allowances and other environmental products are also planned. These financial institutions need to be supported and regulated, similar to other financial exchanges.

In sum, the industry will not, in the short run, make significant strides in the area of environmental sustainability. Yet with some political will and customer pressure, the industry could eventually increase its presence in support of environmental sustainability.

Daniel S. FOGEL
Wake Forest University; EcoLens

See also in the *Berkshire Encyclopedia of Sustainability*: **Accounting; Climate Change Disclosure; CSR and CSR 2.0; Equator Principles; Green GDP; Investment, CleanTech; Investment, Socially Responsible; Risk Management; Social Enterprise; Sustainable Value Creation; Transparency; United Nations Global Compact**

FURTHER READING

American College & University Presidents' Climate Commitment (ACUPCC). (2010). Retrieved January 20, 2010, from http://www.presidentsclimatecommitment.org
The Banker. (2008, October). The Banker investment banking awards 2008. Retrieved August 15, 2009, from http://www.ml.com/media/112394.pdf
Callens, Isabelle, & Tyteca, Daniel. (1999). Towards indicators of sustainable development for firms—a productive efficiency perspective. *Ecological Economics, 28*(1), 41–53.
Carbon Disclosure Project (CDP). (n.d.). Retrieved March 23, 2009, from http://www.cdproject.net/
Charlotte Observer. (2009, February 27). Duke energy to move HQ to tower built for Wachovia. Retrieved March 10, 2009, from http://www.newsobserver.com/business/story/1421353.html
Climate, Community, & Biodiversity Alliance (CCBA). (2008). CCB standards. Retrieved February 18, 2009, from http://www.climate-standards.org/
Coulson, Andrea, & Monks, Vivienne. (1999, April). Corporate environmental performance considerations within bank lending decisions. *Eco-Management and Auditing, 6*(1), 1–10.
CSRWire. (2006, April 6). Wells Fargo invests $5 million in renewable energy fund. Retrieved March 23, 2009, from http://www.csrwire.com/News/5357.html
Deutsch, Claudia H. (2007, July 25). G.E. unveils credit card aimed at relieving carbon footprints. Retrieved March 15, 2009, from http://www.nytimes.com/2007/07/25/business/25card.html?_r=2
Dryzek, John S. (2005). *The politics of the Earth: Environmental discourses* (2nd ed). Oxford, U.K.: Oxford University Press.
Edwards, Pamela; Birkin, Frank; & Woodward, David. (2002). Financial comparability and environmental diversity: An international context. *Business Strategy and the Environment, 11*(6), 343–359.
Enkvist, Per-Anders; Nauclér, Tomas; & Oppenheim, Jeremy M. (2008, April). Business strategies for climate change. *The McKinsey Quarterly, 2*, 24–33.

Environmental Leader. (2007, August 14). Morgan Stanley's carbon bank to provide offset services. Retrieved March 22, 2009, from http://www.environmentalleader.com/2007/08/14/morgan-stanleys-carbon-bank-to-provide-offset-services/

Equator Principles. (2009). Retrieved March 10, 2009, from http://www.equator-principles.com/principles.shtml

Figge, Frank; Hahn, Tobias; Schaltegger, Stefan; & Wagner, Marcus. (2002). The sustainability balanced scorecard—Linking sustainability management to business strategy. *Business Strategy and the Environment, 11,* 269–284. Retrieved August 15, 2009, from http://www.sustainabilitymanagement.net/public/04%20The%20Sustainability%20Balanced%20Scorecard.pdf

Gibbs, Richard. (2007, October).The economics of sustainability risk reporting (SRR). *inFinance, 121*(4), 39–40.

Global Reporting Initiative. (2009). Sustainability reporting guidelines & financial services sector supplement. Retrieved August 15, 2009, from http://www.globalreporting.org/NR/rdonlyres/46FAAF92-F39D-44D4-8EFE-0276FB34A0FC/0/ReportingGuidelinesandFSSSFinal.pdf

Goldman Sachs. (2004, February 24). *Global energy: Introducing the Goldman Sachs energy environmental and social index.* Retrieved April 27, 2009, from http://www.pewclimate.org/docUploads/Goldman%20EESI%20Index.pdf

Gollier, Christian; Jullien, Bruno; & Treich, Nicolas. (2000, February). Scientific progress and irreversibility: An economic interpretation of the "precautionary principle." *Journal of Public Economics, 75*(2), 229–253.

Gray, Rob. (2006). Does sustainability reporting improve corporate behaviour? Wrong question? Right time? *Accounting & Business Research, 36,* 65–88.

Hoffman, Andrew. (2006). *Getting ahead of the curve: Corporate strategies that address climate change.* Retrieved August 15, 2009, from http://www.pewclimate.org/docUploads/PEW_CorpStrategies.pdf

HSBC. (2007). HSBC launches international survey of public attitudes towards climate change. Retrieved March 24, 2009, from http://www.hsbc.com/1/2/sus-index

IBIS World Industry Reports. (2008). Commercial banking in the U.S., December 4. Retrieved January 11, 2010, from http://www.mindbranch.com/about/publisher_info.jsp?pubcode=538

Investor Network on Climate Risk (INCR). (2007). Retrieved March 20, 2009, from http://www.incr.com/Page.aspx?pid=198

Intergovernmental Panel on Climate Change (IPCC). (2007). *Climate change 2007: Synthesis report.* Retrieved January 18, 2010, from http://www.ipcc.ch/pdf/assessment-report/ar4/syr/ar4_syr.pdf

Japan for Sustainability. (2004, July 29). Japanese musicians establish eco-friendly bank. Retrieved March 29, 2009, from http://www.japanfs.org/en/pages/025659.html

Knecht, Frans. (1997). Relevance of environmental performance to corporate value. Paper presented at the Environment and Financial Performance, New York. Cited in Rob Gray (2006), Does sustainability reporting improve corporate behaviour? Wrong question? Right time? *Accounting & Business Research, 36,* 65–88.

Louche, Céline. (2001). The corporate environmental performance–financial performance link: implications for ethical investments. In Jan Jap Bouma; Marcel Jeucken; & Leon Klinkers (Eds.), *Sustainable banking: The greening of finance* (pp. 187–200). Sheffield, U.K.: Greenleaf.

McCammon, A. L. T. (1995). Banking responsibility and liability for the environment: What are banks doing? *Environmental Conservation, 22*(4), 297–305.

Meadows, Donella; Randers, Jorgen; & Meadows, Dennis. (2004). *Limits to growth: The 30-year update.* White River Junction, VT: Chelsea Green.

Melnyk, Steven; Sroufe, Robert; & Calantone, Roger. (2003). Assessing the impact of environmental management systems on corporate and environmental performance. *Journal of Operations Management, 21,* 329–351. Retrieved August 15, 2009, from http://www2.bc.edu/~sroufe/jom2003.pdf

Merrill Lynch. (2009). Environmental sustainability. Retrieved April 14, 2009, from http://www.ml.com/?id=7695_8134_13653_71406

Morales, Alex. (2008, January 21). Eleven multinationals to assess their "carbon footprint." *The Washington Post,* A16. Retrieved August 15, 2009, from http://www.washingtonpost.com/wp-dyn/content/article/2008/01/20/AR2008012002319.html

Mulder, Herman H. (2009). Values-based, sustainable, responsible, banking. Retrieved December 11, 2009, from www.worldconnectors.nl/upload/cms/252_SUSTAINABLE_BANKING.doc

newresourcebank. (2006). Green resources. Retrieved March 23, 2009, from http://www.newresourcebank.com/community/resources.php

Ng, Serena, & Mollenkamp, Carrick. (2009, March 7). Top U.S., European banks got $50 billion in AIG aid. *Wall Street Journal.* Retrieved August 12, 2009, from http://online.wsj.com/article/SB123638394500958141.html?mod=rss_Today%27s_Most_Popular

Nordhaus, Ted, & Shellenberger, Michael. (2007). *Break through: From the death of environmentalism to the politics of possibility.* Boston: Houghton Mifflin.

Orlitsky, Marc, & Benjamin, John D. (2001, December). Corporate social performance and firm risk: A meta-analytical review. *Business & Society, 40*(4), 369–396.

PricewaterhouseCoopers Global. (2009). Financial services. Retrieved March 15, 2009, from http://www.pwc.com/extweb/industry.nsf/docid/79508408741F5B78852570D20076B902

Prince of Wales's Business & the Environment Programme. (2009). Retrieved January 11, 2010, from http://www.cpi.cam.ac.uk/our_work/executives_seminars/bep.aspx

Randjelovic, Jelena; O'Rourke, Anastasia R.; & Orsato, Renato J. (2003). The emergence of *green* venture capital. *Business Strategy and the Environment, 12*(4), 240–253.

Repetto, Robert, & Austin, Duncan. (1999, September 22). Estimating the financial effects of companies' environmental performance and exposure. *Greener Management International, 27,* 97–110.

Riddell, Zoe, & Chamberlin, Brittany. (2007). *Carbon disclosure project—Investor research project.* Retrieved August 13, 2009, from http://www.google.com/search?hl=en&q=Investor+research+project+Riddell+and+Chamberlin&aq=f&oq=&aqi=

Russo, Michael, & Fouts, Paul. (1997). A resource-based perspective on corporate environmental performance and profitability. *Academy of Management Journal, 40*(3), 534–559.

Schaltegger, Stefan, & Figge, Frank. (2000). Environmental shareholder value: Economic success with corporate environmental management. *Eco-Management and Auditing, 7*(1), 29–42.

Schaltegger, Stefan, & Figge, Frank. (2001). Sustainable development funds: Progress since the 1970s. In Jan Jap Bouma; Marcel Jeucken; & Leon Klinkers. (Eds.), *Sustainable banking: The greening of finance* (pp. 203–210). Sheffield, UK: Greenleaf.

Schmidheiny, Stephan, & Zorraquin, Federico. (1996). *Financing change: The financial community, eco-efficiency, and sustainable development.* MIT Press: Cambridge, MA.

Schmid-Schönbein, Oliver, & Braunschweig, Arthur. (2000). *EPI-finance 2000: Environmental performance indicators for the financial industry.* Zurich: E2 Management Consulting AG.

Scholz, Roland; Weber, Olaf; Stünzi, J.; Ohlenroth, W.; & Reuter, A. (1995). *Umweltrisiken systematisch erfassen. Kreditausfälle aufgrund ökologischer Risiken—Fazit erster empirischer Untersuchungen* [The systematic measuring of environmental risk. Credit defaults caused by environmental risk—results of a first study]. *Schweizer Bank, 4,* 45–47.

Securities and Exchange Commission (SEC). (2007). Petition for interpretive guidance on climate risk disclosure (p. F-5). Retrieved December 11, 20009, from http://www.sec.gov/rules/petitions/2007/petn4-547.pdf

Sharma, Sanjay, & Ruud, Aundun. (2003). On the path to sustainability: Integrating social dimensions into the research and practice of environmental management. *Business Strategy and the Environment, 12*, 205–214.

Siddiqul, Firoze, & Newman, Peter. (2001). Grameen shakti: Financing renewable energy in Bangladesh. In Jan Jap Bouma; Marcel Jeucken; & Leon Klinkers (Eds.), *Sustainable banking: The greening of finance* (pp. 88–95). Sheffield, U.K.: Greenleaf.

Stigson, Björn. (2001). Making the link between environmental performance and shareholder value: The metrics of eco-efficiency. In Jan Jap Bouma; Marcel Jeucken; & Leon Klinkers (Eds.), *Sustainable banking: The greening of finance* (pp. 166–172). Sheffield, U.K.: Greenleaf.

Sussman, Francis G., & Freed, J. Randall. (2008). *Adapting to climate change: A business approach.* Arlington, VA: Pew Center on Global Climate Change.

Swiss Re. (2007). Swiss Re announces final close of EUR 329 million European Clean Energy Fund. Retrieved March 24, 2009, from http://www.swissre.com/pws/media%20centre/news/news%20releases%202007/swiss%20re%20announces%20final%20close%20of%20eur%20329%20million%20european%20clean%20energy%20fund.html

Ullmann, Arieh. (1985). Data in search of a theory: A critical examination of the relationship among social performance, social disclosure and economic performance of US firms. *Academy of Management Review, 10*(3), 540-557.

United Nations Environmental Programme (UNEP). (1992). Statement by banks on the environment and sustainable development. UNEP: Rio de Janeiro.

United Nations Environment Programme Finance Initiative (UNEP FI). (2002). CEO briefing on climate change. Retrieved April 27, 2009, from http://www.unepfi.org/fileadmin/documents/CEO_briefing_climate_change_2002_en.pdf

United Nations World Commission on Environment and Development (WCED). (1987). *Report of the world commission on environment and development: Our common future.* Retrieved April 27, 2009, from http://www.un-documents.net/wced-ocf.htm

United States Government Accountability Office. (2009, March 31). Troubled asset relief program: March 2009 status of efforts to address transparency and accountability issues. Retrieved April 27, 2009, from http://www.gao.gov/products/GAO-09-504

van Bellegem, Theo. (2001). The green fund system in The Netherlands. In Jan Jap Bouma; Marcel Jeucken; & Leon Klinkers (Eds.), *Sustainable banking: The greening of finance* (pp. 234–244). Sheffield, U.K.: Greenleaf.

van den Brink, Timo, & van der Woerd, Frans. (2004). Industry specific sustainability benchmarks: An ECSF pilot bridging corporate sustainability with social responsible investments. *Journal of Business Ethics, 55*(2), 187–203.

Weber, Olaf. (2005). Sustainability benchmarking of European banks and financial service organizations. Retrieved August 15, 2009, from http://www.cleanerproduction.com/Training/Banks/Refs/Sustainability%20benchmarking%20in%20Euro%20banks.pdf

Wells Fargo. (2008, December 22). Wells Fargo exceeds $3 billion in environmental financing: Issues progress report on environmental finance activities. Retrieved April 4, 2009, from https://www.wellsfargo.com/press/2008/20081222__Enviromental_Funding

Yunus, Muhammad. (2003). *Banker to the poor: Micro-lending and the battle against world poverty.* New York: PublicAffairs.

Investment, CleanTech

CleanTech *refers to technologies and business models that improve a product or a service's performance, productivity, or efficiency while reducing costs, using less energy and fewer materials, and lessening environmental damage. CleanTech investment in diverse sectors, including energy, water and wastewater treatment, manufacturing, advanced materials, transportation, and agriculture, provides competitive returns for investors and customers. Standardization, legislation, long-term planning, and incentives mediate its risks.*

Since 2004, investment in the venture capital category known as CleanTech has emerged as a new trend that is fundamentally changing the face of the business of sustainability. Such technology—solar power, fuel cells, and aquaculture, for example—drives innovation as it has the potential to become an integral part of corporate value chains. (A "value chain" is a series of activities whose goal is to create value that exceeds the cost of providing a product or service, thereby generating a profit margin.) CleanTech refers to the "clean" technologies and business models that address the source of ecological problems caused by a product or a service's manufacturing or development process. It improves the product or service's performance, its productivity, or its efficiency as it reduces costs, uses less energy and fewer materials, and causes less environmental damage. Such technologies are clustered in diverse industry sectors, including energy (about two-thirds of total investment), water and wastewater treatment, manufacturing, advanced materials, transportation, and agriculture. The products or services cover a wide range including: energy-efficient lighting; wind and solar energy; water filtration; next-generation batteries; advanced materials that make products lighter, stronger, and/or cheaper; nontoxic pesticides; and enabling technologies that improve the performance of smart electricity grids.

Companies are realizing that integrating CleanTech solutions into their operations can potentially "green" their supply chains. It will also reduce their exposure to the uncertainties of climate change and water shortages and pollution, increase market valuations (the amount consumers are willing to pay), and, particularly, develop additional income streams in new markets. The challenge for corporations is to weigh the investment in CleanTech solutions, which often are capital intensive, against the solutions' potential long-term business value. For example, corporations and investors need to contend with the uncertainty of a technology's scalability or robustness and the need for new business models that would allow them to capture the value of the investment. They also need to consider the uncertainties of the financial markets that have hindered debt financing and public offerings, the volatility of oil prices, and the range of proposed policies aimed at adapting to climate change and reducing carbon emissions.

The CleanTech investment space is characterized by high capital investment, long technology-development cycles, a high degree of dependence on government policy, and (as of this early stage) uncertain exit strategies for investors. These characteristics contrast with typical information technology elements (e.g., materials in the solar value chain and smart grids that deliver electricity from alternative power sources), biotechnology (e.g., algae biofuels), and several other more mature investment domains. Hence new business models are needed for CleanTech investments, because investors and businesses that have transitioned from information technology or biotechnology into CleanTech have experienced a significant learning curve, particularly as it pertains to the valuation of companies, the size of investment rounds, and the potential for exit strategies (acquisitions or initial public offerings). The 2009 initial public offering of A123 Systems, which makes lithium-ion batteries that could be used in smart grids, potentially opened a window to access public markets profitably. Acquisitions, however, remain the most likely exit strategy.

Evidence is emerging that corporations are increasingly investing in CleanTech start-ups, joint ventures, and outright acquisitions, particularly in the energy, biofuel, and water-treatment technology areas, for the purpose of strategic differentiation and revenue growth. Examples include Exxon's $600 million investment in Synthetic Genomics during 2009 to develop superior algae strains for biodiesel production, General Electric's 2009 investment in A123 Systems, and Walmart's investment in energy- and water-efficiency companies to reduce carbon and water footprints (Cleantech Group 2009). (Carbon footprints and water footprints measure the amount of greenhouse gases created in the production of goods and services or the amount of freshwater used during daily activities, respectively.) The market for these technologies continues to expand, as more investors and corporations realize how sustainability-driven innovation through investment in CleanTech can better use natural resources in a way that provides economic value. What has fueled this trend, why are companies investing in CleanTech, and how is it related to leading innovations for corporate environmental sustainability?

Growth and Expansion

In the United States, CleanTech dates to the 1970s, when the environmental movement came of age after the Environmental Protection Agency was established. At that time, Congress enacted legislation such as the Clean Air Act and the Clean Water Act in response to public sentiment against environmental pollution and to the widespread evidence of environmental and public health hazards. These events and the oil crisis of 1973 prompted research and technology development for alternative energy generation, water-treatment processes, and "end-of-pipe" environmental treatment technologies that deal with pollution after it happens. Many of these technologies, however, were in an early stage of development, were too expensive, and did not have widespread political support; very few established companies embraced the innovative potential of this sector. This was due, in part, to the cost of these solutions and the absence of business models that would allow investors and companies to capture attractive returns. As a result, environmental technologies were often only implemented in small markets driven by regulatory compliance. Because of these events, the Cleantech Group (which coined and trademarked the term *cleantech*) argues that CleanTech should not be confused with the terms *environmental technology* or *green tech*, commonly used in the 1970s and 1980s.

To date, scores of companies and organizations in the United States and Europe are driving CleanTech business development and helping investors and corporations identify investment and acquisition opportunities. These include Clean Edge, a research and publishing firm dedicated to the CleanTech sector, which targets investors and entrepreneurs; Lux Research, an independent research and advisory firm, which provides corporations and investment funds with strategic advice and ongoing intelligence for emerging technologies; and Cleantech Europe, an advisory firm for entrepreneurs and investors, which canvasses the entire CleanTech space. Aside from business intelligence firms, the financial services industry has embraced CleanTech and focuses on the energy sector by establishing either new specializations within a firm or independent boutique operations.

Even at the start of the twenty-first century, the term *CleanTech* was not in the financial or business community's vocabulary. But since 2004, the sector has matured and gained recognition because it couples new CleanTech products or services with new business models that offer competitive returns for investors and customers. In recent years, this sector has seen a surge in financial innovations that drive businesses and consumers to adopt clean technologies. For example, rooftop solar technology is driven by long-term leasing and purchasing programs. In these programs, the technology is owned and maintained by the solar company, which also negotiates electricity rates with the utility to enable rebates to the consumer. These low-risk value propositions to consumers and peak power–demand mitigation values to utilities are becoming the mainstream for residential and commercial energy production and are being adopted in the waste-to-energy sector. A number of strategic drivers, which determine the success or direction of a company's business strategy, have spurred CleanTech's rapid growth. These drivers include the availability of private and public capital; the decreasing cost of technologies, which affects the scalability of solutions; the competition between governments to build jobs for the green economy; the certainty of climate change, which is influencing companies to disclose and mitigate their exposure risks; a changing consumer base that demands sustainable goods and services; and the resource demands of emerging economies such as India's and China's.

The best evidence that CleanTech has entered the mainstream is that governments around the world have made greening of the economy the centerpiece of their stimulus programs, at a cost that some estimate to be over $500 billion (Edenhofer and Stern 2009). This injection of government capital has accelerated investors' and corporations' interest, resulting in a green technology market rebound of

36 percent in the second quarter of 2009. At that time, more than three thousand venture-backed CleanTech companies were operating globally. Many more were funded through corporate investment, debt-equity financing, wealthy individuals, and government grants. Thus the intent of the technology, and the CleanTech venture based on it, is to mitigate carbon or water footprints through efficiency gains or other means because of their business value. Yet unintended consequences can result when forces other than markets pick which measures will be successes or failures. This has been the case with the ethanol biofuel mandates in the United States and the subsidies and preferential feed-in tariffs for solar and wind energy in Europe. Farmland gave way to energy farms, and food commodity prices spiked as a result. Hence the integration of policies and CleanTech solutions is awkward. Indeed, given the uncertainty of the outcome of the U.N.'s 2009 Copenhagen climate discussions (COP-15), venture firms and entrepreneurs have been positioning themselves to become increasingly less reliant on environmental policies that may have unintended consequences or determine business value.

Impact on Sustainability

Corporations that make targeted investments in internal research and development, joint ventures, and acquisitions of companies that use disruptive technology (advances that improve a product or service in ways that are unexpected by the market) are creating both effective, innovative CleanTech solutions and value in their operations. This is where innovation in clean technologies and sustainability objectives intersect. The rationale is that technology investments help resolve the potential impacts of climate change and water risks on the long-term growth strategies (and thus market valuations) of corporations. Since 2004, disclosures in the financial market of economic, environmental, and social performance have become increasingly common in financial reporting and are important to organizational success. This is evident from corporations' disclosures in their Securities and Exchange Commission (SEC) filings of climate risks to their operations and supply chains and from their innovative solutions to reduce their exposure to the risk.

The Dow Jones Sustainability Indexes (DJSI) have tracked the financial performance of the leading sustainability-driven companies worldwide since 2000, and many organizations such as Ceres, the RiskMetrics Group, and the Carbon Disclosure Project analyze sustainability indicators. For example, Ceres is a national coalition of investors, environmental groups, and other public interest organizations that work with companies to address sustainability challenges such as global climate change. Ceres directs the Investor Network on Climate Risk, a group of more than seventy institutional investors from the United States and Europe that manage over $7 trillion in assets. A 2008 report published by Ceres describes how sixty-three of the largest consumer and technology companies across all industry sectors are positioning themselves to respond to the effects of climate change on their massive operations and supply chains (Risk Metrics 2008, 3). In the responses, the companies plan to reduce their carbon and water footprints. But because sustainability will increasingly become a driver for corporate strategy and differentiation, companies will need next-generation practices that change the existing business paradigms. To develop innovations that lead to next practices, executives must question the implicit assumptions behind their current practices. The Ceres report's recommended actions involve changing pay reward structures, governance systems, and supply chain management; setting renewable energy purchasing targets; and strategically investing in disruptive technologies. CleanTech allows businesses to change the way they operate, because technology differentiation results in strategic differentiation from the competition within and outside their industry sectors.

Many companies focus on the large portion of their carbon and water footprints that are in their supply chains. A number of leading companies began by managing their risks and developing standards to measure their emissions, and then moved forward to identify easy-to-achieve changes and the type of CleanTech investments to target. Consider Nike, whose extensive chain of footwear manufacturing sites accounts for 60 percent of its total carbon footprint. Because it is difficult to measure and control greenhouse gas emissions from raw materials processing, component suppliers, and the transportation of goods, these sites must collaborate with one another and with suppliers. Around 2009, Coca-Cola and Molson Coors started implementing a common industry standard to measure product lifecycle emissions, concentrating on managing their water footprints across the entire supply chain. Dell, Walmart, and several other companies directly engage suppliers in China to ensure that greenhouse gas emissions are assessed and reported.

But many companies go further. Walmart invested in CleanTech companies and technologies that offer solutions for greening their operations. For example, it implemented energy-efficient heating and lighting systems and pervious roofs and parking lot surfaces to restore the hydraulic cycle that moves water through land, the oceans, and the atmosphere. Walmart is even exploring colocating its warehouses with landfill gasification projects to form an off-grid power source. Energy companies such as Exxon and Chevron (alongside venture capital firms) invested heavily in algae biofuel start-up companies because they recognize that algae biodiesel technology may be scalable and produce an alternative to oil. Thus, they explored greening their product mix and tapped into new markets. These companies are particularly focused on the early stages in the value chain, such as the isolation, selection, and genetic engineering of highly efficient strains of algae, and the related extraction process technology. Engineering manufacturing companies such as Bosch and Siemens are diversifying in green technology by investing in start-ups across the solar and wind value chain and through acquisitions. Proponents of improving the corporate value chain believe that core engineering know-how can be directed to improve alternative energy and other technologies. This allows companies to tap into new markets while integrating the innovations into their operations and supply chains.

Risks and Controversies

The investment decisions in the growth and opportunities of CleanTech companies are at the center of a perfect storm: governments are unlocking unprecedented amounts of stimulus funds in order to green economies. Some argue that companies on the DJSI, compared with those not on the list, exhibit an increase of up to 15 percent in price-earnings ratios, indicating that the market values these companies more than it values companies that do not meet sustainability metrics. The market is looking at companies' climate risk disclosures in SEC filings. In addition, climate policies are influencing industry value chains, carbon markets for emissions trading, and consumer behaviors. Yet risks, unintended consequences, and other controversies may affect the future development of CleanTech innovations. Among these impacts are "greenwashing," or incorrectly stating the environmental benefits of a product, technology, or practice; the risk of governments awarding funds and determining policies based on a company's massive investment in targeted innovations; the risk of companies failing to make long-term plans; and the green paradox that policies aimed at curbing emissions may result in the acceleration of oil production.

How can companies and governments address these issues? First, some reporting standards for greening the supply chain and operations are emerging, and analysts are using them. As of the beginning of the twenty-first century, the implementation of climate and water risk reporting within companies is voluntary, and the metrics for various products and services are arbitrary. Increasing the standards of reporting and continuing to release disclosures will aid in the elimination of these risks. If the reporting of climate risks and the proposed mitigation strategies for companies, regardless of sectors, can be standardized, then corporations can hedge their financial risks to climate change and water risk uncertainties. For example, Swiss Re (a leading global reinsurer) and others are piloting weather insurance products that would reduce crop price volatility (affecting the food, beverage, and clothing industries) and transfer risk to financial players (the reinsurers or investors).

Second, the infusion of government capital will have the potential to remake alternative energy and other green technology businesses, influence investment returns, and affect industry value chains. For example, the United States's 2009 "green" economic stimulus plan targets a clean energy future by allotting $117.2 billion, or 12 percent of the $787.2 billion plan (Edenhofer and Stern 2009). It will achieve this through the development of plug-in hybrid cars and renewable energy technology, investment in energy efficiency, and a cap-and-trade program for trading pollution credits in order to reduce greenhouse gas emissions. China's government committed to a circular economy concept that would reduce, reuse, and recycle resources during manufacturing, transportation, and consumption by allotting $218 billion, or 33.4 percent of its budget. This legislation will allow Chinese auto manufacturers to leapfrog automotive technology by a generation and lead the green car revolution. It also identifies an official target for the capacity of installed solar and wind energy plants that well exceeds that of the United States. But history has shown that letting governments rather than markets decide what measures will be successful may be risky. For example, the U.S. government credits for biofuel growers have pushed up commodity prices and caused a food-for-oil trade-off, affecting poor populations and increasing the water footprints of the biofuel industry. The emphasis on hybrid electric or all-electric cars, with their dependence on scarce supplies of lithium-ion batteries, leaves companies exposed to political risk and unsustainable extraction practices.

Third, companies must have a long-term plan that considers the opportunities and sustainability of their investments in CleanTech. The view that CleanTech is a mere add-on with a good cost-benefit ratio is shortsighted. These myopic views may result in companies shedding CleanTech when the market or policy incentives change, meaning the technology's social and environmental impacts will be small. The integration of CleanTech into the company's value structure has a greater potential to shift the company's competitive strategy and have a lasting impact for sustainability.

Finally, the so-called green paradox argues that as governments and companies strive to reduce emissions by reducing fossil fuel consumption (through CleanTech innovations in alternative energy, improved building insulation, and efficient cars), the global extraction of coal, gas, and oil will increase. The argument is that as companies green the economy, they exert a downward pressure on future fossil fuel prices (because less is needed). To maintain profits, owners of oil and gas fields will increase production, thus exacerbating climate change. The implication is that policies need to offer incentives for owners to leave supplies in the ground, rather than attempt to curb demand. The paradox is that curbs on demand have stimulated considerable CleanTech innovation. Taxation disincentives for owners are not politically viable, so a global carbon emissions trading system may be able to cap fuel consumption and slow down extraction rates. This would spur further innovations in carbon financing and bring financial and insurance services up the green value chain. (Carbon financing, as part of the Kyoto Protocol, generally refers to investments in greenhouse gas emission reduction projects and the creation of financial instruments that are tradable on the carbon market. The value chain essentially consists of three major players: project owners, traders or brokers, and buyers of carbon offsets. Even though not all greenhouse gas mitigation projects carry the same value, the carbon markets and their financial services players attempt to authenticate and verify the value of the offsets through financial instruments.)

Future Outlook

The fact that viable business models are generating attractive returns to investors and corporations shows that CleanTech is here to stay, regardless of the market, policy, and technology challenges it poses to corporate operations and value chains. While the United States's 2009 economic stimulus funding will be expended over two years, the impact in the markets of its green investment will take much longer to appear. The traction of SEC filings will continue as more companies participate in the disclosure of climate risks or participate in the Carbon Disclosure Project. With the standardization of measurements coming of age, companies will more easily measure their carbon and water footprints and identify opportunities to mitigate risks. Project financing and insurance pricing are increasingly tied to the climate exposures of corporations, and hence future favorable rates may induce companies to adopt carbon and water management strategies and consider integrating CleanTech solutions into their competitive strategies. In light of the

maturation of the sector since 2004, which was driven by venture capital and private equity, the early twenty-first century will be driven by growth and expansion in the mainstream economy that is fueled by government programs. It is, however, important to differentiate the outlook by technology domain.

Energy will continue to be the main sector for investment, particularly transportation (batteries and fuel cells), biofuels (algae and noncrop plants), and the continued expansion of solar and wind power. In the third quarter of 2009, CleanTech investments for the first time exceeded those in software, biomedical devices, and biotechnology, with 25 percent of the total venture investment occurring in the United States (Cleantech Group 2009, 13). Solar is the top sector, with a 28 percent share of investment, closely followed by transportation (25 percent) and biofuels (9 percent) (Cleantech Group 2009, 10). In the short term, analysts expect major consolidation to occur in the value chains for these industries. The causes are the role of government, private capital shortages, overcapacity in the face of lower energy demand, and decreasing prices for the integrated technology. This consolidation will stimulate investment in energy companies because investors can control the whole supply chain and respond to U.S. mandates under the stimulus package. This trend is already evident for the solar industry and is likely to follow in the wind industry. New financial models and incentives will be needed to ensure the stability of this CleanTech industry. For example, utilities pay feed-in tariffs, or set prices for paying the end users who provide solar power to the power grid. Making these tariffs consistent across all solar projects (as is proposed in China) will reduce costs and make the projects viable, thereby allowing companies to calculate risks and returns. Even though it is hard to project where investments are headed, findings from Deloitte Touche Tohmatsu's 2009 *Global Trends in Venture Capital* report shows that 63 percent of venture capitalists around the globe intend to increase their exposure to the CleanTech category over the next three years—a far higher percentage than any other sector. The trend looks set to continue for some time.

The demand for renewable energy by utilities is growing, as they must comply with state (and most likely federal) renewable portfolio standards (RPSs) by 2020. The doubts some have that the widespread, integral use of solar power in the RPSs are waning. (Even in the oil- and gas-intensive city of Houston, Texas, utilities are buying solar technology.) Global competition is playing a role as well, with capacity targets for installed alternative energy systems in China rapidly eclipsing those in the United States. A major challenge, aside from policy incentives, is the creation of a smart grid that can handle the highly variable production of electricity from renewable energy sources, one that will allow for storage and can track the "green" and "brown" electrons. A smart grid links power production, transmission, and distribution from centralized (e.g., coal-fired power plants) and distributed sources (e.g., wind farms or electric vehicles) with consumer demand. With electricity being generated from traditional coal or oil plants (brown electrons) as well as from the wind, solar energy, biofuels, and batteries (green electrons), an intricate management system needs to be developed. In the United States, many start-up companies in all parts of the value chain are working together to develop enabling technologies and management aspects that meet a federal mandate to create a smart grid. Considering the fixed infrastructure of the current grid, companies will likely locate green smart grids along corridors (e.g., in Arizona and California) to test their feasibility. Bond measures will likely fund their construction in a piecemeal fashion, and business models will be developed to monetize them with attractive returns.

In other sectors, advances in battery technology aside from lithium-ion batteries will fuel the generation of cars that will be developed in the second decade of the century. But first, battery costs must come down and their efficiency must improve. Experience with hybrid technology and General Motors's Volt electric car will prove invaluable to assess market demand for this technology and to drive innovations in electrical grid infrastructure. Experience with hybrid and electric technology might also affect business models pertaining to the purchase, maintenance, and afterlife care of the battery system. Corporations may be highly motivated to move in this direction because of their investments in fuel-efficient fleets, whether on an ownership, lease, or joint venture basis. Future fuel prices, the cost of technology, and government incentives will play a major role in the adoption of this technology. Considering the long development cycles and fragmentation of the industry, these innovations will presumably have a long time on the horizon before they play out in the marketplace.

Finally, conservative deregulation in the water industry sector has seen much innovation and investment or acquisition activity, both for ultrahigh-purity and high-volume applications. For example, General Electric acquired Canada's Glegg Water Company, which developed a superior electrodeionization technology and product (the E-Cell) for ultraclean water treatment. Targeting high-value customers such as the pharmaceutical and semiconductor industries, General Electric's Water and Process Technologies division recognized the opportunity as an acquisition and business opportunity. Two main strategic drivers will increase investments in water technologies: SEC disclosures of corporate water footprints and the energy–water nexus. This nexus includes CleanTech innovations that address the energy used for water conveyance and treatment (e.g., to operate filtration systems, microturbines, and fuel cells). Other innovations address water use for energy production from coal, gas, nuclear, biofuel, and utility-scale solar sources. This water industry sector is moving up the value chain due to a number of factors. First, climate change affects corporate risks to water availability and quality. Second, water costs for corporate users are being renegotiated, and finally, multistakeholder water use is starting to drive new legislation.

Peter ADRIAENS
Ross School of Business, University of Michigan

See also in the *Berkshire Encyclopedia of Sustainability*: **Biomimicry; Cap-and-Trade Legislation; Climate Change Disclosure; Energy Efficiency; Energy Industries—Overview of Renewables; Green-Collar Jobs; Investment, Socially Responsible (SRI); Product-Service Systems (PSSs); Risk Management; Supply Chain Management; True Cost Economics**

FURTHER READING

Alter, Alexandra. (2009, February 17). Yet another footprint to worry about: Water. Retrieved November 16, 2009, from http://online.wsj.com/article/SB123483638138996305.html

Carbon Disclosure Project. (2009). Retrieved November 16, 2009, from http://www.cdproject.net/

Clean Edge. (2009). Retrieved November16, 2009, from http://www.cleanedge.com/

Cleantech Group. (2009). *Cleantech investment monitor: Third quarter 2009*. Retrieved November 16, 2009, from http://www.deloitte.com/view/en_US/us/Services/additional-services/Corporate-Responsibility-Sustainability/clean-tech/article/46dd16e22872521 0VgnVCM100000ba42f00aRCRD.htm

Deloitte Touche Tohmatsu. (2009, June). *Global trends in venture capital 2009 global report*. Retrieved December 8, 2009, from http://www.deloitte.com/view/en_GX/global/article/e79af6b085912210Vgn VCM100000ba42f00aRCRD.htm

Edenhofer, Ottmar, & Stern, Nicholas. (2009). *Towards a global green recovery: Recommendations for immediate G20 action*. Retrieved December 14, 2009, from http://www2.lse.ac.uk/granthamInstitute/publications/GlobalGreenRecovery_April09.pdf

Esty, Daniel C., & Winston, Andrew S. (2006). *Green to gold: How smart companies use environmental strategy to innovate, create value, and build competitive advantage*. New Haven, CT: Yale University Press.

Kammen, Daniel M. (2006). The rise of renewable energy. *Scientific American, 295*(3), 85–93.

Metcalfe, Robert M. (2008, September). Learning from the Internet. Retrieved November 16, 2009, from http://www.sciamdigital.com/index.cfm?fa=Products.ViewIssue&ISSUEID_CHAR=7642E940-3048-8A5E-103FDB5762BAF1D5

Pernick, Ron, & Wilder, Clint. (2008). *The clean tech revolution*. New York: Harper Collins Business.

The power and the glory. (2008, June 19). Retrieved November 16, 2009, from http://www.economist.com/specialreports/displaystory.cfm?story_id=11565685

RiskMetrics Group, & Ceres. (2008, December). *Corporate governance and climate change: Consumer and technology companies*. Retrieved November 16, 2009, from http://www.ceres.org/Document.Doc?id=398

Investment, Socially Responsible (SRI)

Socially responsible investment (SRI) is a process that integrates environmental, social, and community concerns into a traditional financial investment framework. The SRI market's growth, especially in the developing world, depends on development of new research methods, market pressures to encourage further corporate transparency and accountability, and incorporation of SRI into national economies.

Socially responsible investing (SRI) is an investment process that considers social and environmental consequences within the context of traditional financial analysis. Investors—including individuals, institutions, and corporations—use SRI to achieve traditional financial as well as social, environmental, and community returns. They accomplish this by integrating these dimensions onto a traditional financial investment framework. An important goal of SRI is to promote corporate accountability for its social and environmental risks into mainstream financial practices and to engage a wide range of companies in improving their environmental and social responsibility practices.

Origins of Modern SRI

The origins of the modern SRI movement can be traced to the turbulent period in the 1960s when powerful social undercurrents, including environmentalism and antiwar activism, fueled a radical change in the way society viewed faith, values, and commerce. SRI funds were once primarily known as "ethical funds," and given SRI's strong Judeo-Christian roots, this is not at all surprising. The notion of an ethical business is established in Judeo-Christian traditions; examples of it exist in the book of Deuteronomy,

which dates back more than 2,500 years. But it is arguably the Quaker faith that has made the greatest impact in connecting commercial activities and ethical values in the modern age. The Quakers were the first group to practice the "negative screening" of investments when they avoided investments in the military sector by faithfully applying their peace traditions to commercial activities. One of the early examples of what we might call an SRI-like activity is an investment fund established by the Methodist Church in the 1960s that avoided investments in armaments, alcohol, gambling, and tobacco. Since the fund managed by the Methodist Church was closed to outsiders, the first modern example of what we now call an SRI fund was the U.S. Pax World Fund, founded by two Methodist ministers in 1971. The first investment fund that specifically addressed ecological concerns was the Ecology Fund, established by Merlin/Jupiter Company in 1988 (Kreander 2001).

The political unrest in South Africa in the 1960s and 1970s set the stage for another major policy push for SRI and the important connection between ethics and business practices. The Reverend Leon H. Sullivan helped draft a code of conduct (subsequently known as the Sullivan Principles) for companies doing business in South Africa. By the early 1980s the Sullivan Principles became the rallying cry for anti-apartheid activism. In 1982 the state of Connecticut adopted the Sullivan Principles and other social criteria to guide its investment decision making. Just two years later, the California Public Employees' Retirement System (CalPERS), the largest public pension fund in the world, and the New York City Employee Retirement System developed their own investing guidelines in South Africa. In the twenty-first century, corporate divestment and boycott campaigns, addressing issues ranging from the genocide in Darfur, Sudan, to the environmental policies of ExxonMobil, got started in large part due to the success of the South Africa anti-investment campaigners (IFC 2003).

Global SRI Marketplace

The global SRI market in the wealthy countries belonging to the Organisation for Economic Co-operation and Development (OECD) was well established by 2010 and, in the case of Europe, entering a major growth phase. In the United States, US$2.7 trillion, or about 11 percent of the US$26 trillion in total investment assets, is invested in one of the three SRI strategies—screening, shareholder advocacy, and community investing. Although much smaller in size, the European SRI market has grown rapidly in recent years and is now estimated to be €2.7 trillion, accounting for as much as 17.5 percent of the asset management industry (SIF 2008). Even in Japan and the Asia-Pacific region, where awareness of social responsibility concerns lags behind North America and Europe, SRI represents one of the few financial market segments that remain vibrant in terms of market development. In addition, the SRI market in Australia grew 41 percent between 2003 and 2004 alone, twice as fast as that country's retail and wholesale investment market (Eurosif 2008).

Key Global Issues and Trends

As SRI moves to the global financial and business landscape, we can highlight three important trends. The first is the emergence of the investing community, consisting of individual and institutional investors, as a new and powerful actor in global economic and sustainability governance. The second trend attempts to determine the business and sustainability effectiveness of SRI. The third trend focuses on SRI's potential role in the mainstream of emerging and developing economies at the base of the economic development pyramid.

Investing Community's Role

The emergence of investors as important financial actors and the rise of responsible investment since the 1970s highlight the complexities of contemporary global governance. For example, the lines between the domestic and the international have blurred (as investment capital increasingly attempts to link local corporate activities with global responsibilities). Other examples are the expansion of actors from a few dedicated mutual funds (mainly in the United States) to several hundred across the world; the rise of global institutional investors involved in promoting SRI principles in their activities; the emergence of a global civil society attempting to influence financial capital; and the variety of transnational issues motivating capital markets

(from human rights–related concerns, such as apartheid in South Africa, to environmental sustainability and related concerns).

Although SRI investors can technically be anyone in society who has investment capital, institutional investors—including pension funds, investment companies, insurance companies, or those investors with money under professional management—account for the largest percentage of the total SRI market. Individual or retail investors—who owned as much as 93 percent of all U.S. stocks in 1950 and as much as 75 percent in the 1970s—now own a record-low 34 percent of all shares. In contrast, institutional investors quickly gained greater control over the equity markets, with the percentage of their ownership shares increasing from 47 percent in 1987 to over 76 percent in 2007. In 1985, no company had institutional ownership of 60 percent or above, whereas by 2007, seventeen companies had institutional ownership of 60 percent or above, including six with institutional ownership of 70 percent or above (Conference Board 2007; 2008).

The significance of this trend, in terms of SRI, is that institutional investors are starting to have substantial economic, and albeit more subtle, business sustainability influence through the shares they own in particular companies. The equity investments allow institutional investors the right to bring forth shareholder resolutions and exert influence on companies in which they *do not* own equity shares. They can achieve this through creating standards or screens for future potential equity purchases.

Sustainable Impact and Effectiveness

One of the most commonly asked questions, if not one of the most important, is whether SRI portfolio screening and shareholder advocacy / engagement practices have a positive impact on the sustainable behavior of companies. While it is difficult to determine SRI's long-term sustainable impact and effectiveness, some preliminary evidence suggests that SRI is having a sustainability impact on business behavior. When CalPERS announced that it would start employing SRI principles in its investment management decisions in 2001, the practical results of this policy were initially unclear. A year later, after CalPERS decided that it would divest its investments in Thailand, Indonesia, and Malaysia due to unacceptably low levels of labor standards, political stability, and financial transparency

rankings, finance and stock market officials in those respective countries began scrambling to adopt policies to improve business practices in those areas (Aguilera et al. 2006).

The FTSE Group is the global index provider and the parent body of the FTSE4Good Index Series that measures corporations' SRI performances. As part of its five-year review in 2007, FTSE4Good Index Series announced that it had achieved a number of positive impacts on the corporate environmental and social responsibility practices of the companies around the world in which it invests (FTSE Group 2007). Through the enactment of various standards and protocols on supply chain management, bribery, climate change, and others, the FTSE4Good Index Series has pushed companies to adopt, or at least consider adopting, corporate environmental and social responsibility performance measures beyond basic compliance.

What is becoming clear, at least in the North American, European, Japanese, and some segments of the Asian markets, is that mainstream individual and institutional investors are starting to believe that social, environmental, and corporate governance are important factors in the investment decision-making process. Mercer Investment Consulting's 2009 review of thirty-six academic studies that examine the relationship between financial performance and environmental, social, and governance (ESG) factors reveals that twenty studies show a positive relationship (that is, financial and ESG factors are positively correlated), eight studies show a neutral relationship, and six studies show a neutral/negative relationship. Mercer's 2006 survey of 183 large financial institutional investors indicates that as much as 75 percent of the respondents (22 percent of whom were SRI investors) believe that social, environmental, and corporate governance factors can have a material impact on investment performance (Mercer 2006). The question is whether this fact—that twenty out of thirty-six academic studies find a positive relationship between financial performance and ESG factors—represents definitive evidence (Mercer 2009). It is probably safer to conclude that there is strong evidence to suggest a positive relationship between financial performance and ESG factors, albeit with the usual proviso that additional research is required.

SRI and Emerging Economies

The healthy development in the SRI markets of North America, Europe, and to a lesser degree Asia overshadows the almost complete lack of SRI activity in emerging and developing economies, where more than two-thirds of the world's population lives and works. The most recent International Finance Corporation survey (2009) of corporate executives and investment professionals' attitudes toward ESG factors in emerging markets compared their thoughts about the global financial situation before the crisis (2007) and midcrisis (2009). Forty-six percent of the investors surveyed strongly agreed with the statement that ESG issues are an important part of their research, portfolio management, and manager selection, up from 36 percent in 2007. The majority of asset owners (78 percent) also suggested that the importance of ESG factors has been amplified by the late 2007–2009 financial crisis and may result in greater use of ESG criteria over time in emerging markets (IFC 2009).

According to the International Finance Corporation, the sum of SRI assets in emerging markets is approximately US$2.7 billion, or 0.1 percent of the US$2.7 trillion global SRI market. Its most recent figure for emerging market assets held by SRI investors in industrialized countries is anywhere between US$1.5 billion and US$2 billion, while it estimates SRI assets in emerging market capitalization at the most optimistic level of 0.1 percent, or US$5 billion. While the most reliable figures on SRI assets in emerging markets come from a 2003 International Financial Corporation study, what is noteworthy is that the estimated SRI assets in emerging markets is small no matter which benchmark we use for comparison. Although the economic disparity between the wealthy, industrialized developed world and the developing world is always stark, it is nevertheless startling to see such a gap between wealthy countries and developing/emerging countries in terms of sustainable investing. This is clearly one of the many institutional hurdles SRI needs to overcome if it is to become more than just a niche market and realize its potential for sustainability at the Base of the Pyramid.

Future Development

Will SRI realize its full potential as a global sustainable business mechanism and advance sustainable strategic management? The answer to this question may depend in part on the quality and sophistication of future SRI research methodology. Smaller SRI investment companies, without their own research staff, rely on independent research providers like KLD Research and Analytics in the United States or Ethical Investment Research Service in the United Kingdom for most of their research needs. Larger SRI fund companies rely on their own internal staff to conduct research and shareholder advocacy and/ or to engage with companies. While the more simplistic screening of companies from portfolios is still being used, SRI research as a whole is moving toward much more

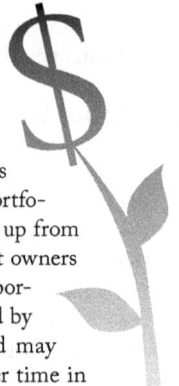

sophisticated techniques, including a myriad of quantitative analyses. Moreover, sustainability business research companies like the U.K.-based Trucost are starting to use sophisticated economic modeling to assess the environmental externalities that may not be captured in conventional financial accounts. The development of global sustainability indexes like the Dow Jones Sustainability Indexes and the FTSE4Good Index Series have become a much-needed investment index to the SRI capital markets and have led to greater pressure on companies to disclose relevant environmental and social indicators.

Another factor in determining the future development of SRI is the degree of market pressure, particularly from institutional investors, for corporate transparency and accountability. The financial crisis that stared in late 2007 has produced a global chorus for transparency in the financial sector, but it remains unclear if this will lead to a fundamental change in how the global financial market, including SRI, will be governed. It is clear, however, that the greater the transparency and accountability pressures, the better it will be for the future growth of the global SRI market. In 2009, a campaign began pressuring the U.S. Securities and Exchange Commission to require companies to disclose their climate change business risks as part of their 10-K corporate filings and other reporting requirements. Similar international policy initiatives like those of the Global Reporting Initiative organization and national/regional government programs are putting increasing regulatory pressure on strengthening disclosures of corporate environmental and social data.

Arguably the most important criterion for determining growth in SRI development worldwide is to what degree SRI becomes a mainstream investment strategy in emerging and developing economies. Just two countries (India and China) constitute 40 percent of the world's population, and China is no longer considered an emerging market. China will become the world's exporter and is expected to replace Japan as the second-largest economy in the world by 2030. Although the current total of SRI assets in emerging economies is a tiny percentage (still less than 1 percent) of the total emerging market capitalization, there are strong signs that institutional shareholder activism and tightening environmental and social regulatory pressures will become the business norm in a certain select number of emerging markets. Case in point: in 2003, the Johannesburg Securities Exchange in South Africa started requiring all companies listed with the exchange to comply with corporate governance codes and to use the Global Reporting Initiative's guidelines for disclosing social and environmental performance. The actual dollar amount may not be as important as the development of the "right" institutional infrastructure and public–private partnerships that steer SRI toward its next phase of green business development and sustainable strategic management, in both the industrialized and emerging/developing economies.

Jacob PARK
Green Mountain College

See also in the *Berkshire Encyclopedia of Sustainability*: **Activism—NGOs; Base of the Pyramid; Corporate Citizenship; CSR and CSR 2.0; Equator Principles; Fair Trade; Financial Services Industry; Human Rights; Investment, CleanTech; Public–Private Partnerships; Risk Management; Supply Chain Management; Sustainable Value Creation; Transparency; Triple Bottom Line; United Nations Global Compact**

FURTHER READING

Aguilera, Ruth V.; Williams, Cynthia A.; Conley, John M.; & Rupp, Deborah. (2006, May). Corporate governance and social responsibility: A comparative analysis of the U.K. and the U.S. *Corporate Governance: An International Review, 14*(3), 147–158.

Conference Board. (2007). *U.S. institutional investors continue to boost ownership of U.S. corporations.* New York: Conference Board.

Conference Board. (2008). *Institutional investment report.* New York: Conference Board.

European Sustainable Investment Forum (Eurosif). (2008). *European SRI study 2008.* Retrieved February 3, 2010, from http://www.eurosif.org

FTSE Group. (2007). *Adding values to your investment: FTSE4Good index series—5 year review.* Retrieved February 3, 2010, from http://www.ftse.com/Indices/FTSE4Good_Index_Series/index.jsp

International Finance Corporation (IFC). (2003). *Towards sustainable and responsible investment in emerging markets.* Washington, DC: IFC.

International Finance Corporation (IFC). (2009). *Sustainable investment in emerging markets.* Washington, DC: IFC.

Kreander, N. (2001). Occasional research paper no. 33: An analysis of European ethical funds. London: Certified Accountants Educational Trust.

Mercer. (2006). *Perspectives on responsible investing.* Toronto: Mercer Investment Consulting.

Mercer. (2009). *Shedding light on responsible investment: Approaches, returns, and impacts.* Toronto: Mercer Investment Consulting.

Social Investment Forum (SIF). (2008). *2007 report on socially responsible investing trends in the United States.* Retrieved February 3, 2010, from http://www.socialinvest.org/pdf/SRI_Trends_ExecSummary_2007.pdfSocial Investment Forum (SIF). (2009). Socially responsible investing facts. Retrieved November 15, 2009, from http://www.socialinvest.org/resources/sriguide/srifacts.cfm

World Bank

The World Bank is an international financial institution concerned with a host of issues at the heart of sustainable development—from environmental and agricultural concerns to the values, ethics, and faith traditions that mobilize around environmental and human development concerns. The World Bank serves as a source of financial and technical assistance to developing countries around the world. It offers loans and grants to support investment in many areas, including environmental and natural resource management.

The World Bank is an international financial institution governed by 185 member states and comprised of the International Bank for Reconstruction and Development (IBRD) and the International Development Association (IDA). The World Bank is concerned with a whole host of issues at the heart of sustainable development—from environmental and agricultural concerns to social and human development and the values, ethics, and faith traditions that mobilize around environmental and human development concerns. Current global crises, such as the energy crisis, concerns about climate change, and agricultural and food shortages, are issues of great concern for the World Bank, and the World Bank is mobilizing its resources to catalyze international cooperation on these issues.

The World Bank is a massive and complex institution, and much has been written about its history and evolution. The international community created the World Bank with the goal of rebuilding Europe after World War II. Since its inception, it has adapted and moved through many stages, with presidents of the institution and regional and country leaders guiding it through various evolutions. The mission of the World Bank—"Our Dream is a World Free of Poverty"—is displayed at its entrance, but the means and style of reaching the goal have changed. Today's World Bank is driven by a holistic view of development, which has evolved through self-conscious reflection on the World Bank's sometimes rocky history and the critique of its critics and partners. Country-level assistance strategies are at the core of the World Bank's work, and it also serves as a think tank on development and global poverty issues.

At the Bank, development no longer means only higher gross domestic products and better economic performance; it also is concerned with the well-being of countries. Development progress is measured by a wide range of benchmarks, including the United Nations' Millennium Development Goals (MDGs), adopted in 2000 by the international community as a common framework for action and a way to track progress on fundamental development goals.

While historically perceived negatively by some for what seemed to be a "one size fits all" approach to economic development, the Bank recently has moved to better understand the "spirit" of sustainability in its work with faith leaders and institutions on development issues. In the 1990s it began to explore ways in which faith and development are connected. The Bank recognized that that some of the best experts on development and poverty eradication are religious leaders living and working in poor communities, where strong ties, local expertise and longevity, and moral authority give them special insight, understanding, and remarkable channels for social service provision. The World Bank's work with faith leaders has included sponsoring an interfaith meeting on AIDS in India in 2004; participating in a two-year structured dialogue on development and poverty issues with the International Monetary Fund (IMF) and the World Council of Churches (WCC); bringing together U.S. Evangelical Christian leaders with Moroccan Muslim leaders to talk about climate change; and working with East Asian countries on environmental and conservation concerns. The dialogue with religious leaders and institutions continues today, grounded in empirical analytical research and with efforts to include faith leaders and institutions in the work of the World Bank.

Marisa B. VAN SAANEN
Yale Law School

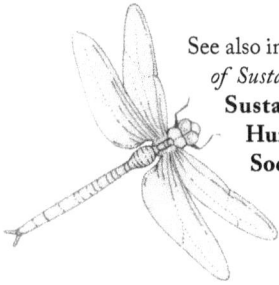

See also in the *Berkshire Encyclopedia of Sustainability*: **Development, Sustainable; Green GDP; Human Rights; Investment, Socially Responsible (SRI);** **Triple Bottom Line; United Nations - Overview of Conventions and Agreements; United Nations Global Compact; World Constitutionalism.**

FURTHER READING

Marshall, Katherine, & Van Saanen, Marisa. (2007). Development and faith: Where mind, heart, and soul work together. Washington, DC: World Bank.

Marshall, Katherine. (2008). The World Bank: From reconstruction to development to equity. New York: Routledge.

The World Bank. (2009). Development dialogue on values and ethics. Retrieved March 25, 2009, from http://go.worldbank.org/HH5UDBBLZ0

THE END IS NIGH . . . PLANT A TREE

World leaders quoted by mainstream media at the September 2009 United Nations meeting on climate change used blunt and unsparing language to paint a dire picture about the fate of the Earth: "We are the very last generation that can take action," said President Nicolas Sarkozy of France. "If things go business as usual, we will not live," stated President Mohamed Nasheed of the Maldives. Oscar Arias Sánchez, president of Costa Rica, depicted the conference itself as "taking place on the brink of a precipice." Martin Palmer and Victoria Finlay, the authors of Faith in Conservation, *describe the long tradition of using scriptural language that evokes end-times or the apocalypse as a tool to foster awareness of crises such as global climate change and the destruction of tropical forests. The book, published by the World Bank in partnership with the Alliance of Religions and Conservations (ARC), challenges stereotypes about world religions and the World Bank itself.*

Imagine you are busy planting a tree, and someone rushes up to say that the Messiah has come and the end of the world is nigh. What do you do? The advice given by the rabbis in a traditional Jewish story is that you first finish planting the tree, and only then do you go and see whether the news is true. The Islamic tradition has a similar story, which reminds followers that if they happen to be carrying a palm cutting in their hand when the Day of Judgment takes place, they should not forget to plant the cutting.

There is a tension in the environmental world between those who wish to tell us that the end is nigh and those who want to encourage us to plant trees for the future. In 1992, for example, we were all told, in any number of press statements before the event, that the Earth Summit held in Rio de Janeiro was "the world's last chance to save itself." And indeed many major reports emerging from environmental bodies paint a picture of terrifying, impending destruction—in a sincere desire to shock people into action.

. . . Such groups often fall back on the vivid language of biblical or Vedic (Hindu) accounts of the end of the world—apocalyptic imagery that encapsulates our deepest terrors more graphically than any chart or statistical breakdown can ever do. Powerfully emotive language is used to make us feel that we are sitting on the edge—that in the words of the Jewish story above, the end of the world is nigh.

Source: Martin Palmer, with Victoria Finlay. (2003). *Faith in Conservation. Washington, DC: World Bank*. Retrieved October 2, 2009, from http://www.arcworld.org/news.asp?pageID=9

Risk Management

Risk management includes all efforts undertaken by a business to minimize and control hazards that threaten its operations. In the past, uncertainties about quantifying risk led to difficulties in evaluating perceived threats and their possible impact on a company's finances. But new models exist, allowing businesses to more accurately measure risk and even gain a competitive edge in markets once considered too risky.

All companies seeking success in the modern marketplace need to maintain balance between minimizing risk and maximizing opportunities. Risk is any event or action that can impede an organization's ability to implement its strategies and achieve its objectives. While companies continuously face myriad risks, from project failure to industrial accidents, some of the most complex risks relate to social, environmental, and political issues, and managing those risks effectively lies at the heart of successful sustainability strategy.

Social risks are challenges to business practices that emerge from concerns of society. These may include diseases that curtail the workforce, environmental issues that create tension within local communities or trigger financial penalties, human rights violations that damage a company's reputation or lead to litigation, and objections by stakeholders (i.e., an individual or group directly or indirectly affected by a company's polices or actions) due to negative perceptions of business practices.

Environmental risk, often considered a subset of social risk, includes those issues stemming from environmental issues that can impact a company. These include concerns about climate change and potential legislation to minimize corporate impact. It can also include concerns about pollution, both as a result of production and of discarding products like computers and cell phones. Companies can

be fined for the pollution generated during manufacturing, and some are held responsible for the proper end-of-life disposal of a product.

Political risk is the exertion of political power in a way that threatens a company's value. This can include the specter of nationalization or forced partnerships facing companies doing business in Venezuela, Bolivia, and other areas of Latin and South America that are drifting farther to the left. It also includes the changed international political landscape heralded by September 11, 2001, and followed by bombings in London, Madrid, and Mumbai, which have impacted the ways in which business is conducted.

The distinction between social and political risk is often blurred. Issues may be experienced differently by different sectors in varied locations—for instance, concerns about climate change may lead to legislation in one geography that can penalize a company but then spur innovation across its manufacturing practices, leading to market success where legislation is not yet in place.

The widely used terms *environmental risk*, *social risk*, and *political risk* are also known as *above-ground risks* (by the mining, oil, and gas industries), *nontechnical risks*, and *noncommercial risks*.

Risk and Sustainability

Issues such as political corruption, child labor, obesity, global terrorism, predatory governments, and environmental pollution pose both challenges and opportunities for business. In fact, setting sustainability objectives is often a result of identifying and seizing opportunities based on the social and political risks facing a company, industry, or region. Corporate sustainability strategy and social and political risk management go hand in hand.

"Leadership" companies view responsiveness to social and environmental issues as assets that produce increased revenues rather than only as liabilities with their associated costs. They recognize that an investment in structures and systems to ensure strong social and environmental performance often pays dividends in terms of improved processes, production quality, efficiency, yields, reputation, and profitability, as well as lower risk. For example, Toyota's leaders tried to envisage what might transform its industry and threaten future market share. They pinpointed climate change and convened a team in 1993 to create the first great car of the twenty-first century, nearly a decade before that century arrived. As a result of a series of technological breakthroughs, manufacturing innovations, and careful marketing, Toyota has sold more than one million Prius gas–electric hybrid cars since introducing them in 1997. That's five times as many hybrid vehicles as its nearest competitor.

Current Practices in Risk Management

Risk management includes all the activities organizations undertake to minimize or control hazards that threaten their objectives. For businesses, access to or analysis of financial information leads to the most rigorous evaluation of options and effective decision making. Companies continue to struggle, however, to integrate social, environmental, and political risks into financial equations in meaningful ways. Failure to consider these risks in investment decisions leaves out critical elements when it comes to allocating resources. According to a 2007 poll by the American Institute of Certified Public Accountants (AICPA), 84 percent of companies don't formally integrate social, environmental, and political risks into financial calculations. Often, therefore, companies make decisions about these risks based on personal biases, or they arbitrarily assign higher risk premiums to projects in unfamiliar locations, failing to focus management's attention on reducing risk. Why? Many analysts mistakenly believe measuring social, environmental, and political risks is not possible. Historically these risks have also been addressed in more descriptive language rather than a format that reflects their financial implications.

Companies have traditionally taken two approaches toward assessing and managing social and political risk—qualitative and quantitative. Neither approach, however, allows companies to use the same formal techniques they employ to evaluate other types of risk, such as business continuity (the risk of disruption to critical functions after a disaster or other unexpected occurrence), information security, or currency fluctuation.

Qualitative Approach

In the 1970s, multinational firms, particularly in the extraction and banking industries, began creating in-house teams to evaluate political and social risks. These teams looked at risk assessment qualitatively, producing detailed briefings that outlined the challenges of conducting business in various parts of the world. Beginning in the 1980s, consultants were often hired to produce similar reports. While providing sound insights about certain risks, such as the likelihood of a coup or a country's use of slave labor, these briefings did not explicitly connect the identified risks to the company's bottom line. Without an understanding of the costs of these risks, executives had no way to integrate the information into business assessments the way they did for other, quantified, data. As a result, important insights contained in those briefs were sometimes relegated to footnotes in the company's business plan.

Quantitative Approach

Realizing the flaws of a purely qualitative approach, some analysts began to quantify political and social risk to make it more relevant to corporate managers. Various methods were developed and put in use.

Scorecards

Indicators of potential political and social risks—such as judiciary independence, corruption, and government turnover—are evaluated and assigned a numerical value. A final "score" is then generated by aggregating and weighting the values of different indicators to calculate a country's overall risk. Such scoring is helpful because it enables a comparison between countries. But it falls short of being directly useful to business decision makers because the risks are not converted into monetary terms.

Statistical Analysis

The emergence of spreadsheet applications, such as Crystal Ball, an analytical tool that automatically generates equations to capture uncertainty, has contributed to quantitative analysis of risk. Results of such software programs show project managers either the most sensitive issues on which to concentrate—sensitivity analysis—or a cumulative probability curve indicating the potential economic performance of a project. The charts, graphs, and dynamic models produced by these calculations, however, cannot be integrated into financial evaluations because they do not generate a return on investment (ROI) number, a political/social risk beta (an indicator used in financial calculations to

compare a company's risk compared to the risk of the overall market), or any monetary results that can be included in financial calculations.

Scenario Analysis

Risk mapping plots the expected degree of exposure to various risks on a graph, with probable frequency on the horizontal axis and expected severity on the vertical axis. Such modeling is beneficial as a communication tool, enabling managers to visualize where to allocate resources, and as a way to measure various types of risk. Mapping as currently practiced does not provide a link to financial statements that are critical for comparisons between competing projects. But, with some modifications, including assignment of monetary values to hypothetical consequences, axis points on such a risk map could correlate to financial data and be integrated into ROI calculations.

Adjusted Discount Rate and Cost of Capital

One method of integrating social and political risks into financial models is to create a discount rate or cost-of-capital calculation that can be used in cash-flow projections. This can be done by creating a social discount rate that employs the weighted average cost of capital (WACC) and the traditional capital asset pricing model (CAPM). (A social discount rate is an important factor in determining the value of contributing funds to a project, such as a school, highway system, or an environmental protection program, that would benefit society in some way.) When dealing with markets that may exhibit hallmarks of social and political risk, this adjusted WACC accounts for social and political factors. Calculations for this risk-adjusted beta, however, have in the past largely relied on the standard country-specific risk-rating methodology generated by political-risk consulting firms, which are too broad to achieve the needed objectives. These ratings are neither industry-, project-, nor company-specific, though social and political risks affect companies and their reputations differently, even those operating in the same country.

Effective Risk Management

Effective risk management involves identifying the sociopolitical and corporate environments that might create risks and then measuring and monitoring them. Reporting these risks in monetary terms is an important step toward integrating them into financial planning and corporate strategies.

One method of monetizing and better managing these nontraditional risks is by including them in slightly modified ROI calculations. Managers commonly calculate ROI, a measure of investment profitability, to make decisions about day-to-day operations and capital investment

planning. ROI is the most popular method for measuring corporate performance because it is the approach CEOs and CFOs are most familiar with. To make such analysis more complete and improve operational and capital investment decisions, political and social risks must be included in the conventional ROI calculation through several phases outlined below, which makes the ROI more explicit and relevant for effective risk management.

Step 1: Generate options. The first step in a modified ROI calculation that incorporates social and political risks is to think about the various options that could potentially minimize risk, such as investing in a range of countries or including a range of suppliers in the supply chain. This thinking is known as "real options." While real options calculations aren't used outside financial settings and stock-option calculations because of their complexity, this type of thinking incorporates financial insights at the strategic stage of project planning rather than as afterthoughts. This helps clarify the risks and their potential repercussions.

Step 2: Calculate benefits and costs. Calculating the savings and costs associated with each issue that could generate social and political risks is the second step. For example, if a corporation considered employing child labor, the savings would be calculated by measuring the wage differential between children and adults. The issue benefit, which is generally assigned a positive value, would be the savings. Next the potential costs associated with the risk of child labor should be calculated, such as lost sales after the public discovers this activity. The reputations of several industries have been seriously damaged by the use of child labor in their supply chains, and some companies have attempted to stop the practice. In 2001, major companies in the chocolate industry like Hershey, Cadbury, and Nestle became aware of kidnappings and forced child labor on cocoa plantations in the Ivory Coast, which tainted their reputations and reduced sales. Had companies in this industry calculated these costs in advance, they may have employed mitigation strategies to avoid sourcing from plantations using these practices. The biggest cost of social and political risk is usually to reputation and lost sales due to consumer boycotts and protests.

Step 3: Estimate probability. After calculating the potential costs of each risk, approximate (in percentages) the likelihood that each risk will occur and hurt the company. This is the *estimated probability*. Assign an estimated probability to each risk identified.

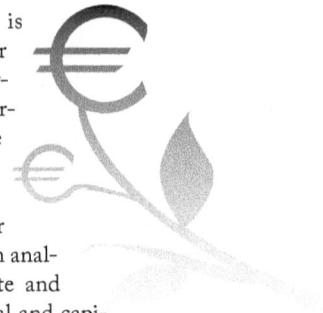

Step 4: Calculate expected value. Calculate the expected value of each risk by multiplying the estimated cost of that risk by the estimated probability it will occur.

Step 5: Calculate net present value (NPV). Calculate the net present value of each risk. Note that each issue has risks that emerge at different times. NPV calculations for social and political risk are determined in the same manner as traditional NPV calculations. Discount back using a set discount rate in the traditional manner used in financial accounting. Carry out these calculations for each social and political risk.

Steps 6: Aggregate NPVs for social and political risks. After calculating all NPVs for social and political risks, add together the social risk NPVs and then the political risk NPVs.

Step 7: Integrate the results into traditional ROI calculations. Insert the social risk NPV and the political risk NPV as line items in the normal ROI calculation. Provide schedules that show the calculations for benefits, costs, probability, and expected value for each social and political risk. This will allow senior managers to see both the results and the processes by which they were obtained.

Defensive and Innovative Risk Management

Identifying and measuring social and political risks, and integrating them into ROI calculations, provides the basis for establishing a comprehensive risk management strategy. While financial risk can be shared or transferred (to joint venture partners, through insurance, or to other entities), this is often impossible with social and political risks. Companies operate in settings where they can be held liable for the misdemeanors of their suppliers or related businesses operating under the same name.

Managing social and political risk includes devising policies and programs to identify, measure, monitor, respond to, and report on issues that generate risk.

There are five methods for managing corporate risk:

- Insuring against risk
- Avoiding risk
- Mitigating risk
- Innovating around risk
- Some combination of the above

Insuring against risk is one of the most conventional methods for managing it. Many insurance policies, however, do not fully cover some of the biggest crises that may arise from political and social issues, such as total expropriation of property, forced joint venture partnerships with the government, or forced renegotiation of contracts. Avoiding certain risks is another option when approaching social and political issues, and it is best achieved by preemptively identifying threats and seeking alternatives. For example, to avoid potential political risks, a company may decide to open operations in a less risky geography. To mitigate a social risk like unpaid overtime, it may implement a working-hours monitoring system in the factories from which it sources its products.

By undertaking the exercise of measuring political and social risk, companies become skilled at recognizing, managing, and even innovating around risk and opening up new business opportunities. In fact, by focusing solely on the downside of risk, companies can overlook opportunities that provide significant possibilities for innovation and creating competitive advantages.

Consider General Electric (GE), which in 2005 launched "ecomagination," its commitment to addressing environmental challenges. The company recognized an opportunity where many others saw only risk. While other companies were litigating and lobbying to avoid liability for their environmental impacts, GE capitalized on growing concerns about the environment by developing products such as energy efficient light bulbs and hybrid locomotives. Ecomagination is a business strategy driving the company's growth—2006 annual revenue from this program exceeded \$12 billion—and GE is not alone. Many companies are discovering opportunities to make money from issues traditionally seen as too risky.

McDonald's is another example of a company that transformed risk into opportunity. While the fast-food industry as a whole has been under attack for contributing to increased obesity, McDonald's recognized that its customers' preferences were changing and it responded with healthier foods. McDonald's began offering salads that were more appealing, and it partnered with Newman's Own to provide all-natural gourmet salad dressing and premium coffee. It now also provides sliced apples in Happy Meals. As a result, McDonald's sales and share price have increased in an age when other fast-food chains are scrambling to respond to the threats of obesity litigation and changing customer preferences.

Innovation is central to companies that identify and seize opportunities where others see only risk. Innovation can be a breakthrough idea; it can also be a new model for doing business in a seemingly risky or inaccessible market.

Outlook in the Twenty-First Century

In an increasingly globalized world, companies are becoming aware of the need to better identify and manage social, environmental, and political risks. These risks can emerge along supply chains and from regions in which companies conduct business. Sometimes the risks are related to products or methods of production and their effects on the environment. Corporations are simultaneously beginning to look at these risks, once considered only threats, and creating strategies to capitalize on the sustainability issues inherent in them: employee issues (strategies to address child labor, worker overtime); consumer issues (strategies to address and capitalize on obesity and eating more healthily); environmental issues (strategies to mitigate pollution, global warming, etc. through better methods of production and green products). To realize benefits, risks must be evaluated and handled within a system that adequately identifies, quantifies, and mitigates them. An increasingly robust treatment of risk issues has enabled some companies to identify opportunities to help them gain a competitive edge. As these successes become more widespread, so likely will the practice of monetizing social, environmental, and political issues for inclusion in financial reports and project plans.

Tamara BEKEFI
Daedalus Strategic Advising

Marc J. EPSTEIN
Rice University

See also in the *Berkshire Encyclopedia of Sustainability*: **Accounting; Climate Change Disclosure; Corporate Citizenship; Fast Food Industry; Financial Services Industry; Human Rights; Investment, CleanTech; Investment, Socially Responsible (SRI); Leadership; Marketing; Performance Metrics; Social Enterprise; Supply Chain Management; Sustainable Value Creation; Transparency**

FURTHER READING

Bekefi, Tamara; Epstein, Marc J.; & Yuthus, Kristi. (2007). *Managing opportunities and risks.* New York: American Institute of Certified Public Accountants.

Bekefi, Tamara & Epstein, Marc J. (2006). *Integrating social and political risk into management decision-making.* New York: American Institute of Certified Public Accountants.

Birkbeck, Kimberley. (1999). Forewarned is forearmed: Identification and measurement in integrated risk management. In *The Conference Board of Canada Report 1999* (pp. 249–299). Ottawa, Canada: Conference Board of Canada.

Campbell, Ashley, & Carment, David. (2002). *The private sector and conflict prevention mainstreaming: Risk analysis and conflict impact assessment tools for multinational corporations.* Ottawa, Canada: Carleton University Press.

Day, George S., & Schoemaker, Paul J. H. (2005, November). Scanning the periphery. Retrieved September 7, 2009, from http://custom.hbsp.harvard.edu/custom_pdfs/DSINTR0511H2005103154.pdf

Gale, Bruce. (2009). Identifying, assessing and mitigating political risk. Retrieved September 7, 2009, from http://knowledge.insead.edu/politicalrisk080204.cfm

Kim, W. Chan, & Mauborgne, Renée. (2005). *Blue ocean strategy: How to create uncontested market space and make the competition irrelevant.* Boston: Harvard Business School Press.

McGee, Kenneth. (2004). *Heads up: How to anticipate business surprises and seize opportunities first.* Boston: Harvard Business School Press.

Minor, John. (2003, March). Mapping the new political risk. *Risk Management. 50*(3), 16–21.

PricewaterhouseCoopers. (2005). Predicting the unpredictable: Protecting retail and consumer companies against reputation risk. Retrieved September 7, 2009, from http://www.pwc.com/en_TH/th/publications/assets/risk_whitepaper_v2c01.pdf

Slywotzky, Adrian J., & Weber, Karl. (2007). *The upside: The seven strategies for turning big threats into growth breakthroughs.* New York: Crown Business.

Wood, Duncan. (2009, May 1). Doing business in a volatile world. Retrieved October 5, 2009, from http://www.treasuryandrisk.com/Issues/2009/May%202009/Pages/Doing-Business-in-a-Volatile-World.aspx

Accounting

In the twenty-first century, many accounting profes-sionals are expected to consider the triple bottom line (TBL)—environmental, social, and financial performance—when preparing statements for businesses; sustainability reports increasingly supplement annual reports. Internal decision makers also rely on analyses that incorporate the TBL. Although formal guidelines do not exist yet, infor-mal accounting and reporting standards are important in helping organizations understand their TBL effect and their stakeholder responsibilities.

A ccountants have long had a role in providing the finan-cial information necessary to assess how an organiza-tion manages its resources, but the need to summarize and measure what matters, and to attest to its veracity, is no longer limited to just financial performance. As investors and other stakeholders demand greater transparency on the triple bottom line, which measures the environmental and social performance of an organization in addition to its economic achievement, the profession has much to offer. This new obligation, however, will require the profession to think beyond generally accepted accounting principles.

External Reporting

Reporting the financial performance of an organization and attesting to its fair and accurate coverage has been a cornerstone of the accounting profession. In response to greater stakeholder activism and demands for more trans-parent disclosure of the triple bottom line, many organiza-tions now augment their annual report with a sustainability report. But as they currently stand, generally accepted accounting principles do not always support or encour-age disclosure that helps stakeholders assess environmen-tal and social performance or helps managers balance the

consequences across the triple bottom line. For example, economic decisions that negatively impact the workforce may provide a short-term boost to financial performance, but they may negatively impact social performance. This creates many important opportunities for the accounting profession.

Sustainability Reporting and GRI

According to a 2007 Social Investment Forum report, 11 percent of the funds under professional management in the United States integrate environmental, social, and gover-nance factors into investment decisions. Sustainability dis-closure, however, is not yet required in the United States (although as of late in 2009 the matter was under discussion), which makes it difficult to assess a company's triple bottom line performance. Numerous institutional investors have petitioned the Securities and Exchange Commission (SEC) to require disclosure of environmental, social, and gover-nance (ESG) risk factors and to adopt the Global Reporting Initiative framework. Speaking for over fifty investment groups on 21 July 2009, the Social Investment Forum—a nonprofit U.S. association dedicated to socially responsi-ble investing—urged the SEC to require ESG disclosure in order to promote long-term thinking and rebuild pub-lic trust. In the letter, the Social Investment Forum (2009) stated that "investors' efforts to incorporate ESG informa-tion into investment decisions have been hindered by a lack of comprehensive, comparable data. Because sustainability reporting among corporate issuers is largely still voluntary, it is far from universal, and often inconsistent and incomplete." This was not the first time such groups have petitioned for more complete disclosure about the risks and opportuni-ties associated with climate change. The group Investors and Business for U.S. Climate Action made a similar petition to the president and members of Congress in 2007.

According to a KPMG International report, over 80 percent of the Global 250 companies issue a separate sustainability report in addition to their annual report (KPMG International 2008). These typically include environmental and social performance indicators, such as tonnes of carbon emissions, pounds of waste recycled, the number of minority-owned supply companies, and working conditions in those companies. Because this is an evolving area still considered voluntary in the United States, the reports are often not audited. Consequently, there may be considerable variability from year to year in company reports and across companies. Another concern is that some companies are using sustainability reports as a public relations tool rather than as meaningful coverage of the company's triple bottom line.

In response to these concerns, the Coalition for Environmentally Responsible Economies and the United Nations Environmental Program founded the Global Reporting Initiative (GRI) in 1997. The GRI framework promotes globally applicable sustainability reporting that discloses economic, environmental, and social dimensions of the organization's activities, products, and services (its triple bottom line). The GRI employs a long-term, multistakeholder process to develop and disseminate sustainability reporting guidelines that can be used by organizations of any size, sector, or location (GRI 2006). The GRI framework relies on fundamental accounting principles such as timeliness, materiality, verifiability, and comparability. Now in its third version, the guidelines are used by over 1,500 organizations. In addition to recommending inclusion of strategy; organizational profile; report parameters; and governance, commitment, and engagement in the sustainability report, the guidelines suggest the inclusion of seventy-nine performance indicators in six different categories: environmental, human rights, labor practices and decent work, society, product responsibility, and economic.

European Union (EU) countries have shown a particularly strong interest in sustainable-development reporting. For example, in France, Germany, Denmark, Sweden, and the United Kingdom, it is mandatory for corporations to disclose some form of environmental and/or social metrics. Sweden, for example, requires all state-owned companies to file independently assured reports that comply with GRI (Waddock 2004). In their 2009 report, the European Sustainability Reporting Association identified an increase in the number of countries requiring sustainability reporting.

In 2006, the GRI moved toward the adoption of XBRL, a standardized business reporting taxonomy that facilitates comparability of its indicators. This should facilitate analysis and intercompany and intracompany comparison. This type of standardization would make triple bottom line analysis easier for research organizations like KLD,

an independent investment research firm. According to its website, KLD (2009) analyzes over ninety positive and negative corporate social responsibility (CSR) indicators for more than 3,000 companies and provides it to over 400 clients. KLD was one of four partners that developed the Newsweek Green Ranking of the 500 largest U.S. companies (McGinn 2009).

Greenhouse Gas Reporting

Two events of the early twenty-first century signal that the United States may soon implement a cap-and-trade program for carbon dioxide. First, California passed Assembly Bill 32: Global Warming Solutions Act in 2006, which required the state to achieve 1990 emission levels by 2020. Second, the conclusion of the May 2009 report of the President's Economic Recovery Advisory Board urged President Obama to support a market-based cap-and-trade system that is both economically sustainable and environmentally sound (Doerr 2009).

Greenhouse gas (GHG) accounting and disclosure standards assist firms in understanding and reporting the firm's effect on global warming. As cap-and-trade legislation becomes increasingly likely, companies will need to reduce their emissions and divulge on their impact. Generally, GHG measurement and reporting is a section of a firm's sustainability report that is based on GRI guidelines, which in turn refer to the World Business Council for Sustainable Development's *Greenhouse Gas Protocol: A Corporate Accounting and Reporting Standard* for guidance. The mission of this standard is to develop internationally accepted greenhouse gas accounting and reporting benchmarks for businesses and to promote its broad adoption. It consists of three key steps: (1) prepare an inventory of greenhouse gases emitted as a result of the firm's existence; (2) set a greenhouse gas target; and (3) develop a plan to reduce greenhouse gases over time. A common approach is to set a deadline to reduce greenhouse gases to a level that existed for the entity at a previous time. For example, BP (British Petroleum) set a goal to reduce annual emissions to 90 percent of 1990 levels by 2010 (Harold and Center 2005).

The standard does not include a verification process, but if the GHG standard is used as part of the GRI reporting guidelines, it will fall under the GRI verification process. In a manner similar to prepared financial statements based on generally accepted accounting principles, the greenhouse gas accounting and reporting standard is guided by principles, such as relevance, consistency, and transparency, rather than rules. Principles-based accounting allows for utilizing judgment, which is useful for new areas of accounting such as triple bottom line. Because of growing international concern about causes of climate change, a business's measurement, reporting, and planned reduction of greenhouse gases helps support sustainability.

There is evidence that such disclosure does impact company actions. As part of the 1986 Emergency Planning and Community Right-to-Know Act, businesses in the United States were required to report the locations and quantities of approximately 650 toxic chemicals. This data was made available through the U.S. Environmental Protection Agency's Toxic Release Inventory. While difficult to navigate since the data was provided by site rather than by company, the information was used to assess impact and develop reduction goals. In another example, the Financial Accounting Standards Board issued Statement of Financial Accounting Standards (SFAS) 148 in 2003, which required companies to recognize stock-based compensation as an expense and a liability at fair market value. As a result, the use of options was reduced, and companies shifted to issuing restricted stock as a result of required disclosure (Carter, Lynch, and Tuna 2007).

Possible future programs related to greenhouse gases include emissions trading programs, such as the European Union Greenhouse Gas Emissions Allowance Trading Scheme that became effective at the beginning of 2005. Three approaches are available to firms to offset and/or reduce their carbon emissions: allowance-based transactions, project-based transactions, and voluntary transactions. In allowance-based transactions, an emission cap is set, and allowances are issued by regulators to organizations included in the regulations. Trading markets are established, which offer a market-based approach for companies to meet their mandated emission levels. If the business emits more than its allowance, it must purchase the right to emit (recognized as an expense). Project-based transactions provide an opportunity for a business to invest in an emission-reduction project, typically in a developing country (for example, ecosystem preservation and/or restoration in the Brazilian rain forest). This is, however, still an emerging market with many players and a great need for independent verification. The Carbon Offset Provider Evaluation Matrix (COPEM) provides guidance on provider selection as well as a description of the various forms of offset mechanisms (Carbon Concierge 2008). Voluntary efforts, such as partnerships to convert waste into energy, are being taken by many values-driven organizations, such as Clif Bar, Inc. and Interface Carpet Company.

Financial Reporting for Emission Rights

Financial reporting of emission credits is related to emission trading programs; it recognizes whether a firm is holding excess emission credits or whether it has an obligation to purchase credits. The accounting treatment for emissions

rights remains unresolved under both International Financial Reporting Standards and generally accepted accounting principles (GAAP) in the United States. Although the International Financial Reporting Interpretations Committee (IFRIC) issued an interpretation on emission rights, IFRIC 3, they withdrew it after intense pressure from the business community and European politicians, who balked at disclosing the financial consequences of applying this interpretation (Deloitte 2008). IFRIC 3 recognized emission credits as intangible assets initially valued at fair value but also required the recognition of the corresponding liability, with the asset and liability shown separately and not offsetting one another (Rogers 2005, 198–199). In the United States, accounting standard setters could not reach consensus on, and subsequently dropped, their 2003 Emerging Issues Task Force project for accounting for emission allowances under a cap-and-trade program, EITF Issue 03-14 (Deloitte 2008, 1).

Regardless, emission credits meet the definition of intangible assets under SFAS 142, Goodwill and Other Intangible Assets. Although a company's emission credits may be reported as an intangible asset, the economic reality is that the obligation to deliver credits to cover actual emissions at the end of a period constitutes a liability (Rogers 2005, 197–199). In the absence of definitive guidance and until formal standards are issued, the Financial Accounting Standards Board and the Securities and Exchange Commission have provided informal guidance on accounting for emissions rights (Deloitte 2008, 4–5).

Accounting for Environmental Liabilities

Liabilities are defined as economic obligations that arise from benefits received in the past and for which the probability, amount, and timing of payment are known with reasonable certainty. In the case of an environmental liability, the benefits received in the past are the products that were produced and/or sold at the time the cause of the environmental liability (e.g., generations of toxic waste) was created. GAAP requires that environmental liabilities be disclosed in the firm's annual report, along with their other liabilities.

Significant reporting challenges arise from environmental liabilities. If there is acknowledgment that an obligation has been incurred, there may be ambiguity about whether the obligation is measurable. Research shows that there is significant variation in the quality of financial statement disclosures on estimated environmental cleanup liabilities. The factors influencing these disclosures include measurability, regulatory enforcement, litigation and negotiation concerns, and capital market concerns (Barth, McNichols, and Wilson 1997). When there is ambiguity with regard to liabilities, management has inherent bias and incentive to understate liabilities to show a healthier financial position (Palepu, Healy, and Bernard 2000). If the obligation is measurable, management records an environmental liability in the financial statements. If is not measurable, the liability will be disclosed as a note to the financial statements. From management's perspective, disclosure may be used as evidence of acknowledgment of the liability in legal proceedings and may put the company at greater risk of losing in court.

Resources exist for the company that wants to better understand its environmental impact. ISO 14000 standards, international management standards developed by the International Organization for Standardization (ISO), provide guidance on how to implement an environmental management system and measure the results. As previously mentioned, the GRI framework includes thirty environmental indicators, such as energy consumed, waste generated, greenhouse gas emissions, water withdrawal, and biodiversity impact. The disclosure of environmental liabilities makes company environmental performance more transparent and may discourage management from engaging in economic activities that damage the environment. For preexisting environmental damage, mandatory disclosure may force firms to recognize the need to account for the damage. Disclosure of current environmental impact may discourage management from engaging in economic activities and operating practices that damage the environment. For example, implementation of sustainable operating practices that reduce the amount of energy consumed reduces expenses as well as environmental risk, which in turn will reduce environmental liabilities.

Financial Reporting of Intangible Sustainable Assets

If GAAP allowed sustainable practices to be reported as intangible assets, management would have incentive over and above the sustainable business strategy incentive to engage in economic activities that give rise to assets that reflect sustainable practices. Examples of sustainable practices that could be recorded as intangible assets include an organization's reputation for sustainable practices, sustainable intellectual capital, a specific strategy to reduce greenhouse gas emissions, energy conservation policy, sustainable component of a company brand, and emission credits. Positive sustainability attributes, such as the examples listed above, can significantly increase the value of an organization (Rogers 2005, 174–175).

If the firm purchases assets that will lead to sustainable practices, they are reported as assets on the balance sheet, either as tangible assets such as plant improvements or as an intangible asset called goodwill. But under International Accounting Standard 38 and U.S. GAAP, specifically SFAS 142, a publicly held firm generally cannot report internally generated sustainable practices as assets. For example, if a firm redesigns a production process to use less water or produce less waste, the expenditures would be handled similarly to research-and-development costs and expensed. Conversely, investment in energy-saving equipment, such as the installation of solar panels, would be capitalized. Expenditures related to developing these assets are normally expensed rather than capitalized. Although the firm creates value from sustainable practices over time, the related asset cannot be recorded because of accounting measurement and objectivity issues. Because accountants historically value reliability over relevance in financial statements (Financial Accounting Standards Board 1980), GAAP does not allow them to record internally generated assets. If a company is purchased at a price that is greater than the fair market value of the identifiable assets because of sustainable practices, this excess is recorded as an intangible asset.

As of 2009, the Financial Accounting Standards Board in the United States and the International Accounting Standards Board do have a convergence project in progress. One of the issues for deliberation is treatment of internally developed intangible assets. It is expected that the future standard (developed jointly by these two boards) would require recognition of internally developed intangible assets.

Full Cost Accounting

In a traditional product pricing model, an organization considers the direct costs (material and labor) of producing goods and adds a charge to cover the indirect costs (manufacturing infrastructure, selling, development, administrative costs, and cost of capital). This approach captures internally generated costs, but it disregards externalities, such as the environmental costs associated with hazardous waste generated during the production process. Beginning in the 1970s, environmental regulations in the United States—the Clean Air Act, the Clean Water Act, and the Comprehensive Environmental Response Compensation and Liability Act—and the Toxic Release Inventory required firms to report their environmental impact. These regulations caused firms to consider the impact their methods of production had on the environment.

In 1995, the U.S. Environmental Protection Agency (EPA) provided guidance for how to "full cost" a product to include environmental costs (U.S. EPA 1995). Recognizing that the "full cost" of providing a product to a customer should include environmental and social costs helps management determine what products to offer and how to price them. On balance, sustainable products are less expensive in the long run because they reduce the risk of costs related to future environmental and social regulation.

In some countries, firms are responsible for the environmental and social costs of their products throughout the product's entire life cycle. For example, two European Union (EU) orders, the Restriction of Hazardous Substances Directive (effective 2006) and the Waste Electrical and Electronic Equipment Directive (effective 2003), require firms to eliminate certain hazardous materials in the design/production phase and to be responsible for the end-of-life disposal/recycling costs of their products. A third EU regulation titled Registration, Evaluation, Authorization and Restriction of Chemicals (REACH), which became effective in 2007, requires companies to provide full disclosure on the chemicals used during the production of its products.

While there have been considerable advances on understanding and reporting environmental impact, assessing social impact has proved more challenging. Earlier efforts tended to focus on employee attributes such as safety records, compliance with Occupational Safety and Health Administration (OSHA) standards, and the percentage of management meeting certain criteria. The GRI framework expands coverage to include community, customer, and cultural sensitivity indicators that encompass the entire value chain. With a planned release of ISO 26000 in 2010, the International Organization for Standardization (ISO) will provide guidance to companies that want to measure and report on their social impact. In triple bottom line terminology, ISO 26000 addresses the social aspect, while the ISO 14000 family addresses the environmental aspect of business operations.

Increasingly, companies are including such criteria in supplier contracts and providing data to their customers. For example, in July 2009, Walmart announced plans to work with universities, nongovernmental organizations, governments, suppliers, and retailers to develop a research-based sustainability product index. The process will require all 100,000 Walmart suppliers to assess and report on their energy, water, resource, and social impact. Walmart's ultimate goal is to provide customers with the information they need to make sustainable purchases.

Numerous firms have begun to report on their efforts to better understand costs. For example, Ford's 2008–2009 Sustainability Report provides a good example of the company's analysis of environmental and social costs incurred along its value chain. Interface, Inc., the world's largest manufacturer of modular carpet, developed their own measurement systems: EcoMetrics to measure their progress towards zero waste, and SocioMetrics to better understand their impact on people (Interface 2008). Included in Interface's report are the cost savings as a result of their sustainability initiatives. Interface also provides an excellent example of the benefits of working with independent organizations to develop standards and metrics by which to assess social and environmental impacts. Interface partnered with NSF International (a nonprofit, nongovernmental organization) using a multistakeholder process to develop the NSF/ANSI 140 standards that define sustainable carpet and establish levels of certification.

Finally, Toyota's approach to understanding the environmental and social costs of producing a product demonstrate the impact this topic can have on making sustainable decisions. Toyota (2008) classifies their environmental accounting into environmental investments, maintenance costs, and eco-efficiency to better understand product costing. These examples illustrate the breadth and depth of environmental accounting.

Outlook for the Future

For external stakeholders, financial disclosures are extended to include environmental and social performance so a more informed analysis of how a company manages its resources and its impacts can be made. Internal stakeholders can better allocate resources and determine how the company's outputs impact external stakeholders when full cost accounting is considered.

To date, much of the leadership on accounting for sustainability has come from EU-based organizations. If the focus of organizations like the International Federation of Accountants (IFAC) and The Prince of Wales Accounting for Sustainability Project (PWAS) is any indication, the world will continue to look to the EU for future guidance. The IFAC (n.d.) has identified five roles for the professional accountant in changing business for a more sustainable future:

- Challenging conventional assumptions of doing business
- Redefining success
- Establishing appropriate performance targets
- Encouraging and rewarding the right behaviors
- Ensuring that information flows to support decisions and to monitor and report performance go beyond the traditional ways of thinking about economic success

Being sustainable requires an organization to take full account of its impact on the planet and its people. The PWAS (2009) mission statement suggests a similar focus: "The Prince's Accounting for Sustainability Project works with businesses, investors, the public sector, accounting bodies, NGOs and academics to develop practical guidance and tools for embedding sustainability into decision-making and reporting processes."

Extending assessment and disclosure to include environmental and social impact so stakeholders both within and outside of corporate walls are better able to make informed decisions is much needed. Accounting professionals, with their collective expertise in performance metrics, analysis, and using numbers to tell a story have much to offer as we challenge conventional assumptions of business and reframe our future to consider environmental and social implications of business and consumption decisions. In the words of former U.S. secretary of the interior Stewart Udall from a much-quoted speech given in 1970: "Over the long haul of life on this planet, it is the ecologists, and not the bookkeepers of business, who are the ultimate accountants."

Doug CERF, Kate LANCASTER, and Arline SAVAGE
California Polytechnic State University, San Luis Obispo

See also in the *Berkshire Encyclopedia of Sustainability*: **Cap-and-Trade Legislation; Climate Change Disclosure; Ecosystem Services; Global Reporting Initiative (GRI); Green GDP; Performance Metrics; Stakeholder Theory; Transparency; Triple Bottom Line; True Cost Economics**

FURTHER READING

Barth, Mary E.; McNichols, Maureen F.; & Wilson, G. P. (1997). Factors influencing firms' disclosures about environmental liabilities. *Review of Accounting Studies 2*(1), 35–65.

Carbon Concierge. (2008). *Carbon Concierge introduces COPEM carbon offset provider evaluation matrix.* Retrieved August 10, 2009, from http://carbonconcierge.com/learn/COPEM-Final.pdf

Carter, Mary Ellen; Lynch, Luann; & Tuna, Irem. (2007). The role of accounting in the design of CEO equity compensation. *The Accounting Review, 82*(2), 327–357.

Deloitte. (2008, February 6). *Accounting for emission rights.* Retrieved June 23, 2009, from http://www.deloitte.com/assets/Dcom-Australia/Local%20Assets/Documents/Deloitte_Accounting_Emissionright_Feb07.pdf

Doerr, John. (2009). Proposed memorandum for the President's Economic Recovery Advisory Board. Retrieved June 25, 2009, from http://www.whitehouse.gov/assets/documents/PERAB_Climate_Policy_5-19-09.pdf

European Sustainability Reporting Association. (2009). *The state of sustainability reporting in Europe: Commission statement.* Retrieved July 21, 2009, from *http://www.sustainabilityreporting.eu/general/downloads/ec08.pdf*

Financial Accounting Standards Board. (1980, November). *Financial reporting and changing prices: Specialized assets—timberlands and growing timber (A supplement to FASB statement no. 33).* Retrieved August 11, 2009, from http://www.fasb.org/pdf/fas40.pdf

Financial Accounting Standards Board. (2001). *Statement of financial accounting standards no. 142: Goodwill and other intangible assets.* Retrieved August 11, 2009, from http://www.fasb.org/pdf/aop_FAS142.pdf

Ford. (2009). Sustainability report 2008/9: Our value chain and its impacts. Retrieved June 24, 2009, from http://www.ford.com/microsites/sustainability-report-2008-09/operations-value

Global Reporting Initiative (GRI). (2006). *Sustainability reporting guidelines: Version 3.0.* Retrieved June 24, 2009, from http://www.globalreporting.org/NR/rdonlyres/A1FB5501-B0DE-4B69-A900-27DD8A4C2839/0/G3_GuidelinesENG.pdf

Harold, Jacob, & Center, Rebecca. (2005). *The MBA's climate change primer.* Retrieved June 27, 2009, from http://www.gsb.stanford.edu/PMP/pdfs/ClimateChange_2005PMI.pdf

Interface, Inc. (2008). Metrics: What gets measured gets managed. Retrieved June 24, 2009, from http://www.interfaceglobal.com/Media-Center/Ecometrics.aspx

International Federation of Accountants (IFAC). (n.d.). Sustainability framework. Retrieved June 29, 2009, from http://web.ifac.org/sustainability-framework/overview

KLD. (2009). KLD stats. Retrieved September 2, 2009, from http://www.kld.com/research/stats/index.html

KPMG International. (2008). *KPMG International survey of corporate responsibility reporting 2008.* Retrieved June 25, 2009, from http://www.kpmg.com/SiteCollectionDocuments/International-corporate-responsibility-survey-2008_v2.pdf

McGinn, Daniel. (2009, September 28). The greenest big companies in America. *Newsweek,* 34–54. Retrieved September 27, 2009 from http://www.newsweek.com/id/215577

Palepu, Krishna; Healy, Paul; & Bernard, Victor. (2000). *Business analysis and valuation: Using financial statements, text and cases* (2nd ed.). Cincinnati, OH: South-Western College.

The Prince's Accounting for Sustainability Project (PWAS). (2009). Current activities. Retrieved June 29, 2009, from http://www.accountingforsustainability.org/output/page136.asp

Rogers, C. Gregory. (2005). *Financial reporting of environmental liabilities and risks after Sarbanes-Oxley.* Hoboken, NJ: Wiley.

Social Investment Forum. (2007). 2007 *Report on socially responsible investing trends in the United States.* Retrieved July 27, 2009, from http://www.socialinvest.org/pdf/SRI_Trends_ExecSummary_2007.pdf

Social Investment Forum. (2009). *Letter to SEC Chairman Shapiro.* Retrieved July 21, 2009, from http://www.socialinvest.org/documents/ESG_Letter_to_SEC.pdf

Toyota. (2008). *Sustainability report 2008.* Retrieved June 24, 2009, from http://www.toyota.co.jp/en/csr/report/08/download/pdf/sustainability_report08.pdf

United States Environmental Protection Agency (EPA). (1995). *An introduction to environmental accounting as a business management tool: Key concepts and terms.* Retrieved June 25, 2009, from http://www.epa.gov/oppt/library/pubs/archive/acct-archive/pubs/busmgt.pdf

Waddock, Sandra. (2004). *Social and environmental disclosure: Should there be a mandatory requirement?* Retrieved June 24, 2009, from http://www.bcccc.net/index.cfm?fuseaction=Page.viewPage&pageId=1172&nodeID=3&parentID=1170&grandparentID=885

World Business Council for Sustainable Development. (2004). *The greenhouse gas protocol: A corporate accounting and reporting standard* (Rev. ed.). Retrieved June 25, 2009, from http://www.wri.org/publication/greenhouse-gas-protocol-corporate-accounting-and-reporting-standard-revised-edition

Transparency

Transparency, as it relates to sustainability, entails the disclosure of information. Transparency increasingly has been seen globally as an essential component in efforts to hold governments and private industry accountable for their actions on environmental issues. But the lack of definitive research about whether or not such disclosures reach their targeted audience raises questions about transparency's effectiveness as a sustainability tool.

In the search for sustainability, the idea of *transparency* has gained increasing favor as a means to achieve desired results. More and more it is being looked upon as an essential component for holding both government and private industry accountable. Transparency means many things to many people—general openness, "opposite of secrecy" (Florini 1998), greater flow of information. Here it means *information disclosure*, a phenomenon increasingly central to a diverse range of sustainability initiatives.

Accompanied by freedom of information legislation, the "right to know" movements spreading across the globe reflect an embrace of transparency (Florini 2007). In the context of industrialized countries, transparency underpins what foreign policy expert Ann Florini (1998) calls "regulation by revelation" to address issues such as air pollution, food safety, and vehicle safety. The most prominent example of regulation by revelation is the Toxic Release Inventory (TRI), a chemical release registry established by the United States Emergency Planning and Community Right to Know Act of 1988. The act mandates that companies disclose information about their toxic emissions, with the goals of informing communities exposed to pollutants, holding the companies accountable, and eventually leading to reduced emissions. The TRI has been hailed as a successful sustainability initiative and served as a model for other countries, resulting in a spread of pollutant emission registries across the globe, not only in Europe but also in Mexico, South Korea, and China (Fung, Graham, and Weil 2007; Graham 2002; Stephan 2002; Weil et al. 2006).

In the context of global sustainability, information disclosure as a means of governance includes both mandatory state-led and voluntary private initiatives (Gupta 2008; Langley 2001). For example, a belief in the power of transparency underpins the June 1998 Convention on Access to Information, Public Participation in Decision-Making and Access to Justice in Environmental Matters (the Aarhus Convention), negotiated under the auspices of the United Nations Economic Commission for Europe (UNECE), which is intended to enhance citizens' right to know about environmental decisions (Mason 2008). Transparency is also central to various multilateral treaties governing trade in pesticides, hazardous waste, and genetically modified organisms, such as the Cartagena Protocol on Biosafety under the Convention on Biological Diversity, and the Basel Convention on Trade in Hazardous Waste. Privately initiated ecolabeling programs in forestry, fisheries, and organic foods, such as the Forest Stewardship Council and the Marine Stewardship Council, also rely upon information disclosure as a way to promote sustainable choices and enhance sustainable resource use. Various efforts to promote corporate sustainability also rely on information disclosure and transparency, for example: the Global Reporting Initiative (calling for sustainability reporting by private corporations); the Carbon Disclosure Initiative (calling for disclosure of carbon emissions); or the Publish What You Pay initiative (calling for disclosure of earnings from extractive—oil, gas, and mining—industries operating in resource-rich developing countries).

As evident from this range of examples, transparency can be invoked to help fulfill a variety of sustainability-related aims. This suggests that there are multiple architects of transparency in a global and national context: those in the private sector, for instance, who voluntarily promote transparency to further corporate sustainability goals, improve their public image, and/or avoid government intervention; and those in the public sector who, while promoting transparency to remedy perceived and real deficiencies in their environmentally related decision making, aim to ensure political accountability and greater citizen participation. The diverse motives underlying transparency can thus range from a desire to extend the regulatory reach of the state to scaling back its reach; and from furthering a moral "right to know" (thereby holding government and private sectors accountable) to promoting individual lifestyle choices and market-based solutions (Mason 2008).

Impact on Sustainability

Given diverse reasons to deploy transparency, how effective is it as a tool of sustainability? Answering that question requires a systematic and comparative analysis of transparency-based sustainability initiatives, and that research remains largely undone (Gupta 2008).

The Global Reporting Initiative (GRI) provides an example of how transparency has been perceived to impact corporate sustainability to greater or lesser degrees. The GRI has been lauded by scholars and corporate sustainability practitioners alike for its comprehensive,

stakeholder-driven process of generating reporting guidelines for use by private companies (Dingwerth 2007; Brown, de Jong, and Levy 2009). But emerging research into its effectiveness suggests that despite time-consuming and resource-intensive efforts to generate large amounts of data and disclose it, certain controversial data (about unintentional releases of genetically modified organisms, for example) is not being disclosed (Clapp 2007) and therefore never reaches its intended beneficiaries. Or alternately, disclosed information is inaccessible and/or irrelevant for those it is intended to benefit, hence resulting in few users of disclosed information (Brown, de Jong, and Levy 2009).

Such findings can relate to various components of transparency-based reporting, ranging from *design of disclosure*, such as the means by which information is to be disclosed (whether electronic or otherwise), to the *attributes of information* disclosed, such as whether it is standardized, comprehensive, and comprehensible. Those with alternative motives sometimes turn the standard intent of transparency on its head by overwhelming reporting authorities and the public with information, a practice called "drowning in disclosure" (Gupta 2008; Mason 2008; Graham 2002; Fung, Graham, and Weil 2007). Finally, newly emerging *intermediaries of transparency*—auditors, verifiers, and certifiers of disclosed information—are becoming more important, and their degree of involvement can vary depending on the potential ramifications the disclosure. These intermediaries are likely to be increasingly significant in shaping the impact of transparency in sustainability governance (Langley 2001).

Outlook: Struggles over Transparency

Many analysts of transparency begin with an optimistic view of its promise only to subsequently highlight various perils in relying on disclosure in the quest for sustainability (Mol 2008). While most would concur that transparency is no panacea in the search for sustainability, discussions about transparency seem destined to take place in the context of larger societal conflicts, particularly in a global context characterized by North–South disparities in capacities to access and use information.

This is also related to the fact that pressing global sustainability challenges, such as climate change or safe use of biotechnology, are characterized by fundamental conflicts over what is valid knowledge and whose information is credible. In such areas, therefore, agreeing on what constitutes "more and better" information, that is, on the scope and content of transparency, will itself become a site of conflict (Gupta 2008). In short, we can conclude that both the quest for transparency and struggles over it are likely to be defining features of future sustainability politics.

Aarti GUPTA
Environmental Policy Group, Wageningen University

See also in the *Berkshire Encyclopedia of Sustainability*: **Accounting; Climate Change Disclosure; Corporate Citizenship; Financial Services Industry; Global Reporting Initiative (GRI); Performance Metrics; True Cost Economics**

FURTHER READING

Brown, Halina Szejnwald; de Jong, Martin; & Levy, David L. (2009). Building institutions based on information disclosure: Lessons from GRI's sustainability reporting. *Journal of Cleaner Production, 17*(6), 571–580.

Clapp, Jennifer. (2007). Illegal GMO releases and corporate responsibility: Questioning the effectiveness of voluntary measures. *Ecological Economics, 66*(2–3), 348–358.

Dingwerth, Klaus. (2007). *The new transnationalism: Transnational governance and democratic legitimacy.* Basingstoke, U.K.: Palgrave MacMillan.

Florini, Ann. (1998, Summer). The end of secrecy. *Foreign Policy, 111,* 50–63.

Florini, Ann. (Ed.). (2007). *The right to know: Transparency for an open world.* New York: Columbia University Press.

Fung, Archon; Graham, Mary; & Weil, David. (2007). *Full disclosure: The perils and promise of transparency.* Cambridge, U.K.: Cambridge University Press.

Graham, Mary. (2002). *Democracy by disclosure: The rise of technopopulism.* Washington, DC: Brookings Institution Press.

Gupta, Aarti. (2008). Transparency under scrutiny: Information disclosure in global environmental governance. *Global Environmental Politics, 8*(2), 1–7.

Kolk, Ans; Levy, David; & Pinkse, Jonatan. (2008). Corporate responses in an emerging climate regime: The institutionalization and commensuration of carbon disclosure. *European Accounting Review, 17*(4), 719–745.

Langley, Paul. (2001). Transparency in the making of global environmental governance. *Global Society, 15*(1), 73–92.

Mason, Michael. (2008). Transparency for whom? Information disclosure and power in global environmental governance. *Global Environmental Politics, 8*(2), 8–13.

Mol, Arthur. (2008). *Environmental reform in the Information Age: The contours of informational governance.* Cambridge, U.K.: Cambridge University Press.

Pattberg, Philipp, & Enechi, Okechukwu. (2009). The business of transnational climate governance: Legitimate, accountable, and transparent? *St Anthony's International Review, 5*(1), 76–98

Stephan, Mark. (2002). Environmental information disclosure programs: They work but why? *Social Science Quarterly, 83*(1), 190–205.

Weil, David; Fung, Archon; Graham, Mary; & Fagotto, Elena. (2006). The effectiveness of regulatory disclosure policies. *Journal of Policy Analysis and Management, 25*(1), 155–181.

Applications

Sustainable Value Creation

In business, the meaning of sustainability has changed since the 1980s. Originally it indicated the ability to remain profitable over time; it now includes social and environmental issues as well as economic ones. The global context has changed, and, with many major corporations leading the way, businesses that promote sustainability must acknowledge their responsibility to both shareholders and stakeholders to succeed.

In the business world, the term *sustainable* has long been associated with economic viability. *Sustain-ability* is usually taken to be the ability to sustain shareholder returns above the cost of capital. A sustainable company is one that is profitable over time.

The terms *society* and *ecology*, when used in the context of business, have long been associated with compliance to government regulations and the moral obligation of companies to be environmentally and socially responsible. They represent the obligatory costs of doing business.

This backdrop of meanings has contributed to confusion and even rejection by business managers of the composite term *environmental and social sustainability*. Executives everywhere are confronted with it, yet they do not understand what it means for their company, and they certainly don't see it as a source of strategic advantage. They don't see how growing societal constraints can be a matter for the CEO agenda.

Yet the global competitive context has changed to make environmental and social sustainability a huge business opportunity—for those executives who have the right knowledge and competencies. *Sustainable value*, a term coined by Chris Laszlo in his 2003 book *The Sustainable Company*, implies that a company can address the "social and environmental dimensions of their business activities" (Laszlo 2008, 119) and create value for both shareholders and stakeholders. Leading companies are jumping on the sustainability bandwagon: just a few global players who have recently done so include DuPont, General Electric, Walmart, Marks & Spencer, Toyota, Unilever, Danone, Alcoa, Philips, and JPMorgan Chase. They are not only "doing well by doing good," they are doing better as a result (Laszlo 2008).

A New Competitive Context

Since the 1990s, massive changes in the competitive landscape have increased the influence of a broad range of stakeholders, from nongovernmental organizations (NGOs) and activist bloggers to the media and government regulators (Assadourian 2005). Low-cost communications and the sheer availability of information have educated the general public and increased its awareness of environmental and social issues. Corporate disasters from Bhopal to Enron have sown a mistrust of big business, while tougher government regulations and new environmental laws have raised the requirements (and costs) of operations. Companies find it increasingly difficult to hide environmental and social transgressions, even in far-flung markets where the risk of discovery—and subsequent YouTube exposure—is ever present.

As a result of these trends, stakeholders instantly and globally access information about a company, mobilizing against those seen as doing wrong and enhancing the reputation of those seen as leading positive change.

A separate but immensely important development is the rise of intangible value as a component of stock price performance. The economist Baruch Lev (2001) has shown the extent to which accounting value has fallen as a driver of market capitalization—from 70 percent in 1900 to 30 percent in 2000—while intangibles such as goodwill, knowledge, brand value, and strategic relationships have risen accordingly (Low and Kalafut 2002).

A growing number of CEOs understand that their company's environmental, social, and governance performance affect their ability to attract and retain talented employees, drive innovation, and enhance corporate reputation. Such intangibles help in turn to differentiate their company's offering, leading to superior earnings and share price. Today the value created or destroyed for stakeholders carries strategic business risks or opportunities, demanding that business leaders rethink environmental and social sustainability in terms of value creation.

The Sustainable Value Framework

Stakeholder value requires managers to think "outside-in" about how their companies create and sustain competitive advantage. Outside-in thinking, which sees the world from the perspective of stakeholders, is a powerful new lens through which managers can discover new business opportunities and risks. Leaders who engage stakeholders and proactively address stakeholder issues can better anticipate changes in the business environment, reducing the risk of being unpleasantly surprised by emerging societal

expectations. Ultimately, stronger stakeholder engagement allows leading companies to discover new sources of value through innovation.

Figure 1 describes company performance along two axes—shareholder value and stakeholder value. Shareholder value is exemplified by increased dividends and stock prices for company "owners"; stakeholder value emphasizes responsibility to all the stakeholders—employees, customers, community, and shareholders—over profitability and "is created when a business adds to the capital or well-being of its stakeholders" (Laszlo 2008, 120). Managing in two dimensions represents a fundamental shift in how managers think about business performance. In this framework, companies that deliver value to shareholders while destroying value for other stakeholders have a fundamentally flawed business model, while those that create value for stakeholders are cultivating sources of extra value that can fuel competitive advantage for years to come. Sustainable value occurs only when a company creates value that is positive for its shareholders and its stakeholders.

Starting in the upper left of Figure 1 and moving counterclockwise, consider the following four cases of value creation.

Figure 1. The Sustainable Value Framework

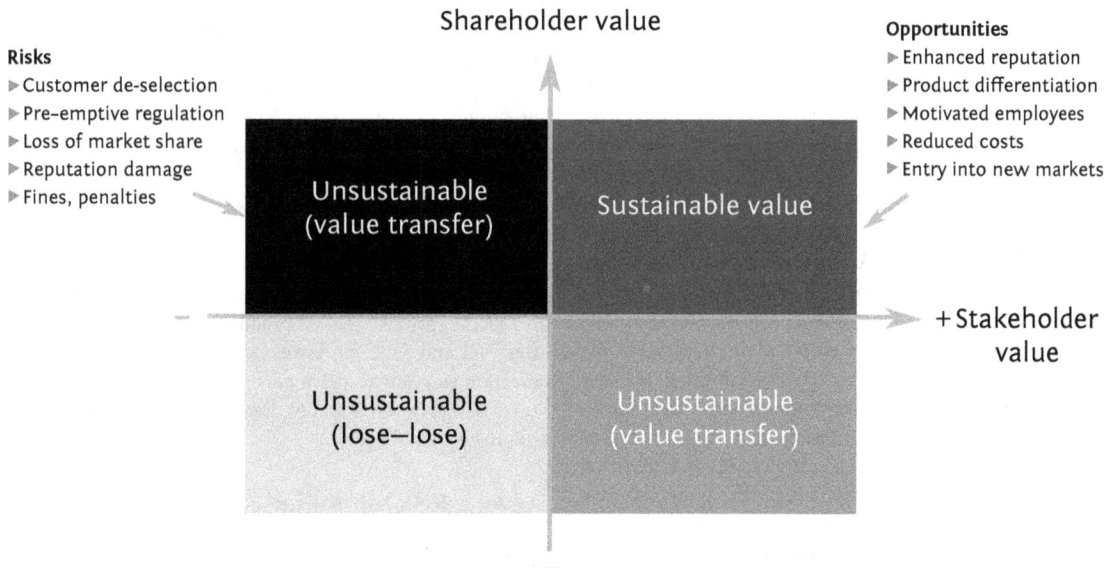

Source: Laszlo 2003, 126.

Sustainable value (top right) is created only when both shareholder and stakeholder values are incorporated by business, resulting in positive opportunities for all interested parties. Unfocused charity and action by well-intentioned environmentalists (for instance, actions that cause a business to go bankrupt) fall into the bottom right sector. A business that pays no heed to societal or environmental concerns and pays the price in lost customers falls into the top left sector. Actions that benefit neither the shareholders nor the stakeholders (the least desirable situation) fall into the bottom left sector.

Upper left quadrant: When value is transferred from stakeholders to shareholders, the stakeholders represent a risk to the future of the business. Leaded paint and asbestos are historical examples; today, carbon dioxide emissions from coal-fired power plants, phthalates in cosmetics, toxic additives in children's toys, volatile organic compounds in carpet adhesives and paints, heavy metals in fabric dyes, and lead solder and brominated flame retardants in consumer electronics are examples of products that create risks to employees, customers, and society even while they create value for shareholders. Companies that avoid environmental regulations in their home markets by exporting production to countries with lower regulatory standards create similar risks. Also in this quadrant are firms that create shareholder value through a low-cost strategy that tolerates management actions to cut expenses by avoiding overtime pay, undertraining on employee safety, or discriminating on the basis of gender and ethnic background. Shareholder value in these cases is created "on the backs" of one or more stakeholder groups, thereby representing a value transfer rather than true value creation.

Bottom left quadrant: When value is destroyed for both shareholders and stakeholders, this represents a lose-lose situation of little interest to either. Monsanto and its European competitor Aventis lost large sums of money by underestimating consumer and farmer resistance to their genetically modified (GMO) crop products. Before Aventis sold its CropSciences division to Bayer in 2001, it is estimated to have lost $1 billion in buyback programs and other costs associated with its genetically modified corn, StarLink, which was approved only for use in animal feed but was found by NGOs to have contaminated a number of human food products.

Bottom right quadrant: When value is transferred from shareholders to stakeholders, the company incurs a fiduciary liability to its shareholders. Actions intended to create stakeholder value that destroy shareholder value put the company's viability into question. Environmentalists often unintentionally pressure companies to take actions in this quadrant without realizing that the pursuit of activities that generate losses is not sustainable either. It is interesting to note that philanthropy, when it is unrelated to business interests and represents pure charity, is also located in this quadrant. Unfocused philanthropy is implicitly a decision to take financial value from the company's shareholders and transfer it to one or more of its stakeholders (Porter and Kramer 2002).

Upper right quadrant: When value is created for stakeholders as well as shareholders, stakeholders can represent a potential source of hidden business value. Sustainable value is created only in this case. When companies design manufacturing facilities that cost less to build and operate than conventional facilities and that use less energy for heating and lighting, they are creating sustainable value. The same

is true when they eliminate packaging waste by rightsizing their products, or when they add environmental intelligence to their products by making them more recyclable, reusable, biodegradable, less toxic, or otherwise healthier. Sustainable value is also created when companies find ways to profitably meet unmet societal needs, for example, by providing nutrition and clean water to the poor. The key is to provide environmental and social benefits to stakeholders without asking customers to accept higher prices or worse quality. Companies that are global industry leaders cannot afford to require their customers to pay the "green premium" that specialty companies have historically charged for their products. Only through process or product redesign and innovation can leading companies create new business and societal benefits without consumer trade-offs.

Managers assessing opportunities to create shareholder and stakeholder value (in other words, opportunities that drive a company further into the upper right-hand quadrant of figure 1) need to make the business case for taking action. Without a clear articulation of business value, managers will be unable to obtain the approval needed to obtain the required resources. The six levels of strategic focus described in the following section is an essential tool used to apply the sustainable value framework.

Six Levels of Strategic Focus

The six levels of strategic focus shown in figure 2 on the following page constitute an important tool for managers seeking to identify how business value is created from sustainability projects. The six levels represent distinct types of sustainability-related business value that can be found in every sector.

Companies have made great strides in compliance-oriented risk mitigation (level 1) and process cost reduction (level 2) through eliminating waste and improving energy efficiencies. Relatively few have focused on top-line (gross revenues) growth based on product or brand differentiation (levels 3 and 5). Even fewer have used stakeholder value creation as a way to drive new markets and business context change (levels 4 and 6). Each of the levels is described in greater detail below.

Level 1: Risk Mitigation

Actions that companies take to comply with government regulations and industry standards (one of the earliest examples being Responsible Care in the chemicals industry, adopted in 1988 by the American Chemistry Council) have historically been seen as a financial burden: they are the necessary cost of doing business and of maintaining license to operate. Yet efficient risk mitigation strategies can create significant value to both shareholders and stakeholders.

Figure 2. The Six Levels of Strategic Focus

Source: Laszlo (2003, p. 140).

Implementing the six types of business value, which are applicable to every business sector, is an important tool in creating sustainable value.

They include the avoidance of penalties and fines, reduced legal fees, and reduced site-remediation costs.

Level 2: Process Cost Reductions

Process cost reductions are often one of the first sustainability initiatives a company undertakes. Reducing energy consumption, eliminating waste, and minimizing materials intensity are all initiatives that save the company money while reducing environmental, health, and safety impacts on stakeholders.

Level 3: Product Differentiation

The growing segment of consumers for whom social and environmental attributes are important criteria provides an opportunity for leading companies to differentiate themselves on a dimension other than price or technical performance. Al Gore's film, *An Inconvenient Truth* (David and Guggenheim 2006), along with a changing political

awareness of climate change, is helping to push sustainability issues into the forefront of public consciousness. On the supply side of the equation, mainstream players such as Walmart and General Electric are democratizing green products by bringing unit costs in line with the products' traditional (non-green) counterparts. It is now possible to buy an organic cotton shirt at Walmart for about the same price as one made from conventionally grown cotton.

When consumers are not asked to pay more for environmental and social benefits, and when they are not forced to compromise quality or performance, sustainability attributes become a "plus one." The recent experience of leading companies, including Unilever, Toyota, JPMorgan Chase, and Aviva, shows that consumers prefer green products and services if they do not have to give up anything in return.

Level 4: New Markets

Technological innovation that creates stakeholder value increasingly opens up new markets. Examples include

DuPont's push into soy-based nutritional products and Procter & Gamble's development of water purification products in emerging markets. Aviva, one of the world's largest insurance companies, has begun selling life insurance in rural India for households where the disability or death of the principal wage earner can be devastating. Celanese AG has parlayed its expertise in plastic polymers to develop high-temperature membrane electrode assembly (MEA) for fuel cells suitable for use in cars—itself a new market driven by climate change–related concerns. The French materials giant, Saint-Gobain, is finding new applications for its high-performance materials from particulate filters in diesel cars to solar panel components and windmill tips.

Level 5: Enhancing Corporate Image

DuPont, Walmart, Unilever, General Electric, Alcoa, and many other leading companies are finding that a brand/culture based on creating stakeholder value is rapidly becoming a source of competitive advantage. Among other business benefits, a sustainability image draws in higher-income consumers, attracts and retains talented people, and can ease negotiations with government regulators concerned about industry impacts. It contributes to an image of innovation—in some cases attached to a single product, such as Toyota's Prius—that confers reputation benefits to the entire company.

Level 6: Business Context

At this level, companies attempt to shape the regulations, practices, and rules that govern how business can be conducted in their favor. An example is the U.S. Climate Action Partnership (2007), which began by urging President George W. Bush to support mandatory reductions in greenhouse gas emissions and to propose federal reduction targets. Rather than slowing down climate change legislation, industry leaders are encouraging it. They see their efforts to reduce emissions, reduce energy use, and provide climate change solutions as a source of future comparative advantage in a carbon-constrained world. These companies don't want the price of oil to fall back to twenty dollars a barrel, since they would lose that advantage relative to competitors who are less energy efficient and who have a higher intensity of greenhouse gas emissions. Influencing the business context is not only about lobbying government; increasing

the overall stakeholder value in an industry can create goodwill for the entire industry. Conversely, negative stakeholder value can shrink the potential market size and reduce the ability of players in the industry to make enduring profits.

Companies can use the sustainable value framework to think in strategic terms about their existing portfolio of products and services. With the framework, managers are able to assess the business value and obtain the resources for sustainability-related initiatives. Perhaps the single biggest obstacle to taking action, however, is not making the business case for the initiatives, but establishing the leadership mindset required to even consider sustainability as a business opportunity.

Leadership Challenge

Sustainability-related business opportunities are often poorly managed in companies that are otherwise global industry leaders, even where a great many strategic business opportunities exist. Several factors can contribute to this situation. An incomplete awareness exists about the company's impacts on stakeholders and how these might in turn affect future business value. Responsibility for social and environmental issues are typically fragmented across the organization and often delegated to those outside the core management team. Line managers are naturally focused on short-term drivers of shareholder value and view stakeholder-related issues as a distraction from their business objectives.

These factors are usually symptoms of what is the most critical barrier to effectively managing stakeholder value—our mental models. A new leadership mind-set is needed to capture the systemic interrelationships between a company and its societal context. In this mind-set, the goal is not only competing with industry rivals, but also meeting the changing expectations of an ever-growing and diverse set of stakeholders.

Capturing sustainable value requires the CEO and leaders with profit-and-loss (P&L) responsibility to see stakeholder value as essential to the growth of their companies. The primary barrier to adopting a stakeholder perspective stems from the leader's mind-set, not from whether there is business value to be found. Mind-set can be understood

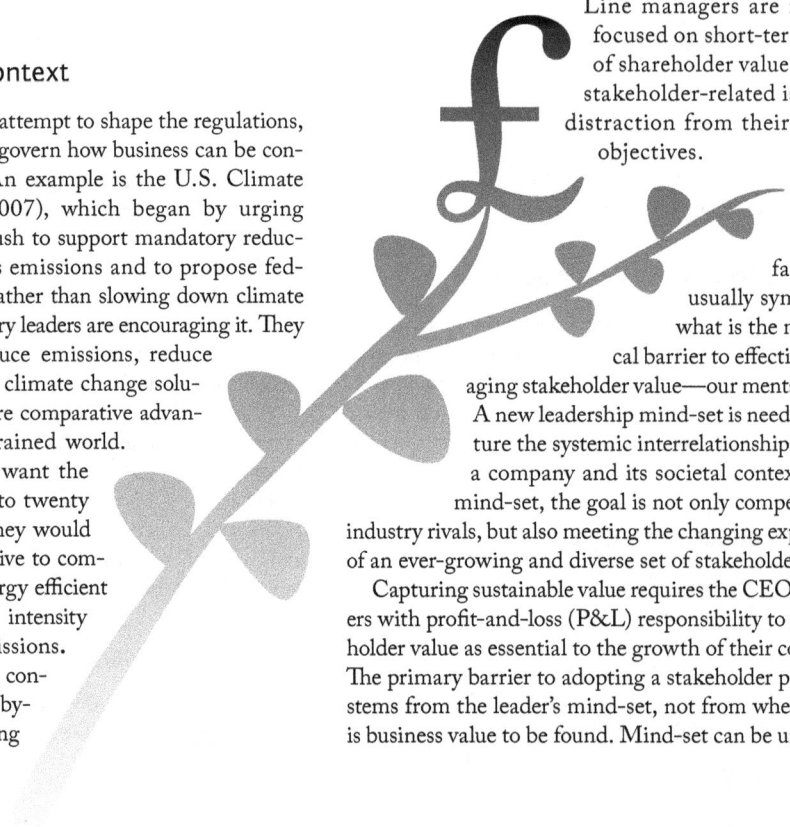

as the hidden set of beliefs about the individual, others, and the world. Much as computer operating systems allow only certain software applications to run, our mind-sets dictate the range of possibilities we draw upon to solve problems (Senge 1994). For instance, if an executive believes that an NGO's primary commitment is to put his or her company out of business, the actions to engage with them will be very different than if the executive believes both are committed to solving a common problem.

Historically, the mind-set required to rise to the top of a large corporation has run counter to adopting a stakeholder perspective in the process of value creation. Executives have tended to focus narrowly on maximizing shareholder value. They have privileged activities that, often unintentionally, externalize negative social and environmental impacts. They have risen to their positions of power precisely because they are able to create shareholder value by maximizing "efficiencies" that legally drive externalities elsewhere.

The idea that maximizing the value of *all* key stakeholders is of interest (much less essential) for business success is quite heretical to what has made leaders successful in the past. Yet stakeholder power is now a reality in the new global business environment. Business leaders who fail to adopt a new mind-set risk putting their companies and careers at risk.

Outlook for the Future

In the past, managers often felt forced to choose between two perspectives: business has a moral responsibility to society, *or* it has a fiduciary responsibility to its shareholders. Those who believe in the profit motive consider moral questions in the workplace to be a distraction. Those who believe in a societal role for business consider the single-minded focus on short-term profits to be irresponsible.

In the new global business environment, companies can pursue both simultaneously. Indeed, they must if they want to succeed. Companies that deliver profits to shareholders while destroying value for society are incurring liabilities; those that offer solutions to environmental and social challenges are discovering huge profit opportunities. The corporate path to doing well by doing good has become the smart way to do business, if you have the knowledge and competencies required for it.

Chris LASZLO
Case Western Reserve University; Sustainable Value Partners

See also in the *Berkshire Encyclopedia of Sustainability*: **Base of the Pyramid; Corporate Citizenship; CSR and CSR 2.0; Education, Business; Equator Principles; Financial Services Industry; Leadership; Natural Capitalism; Social Enterprise; Stakeholder Theory; Transparency; Triple Bottom Line**

FURTHER READING

Assadourian, Erik. (2005). The role of stakeholders. Retrieved September 25, 2009, from http://www.worldwatch.org/node/585

David, Laurie (Producer) & Guggenheim, Davis (Director). (2006). *An Inconvenient Truth* [Motion picture]. United States: Paramount Home Entertainment.

Laszlo, Chris. (2003). *The sustainable company: How to create lasting value through social and environmental performance*. Washington, DC: Island Press.

Laszlo, Chris. (2008). *Sustainable value: How the world's leading companies are doing well by doing good*. Stanford, CA: Stanford University Press.

Lev, Baruch. (2001). *Intangibles: Management, measurement, and reporting*. Washington, DC: The Brookings Institution Press.

Low, Jonathan, & Kalafut, Pam Cohen. (2002). *Invisible Advantage: How intangibles are driving business performance*. Cambridge MA: Perseus Publishing.

Porter, Michael E., & Kramer, Mark R. (2002, December 1). The competitive advantage of corporate philanthropy. Retrieved September 26, 2009, from http://custom.hbsp.harvard.edu/b01/en/implicit/p.jhtml?login=FSGS030708S&pid=R0212D

Senge, Peter M. (1994). *The fifth discipline: The art and practice of the learning organization* (Rev. ed.). New York: Doubleday Business.

U.S. Climate Action Partnership. (2007). *A call for action*. Retrieved September 25, 2009, from http://www.us-cap.org/USCAPCallForAction.pdf

Consumer Behavior

Researchers have found that social, economic, and biological factors contribute to consumer behavior. Consumption of consumer goods has increased since the beginning of the twentieth century, largely because of social factors (desire for social and sexual status, displays of wealth, personal identity, and symbolic meaning). The increase affects sustainable consumption, and policy makers need to examine social contexts when addressing pro-environmental behavioral change.

Understanding mainstream consumer behavior is a prerequisite for understanding how to motivate or encourage pro-environmental consumer behavior. Although the terminology and the context of sustainable consumption were developed during the twentieth century, the debates about consumption, consumer behavior, and consumerism are much older and much deeper.

Consumption, in the words of the social scientist Daniel Miller (1995), has become the "vanguard of history." To question consumption is, at one level, to question history itself. To engage in attempts to change consumption patterns and consumer behaviors is to tinker with fundamental aspects of our social world. To proceed without acknowledging this degree of complexity and sophistication, many thinkers believe, is to invite an inevitable failure.

The wider debates on consumption can be traced back (at least) to classical philosophy. They encompass the critical social theory of the nineteenth and early twentieth centuries, the consumer psychology and "motivation research" of the early postwar years, the "ecological humanism" of the 1960s and 1970s, the anthropology and social philosophy of the 1970s and 1980s, and the sociology of modernity, popularized in the 1990s. Each different avenue of exploration asks slightly different questions about consumption and consumer behavior.

Consumption and Well-Being

Consumption can be viewed as a functional attempt to improve individual and collective well-being by providing the goods and services necessary to meet people's wants and desires. This linear view of consumption is generally the one encoded in conventional economics (Mas-Colell, Whinston, and Green 1995; Begg, Fischer, and Dornbusch 2003). (See figure 1 on page 20.) Stressing the "insatiability" of consumer desire and the "sovereignty" of consumer choice, economics takes a broad, utilitarian approach to evaluating consumer goods and services.

A consumer buys a particular commodity because it offers certain useful functionalities. A new car gets a person from A to B more efficiently, cheaply, and pleasantly than an old car does. A wide-screen plasma TV is easier to see and hear. People are willing to spend more money on these purchases because they value these additional services. But a consumer can never be considered entirely satiated, because new and better products and more and different ways of satisfying appetites and tastes will always be offered.

Though based on the assumption that consumers have a certain set of preferences or tastes, the economic view of consumption does not address the underlying motivations for them. The economic view goes only so far as to "reveal" the ways in which consumers spend their money in the market. Economics makes key assumptions about the rationality of consumers' ability to choose products that offer them utility and thereby contribute to their well-being.

Figure 1. A "Supply Chain" View of Well-Being

The "supply chain" view of consumption illustrates the inherent unsustainability of depending on material things for a feeling of well-being.

Consumption and Needs

Over the years, numerous critics have attacked the conventional economic position on consumption and needs. One of the most telling critiques draws heavily on the concept of human needs. Needs theorists suggest that, in contrast to the "insatiability" of desire, "true" human needs are finite, few, and universal (Max-Neef 1992; Maslow 1954, 1968).

Classifications and typologies of human needs tend to distinguish between material needs (such as subsistence and protection) and social or psychological needs (such as self-esteem, autonomy, and belongingness). They also distinguish between needs themselves and satisfiers, things that produce satisfaction. They suggest, crucially, that not all satisfiers are equally successful at meeting the underlying needs. Food, for example, is a satisfier of the need for subsistence. But not all foods have equal nutritional value, and some are positively bad for us in anything more than very small quantities.

The possibility that some of what we consume does not satisfy our needs provides the basis for a long-standing critique of consumer society (Springborg 1981). Social critics maintain that, far from meeting our needs, commercial interests in modern society have created sets of "false" or "unnatural" needs that have come to alienate consumers from their own well-being, and in the process threaten the environment (Fromm 1976; Illich 1978; Marcuse 1964;

Scitovsky 1976). According to this critique, the consumer way of life is deeply flawed. It neither serves our own best interests nor protects the environment. Proponents of this argument call on the so-called life-satisfaction paradox in defense: real consumer expenditure has more than doubled in the last thirty years, but reported life satisfaction has barely changed (Donovan, Halpern, and Sargeant 2002).

The debate about human needs has generated protracted and sometimes fierce disagreements. Cultural theorists and sociologists tend to be skeptical of this discourse on needs, arguing that it is naive, rhetorical, and moralistic. Nonetheless the language of needs has popular appeal, and it links with the discourse of sustainable development. Indeed this needs-based critique of consumer society appears to offer considerable hope for achieving sustainable consumption. If social and psychological needs really are ill served by modern commodities, then it should be possible to live better by consuming less, and in the process reduce our impacts on the environment.

On the other hand, if consumerism fails to satisfy, why do we continue to consume? The social critique of consumer society tends to point to the power of commercial marketers—the "hidden persuaders" in the sociologist Vance Packard's (1956) terminology—to "dupe" consumers into buying things that do not serve their needs. But there are a number of other equally powerful and sometimes more sophisticated responses to the question.

Consumption and Desire

One response to the question of why we continue to consume is that human needs have been overemphasized. Consumers are not driven much by coherent attempts to satisfy well-defined sets of needs and wants, according to this view. Instead many of our tastes and preferences are informed by desire. And desire, it is argued, has a different character from need. Desire is associated with powerful emotional or sexual drives and motivations, rather than with "rational" efforts to match the functional character of goods with specific personal or social requirements.

The idea that consumption is connected to sexual desire is supported by ethnographic research (Belk, Güliz, and Askegaard 2003) and bolsters the wisdom of advertising executives that "sex sells." From cigarettes to chocolate, and from underwear to cars, sexual connotation has been widely employed in advertising, both directly and indirectly, to render goods and services attractive to prospective consumers. But this association of objects with sexual desire is not an arbitrary or artificial device concocted by marketers. If it were, it would be highly unlikely to succeed. What advertising attempts to exploit is a widespread association of material commodities with sexual and social status. Therefore, for well over a century, sociological and psychological discourses on consumption have focused on displays of wealth and income and the status they bring.

This is where accounts of consumer desire sometimes call on evolutionary biology to explain and understand display- and status-oriented consumption (Wright 1994; Ridley 1994). The theory of evolution suggests that animal behaviors are the result of evolutionary adaptation under pressure from the forces of natural selection and sexual selection. (Natural selection is inter- and intraspecies competition for scarce resources, and sexual selection is intraspecies competition for sexual partners). This explanation suggests that consumer behavior is conditioned, at least partly, by social and sexual competition. It also suggests a biological basis for consumption that makes behavioral changes in consumption difficult.

Ordinary and Inconspicuous Consumption

Sociology studies suggest that the conspicuous and status-seeking aspects of consumer behavior have been overemphasized. According to this view, a great deal of consumption takes place inconspicuously as a part of the ordinary, everyday decision making of millions of individual consumers.

Ordinary consumption, argue these studies, is not oriented toward individual display. Rather it is about convenience, habit, practice, and individual responses to social norms and institutional contexts (Gronow and Warde 2001; Shove 2003; Shove and Warde 1997). Instead of acting as willing partners in the process of consumerism, consumers are "locked in" to a process of unsustainable consumption over which they have little individual control (Sanne 2002).

The concept of *inconspicuous consumption* is important to understanding consumer behavior. In particular, it connects with our day-to-day experience of consuming. Shopping for high-fashion goods may explicitly engage our display motivations on selected occasions. Apart from compulsive or addictive shoppers, however, we do not as a rule spend our day-to-day life engaged consciously in this kind of consumption. Much everyday consumption is almost invisible, even to ourselves. The regular payments that leave our bank accounts to cover our mortgages, insurance payments, utility bills, and local taxes do not appear to be associated with display or status. Even when we change electricity or gas suppliers, for example, few of us are motivated to choose a new supplier by any attempt to improve our social standing.

In this analysis, consumers are a long way from being willing actors in the consumption process, capable of exercising either rational or irrational choice in satisfying their own needs and desires. More often they find themselves locked in to unsustainable patterns of consumption, either by social norms that lie beyond individual control or by institutional constraints in which individual choice is negotiated.

Consumption and Identity

There is a broad agreement that, in modern society, consumption is in some sense inextricably linked to personal and collective identity. According to Yiannis Gabriel, a former professor of organizational theory, and Tim Lang, a food-policy professor, identity is the "Rome to which all discussions of modern Western consumption lead, whether undertaken by Marxist critics or advertising executives, deconstructionists or liberal reformers, advocates of multiculturalism or radical feminists" (1995, 81).

Certain sociologists and social philosophers believe that consumer goods are important to processes of identity creation, a belief that forms the basis for a specific view of consumer society. According to this view, the individual consumer is engaged in a continuous process of constructing and reconstructing personal identity in a continuously renegotiated universe of social and cultural symbols.

Authors take different positions on the extent to which this relationship between identity and consumerism is a good or a bad thing. The sociology professor Colin Campbell (1997) argues that an open choice of consumer goods is vital to enabling consumers to be autonomous individuals in modern society. The historian and psychotherapist Phillip Cushman (1990) argues that the "empty self" of the modern consumer, which constantly needs "filling up," is a cultural artifact, or human-made object, generated explicitly by and for the commercialism of modern society. The philosopher Jean Baudrillard (1998) condemns the "social logic" of consumption, in which people consume for status, as a "luxurious and spectacular penury."

Despite these differences, the link between the consumption of material goods and the construction and maintenance of personal identity is one of the most prominent and perhaps most important elements in modern understanding of consumer behavior. Whereas in earlier times we were what we did (or sometimes who we knew), in modern society we are what we consume.

Symbolic Role of Consumer Goods

Embedded within the idea that consumption and identity are linked lies an important insight into our relationship to consumer goods: consumer goods play vital, symbolic roles in our lives. We value goods for what they can do, but also for what they represent to us and to others. Without this belief, it is doubtful that plain "stuff" could serve such a key role in our lives. This insight resonates with popular psychology about our relationship with material possessions (artifacts). A favorite teddy bear, a wedding dress, a favorite set of golf clubs, the souped-up sports car: all these examples suggest that more is at stake in the possession of material artifacts than simple functional value.

Over the second half of the twentieth century, this popular wisdom was given more credence. The symbolic importance of consumer goods has been underlined by a wide range of intellectual sources; the evidence from anthropology is perhaps the most convincing. Societies throughout the ages have used material commodities (things of value to exchange or sell, such as cattle, for example, in early societies) as symbolic resources to denote a wide variety of different meanings in a wider variety of situations and contexts.

The lesson from the huge body of literature on the symbolic roles of goods is clear: material commodities are important to us, for what they do and for what they signify to others and to ourselves about us and about our lives, loves, desires, relationships, successes, and failings. Material commodities are not just artifacts. Nor do they offer purely functional benefits. They derive their importance, in part at least, from their symbolic role in mediating and communicating personal, social, and cultural meaning.

The symbolic role of material artifacts is not unique to modernity. In the light of the anthropological evidence, we must see the symbolic role as an essential feature of human societies with long roots in antiquity. Any understanding of consumer behavior not built on this insight likely underestimates the social and psychological importance of consumer goods and services.

Consumption as Social Conversation

The symbolic function of consumer goods allows them to play a key role in "social conversations"—the continuing social and cultural dialogues and narratives that keep societies together and help them function. "Forget that commodities are good for eating, clothing and shelter," argue the anthropologist Mary Douglas and the economist Baron Isherwood (1996). "Forget their usefulness and try instead the idea that commodities are good for thinking; treat them as a non-verbal medium for the human creative faculty."

Douglas and Isherwood draw attention to the importance of material goods in providing "marking services." These are social rituals—dinner parties, work functions, or festive celebrations, for example—that embed people in their social group, cement social relations, and help maintain information flows within the social group. These information flows, claim Douglas and Isherwood, go far beyond the "display consumption" mentioned in the above discussion about status- and display-oriented consumption. Information flows are crucial to helping the individual maintain and improve social resilience in the face of cultural shifts and social shocks, and in helping the group maintain its social identity and negotiate intergroup relationships.

Consumption and the Pursuit of Meaning

The ability of consumer goods to operate as a form of social conversation means that they become embedded in a wide variety of different personal, social, and cultural narratives. The anthropologist Grant David McCracken (1990) argues that one of the most pressing problems a culture must deal with is the "gap between the 'real' and the 'ideal' in social life," the distance between our aspirations (for ourselves, for our society, and for human nature) and daily reality. He suggests that consumer goods help overcome this problem. Material artifacts, he says, are "bridges" to displaced

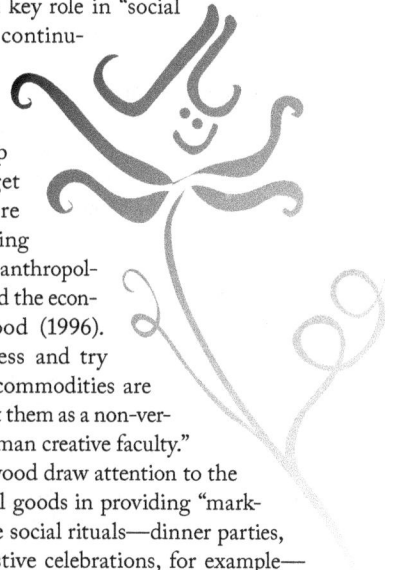

meaning (a coping strategy people use to sustain hope). Designer sunglasses, the new car, the wedding outfit, the seaside vacation are more than satisfiers of functional needs. They are bigger than the objects themselves or even than their use value. They are material representations of our expectations for the future, of the status to which we aspire, of the comforts that we deserve, of the rewards that we fervently hope will be showered upon us. They are bridges to our displaced ideals.

The concept of the pursuit of meaning is vital to understanding consumption. No purely functional account of material goods will deliver a robust model for understanding consumer behavior, because functionality is not the point (or not exclusively the point). We consume not just to nourish ourselves or protect ourselves from the elements or maintain a living; we consume in order to identify ourselves with a social group, to position ourselves within that group, to distinguish ourselves with respect to other social groups, and to communicate allegiance to certain ideals. We consume in order to communicate. Through consumption, we communicate not only with each other but with our past, with our ideals, with our fears, and with our aspirations. We consume, partly, in pursuit of meaning.

Implications for Behavioral Change

The psychological, sociological, and anthropological literature on consumption is rich. Its richness has long been recognized in marketing, consumer studies, and motivation research. Business and commercial interests have drawn widely on this depth to design products and devise strategies for persuading people to buy them. Importantly, the same literature is a resource for policy makers attempting to deal with the problem of unsustainable consumption. But the vast literature is dogged with disagreements and intellectual tensions, and its understandings straddle some well-entrenched and rather intractable debates with very long histories. Nonetheless, it is possible to draw out two or three important themes in relation to understanding unsustainable consumption.

The first theme is that we are living in a consumer society. There has been a massive expansion in the availability of consumer goods in developed economies since the mid-twentieth century. These economies have a structural reliance on consumption growth, and previously public goods and services have been extensively commercialized.

Fundamental aspects of our modern cultural identity are different than they were in the nineteenth century. Modern consumer society has its own logic, its own dynamics, its own epistemologies and ethics, its own myths and cosmologies. All of these are different from those of other times

and places. Policy makers addressing the large-scale shifts in consumption patterns will be well served to examine the history of consumption.

In certain respects, however, modern consumer society is much like any other society before it. The second theme to be drawn from the consumption literature is that material artifacts have important symbolic roles and, accordingly, can negotiate crucial psychological and social functions in our lives. The main objective of consumption by the individual is, in Mary Douglas's words (1976), "to help create the social world and to find in it a credible place."

The symbolic role of material artifacts appears to be shared by every society for which there is anthropological evidence. But modern society's extensive appropriation of this symbolic role for key social and psychological purposes does appear to be a distinguishing feature of modernity. The social-psychological and cultural complexity associated with this relationship is a main reason for the apparent difficulty in analyzing consumer behavior and consumption patterns.

The third theme is equally important, because the evidence indicates that consumer motivations are often embedded in a variety of ordinary, routine, and habitualized behaviors. The behaviors are heavily influenced by social norms and practices and constrained by institutional contexts. These factors emphasize that consumers are not able to exercise free choice in the selection of goods and services, and they often find themselves locked in to specific consumption patterns by a variety of social, institutional, and cognitive constraints.

These understandings highlight the difficulty and complexity associated with negotiating pro-environmental behavioral change. They also point to the importance of understanding and influencing the social context within which consumer choice is negotiated. Policies that seek to promote pro-environmental behavioral change will need to engage the social context that shapes and constrains social action and the mechanisms of individual choice equally.

Tim JACKSON
University of Surrey

This article is based on chapter two of *Motivating Sustainable Consumption: A Review of Evidence on Consumer Behaviour and Behavioural Change*, a report to the Sustainable Development Research Network (2005) by Tim Jackson. That chapter, in turn, draws from an earlier paper published by the Sustainable Development Commission (Jackson and Michaelis 2003).

See also in the *Berkshire Encyclopedia of Sustainability*: **Development, Sustainable; Green GDP; Marketing; True Cost Economics**

FURTHER READING

Baudrillard, Jean. (1998). *The consumer society: Myths and structures*. London: Sage Publications.

Begg, David; Fischer, Stanley; & Dornbusch, Rudiger. (2003). *Economics* (7th ed.). Maidenhead, U.K.: McGraw-Hill.

Belk, Russ; Güliz, Ger; & Askegaard, Søren. (2003). The fire of desire: A multi-sited inquiry into consumer passion. *Journal of Consumer Research, 30*(3), 325–351.

Campbell, Colin. (1997). Shopping, pleasure and the sex war. In Pasi Falk & Colin Campbell (Eds.), *The shopping experience* (pp. 166–176). London: Sage Publications.

Cushman, Philip. (1990). Why the self is empty: Toward a historically constituted psychology. *American Psychologist, 45*(5), 599–611.

Donovan, Nick; Halpern, David; & Sargeant, Richard. (2002, December). *Life satisfaction: The state of knowledge and implications for government*. Retrieved September 28, 2009, from http://www.cabinetoffice.gov.uk/media/cabinetoffice/strategy/assets/paper.pdf

Douglas, Mary. (1976). Relative poverty, relative communication. In A. H. Halsey (Ed.), *Traditions of social policy: Essays in honour of Violet Butler*. Oxford, U.K.: Basil Blackwell.

Douglas, Mary, & Isherwood, Baron. (1996). *The world of goods: Towards an anthropology of consumption* (Rev. ed.). London: Routledge.

Fromm, Erich. (1976). *To have or to be?* New York: Harper & Row.

Gabriel, Yiannis, & Lang, Tim. (1995). *The unmanageable consumer: Contemporary consumption and its fragmentations*. London: Sage Publications.

Giddens, Anthony. (1991). *Modernity and self-identity*. Stanford, CA: Stanford University Press.

Gronow, Jukka, & Warde, Alan. (2001). *Ordinary consumption*. London: Routledge.

Illich, Ivan. (1978). *Toward a history of needs* (1st ed.). New York: Pantheon Books.

Jackson, Tim, & Michaelis, Laurie. (2003). *Policies for sustainable consumption*. Retrieved September 28, 2009, from http://www.sd-commission.org.uk/publications/downloads/030917%20Policies%20for%20sustainable%20consumption%20_SDC%20report_.pdf

Marcuse, Herbert. (1964). *One-dimensional man: Studies in the ideology of advanced industrial society*. Boston: Beacon Press.

Mas-Colell, Andreu; Whinston, Michael D.; & Green, Jerry R. (1995). *Microeconomic theory*. New York: Oxford University Press.

Maslow, Abraham H. (1954). *Motivation and personality*. New York: Harper & Row.

Maslow, Abraham H. (1968). *Toward a psychology of being* (2nd ed.). Princeton, NJ: Van Nostrand Reinold.

Max-Neef, Manfred. (1992). Development and human needs. In Paul Elkins & Manfred Max-Neef (Eds.), *Real-life economics: Understanding wealth creation* (pp. 197–213). London: Routledge.

McCracken, Grant David. (1990). *Culture and consumption: New approaches to the symbolic character of consumer goods and activities*. Bloomington: Indiana University Press.

Miller, Daniel (Ed.). (1995). *Acknowledging consumption: A review of new studies*. London: Routledge.

Packard, Vance. (1956). *The hidden persuaders*. New York: D. McKay.

Ridley, Matt. (1994). *The red queen: Sex and the evolution of human nature* (1st American ed.). New York: Maxwell MacMillan International.

Sanne, Christer. (2002). Willing consumers—or locked in? Policies for sustainable consumption. *Ecological Economics, 42*(1–2), 273–287.

Scitovsky, Tibor. (1976). *The joyless economy: An inquiry into human satisfaction and consumer dissatisfaction*. London: Oxford University Press.

Shove, Elizabeth. (2003). *Comfort, cleanliness and convenience: The social organization of normality*. Oxford, U.K.: Berg Publishers.

Shove, Elizabeth, & Warde, Alan. (1997, April). *Noticing inconspicuous consumption*. Paper presented at the European Science Foundation TERM programme workshop on Consumption, Everyday Life and Sustainability, Lancaster University, U.K. Retrieved September 28, 2009, from http://www.lancs.ac.uk/fass/projects/esf/inconspicuous.htm

Springborg, Patricia. (1981). *The problem of human needs and the critique of civilisation*. London: Allen & Unwin.

Wright, Richard. (1994). *The moral animal: Why we are the way we are: The new science of evolutionary psychology*. New York: Pantheon Books.

Smart Growth

Smart growth describes development models designed to limit urban sprawl by creating more compact living zones that incorporate all aspects of daily life: residences, business, industry, entertainment, shops, and recreation. Smart growth is considered more sustainable because, in theory, it reduces land use and offers public transportation as an alternative to automobiles, thus cutting down on greenhouse gas emissions.

The term *smart growth* can be understood as a collection of urban planning theories and policies created to counter environmental and social problems linked to urban sprawl (uncontrolled urban growth). Inasmuch as it is reactionary, smart growth is defined by the problems it is intended to affect, and as a result takes different forms and is used to different purposes from country to country, and even from city to city. Similarly, it is often described by different names that are used interchangeably or in conjunction with broad concepts such as the *compact city, new urbanism*, and *transit-oriented development*. For instance, since the 1970s growth has been managed in the Netherlands according to a policy called *clustered urbanization*. In Japan it can be found in a national policy called *urban renaissance* and in local initiatives called *machi-zukuri* (literally, "town-making"). In the United States smart growth policies can be found in initiatives to promote walkable neighborhoods and urban revitalization, and it has also been called *land-use control* and *growth management*.

As cities expand, they inevitably consume land, but they also require the investment of a significant amount of new infrastructure, such as roads, sewage systems, electrical power, and gas lines for heating and cooking, as well as a broad range of basic public services, including schools, fire stations, and police stations. When these resources and services are provided at low densities, as in suburban developments, the environmental, economic, and social consequences can be significant. Dependence on automobiles is especially problematic for both environmental and social reasons. Automobiles create congestion, are responsible for the consumption of large amounts of fossil fuels, and can be a barrier to participation in society for those unable to drive if public transit alternatives are not available. This latter is a measurable problem in nations such as Japan, where the population is aging rapidly and residents of older suburbs are already being excluded from a range of activities. Lacking access to a vehicle can make it difficult to undertake simple tasks such as grocery shopping or visiting a doctor without relying on family members or outside assistance.

In order to overcome these issues, smart growth promotes the use of controls on the way cities grow and change over time. Broadly speaking, the intent is to ensure the social and environmental consequences of urban form are given equal weight with financial concerns in the development process.

Origins

The beginnings of smart growth parallel a change in perspective on what constitutes desirable urban form. Its conceptual origins can be traced back to the late nineteenth-century Garden City Movement, the inspiration of the social theorist Ebenezer Howard (Hall 2002, 414–415; Hayden 2003, 202). Howard advocated the creation of self-supporting communities located outside the overcrowded industrial cities of his age, where businesses and residences could coexist in a setting that combined the best of urban and rural elements. Greenbelts and communal ownership of land were included to ensure a degree of social equity and to place a limit on growth. Unfortunately his vision was quickly transformed into one of garden suburbs rather than cities, and the relationship between city center and periphery became one in which functions were segregated rather than integrated. Even in Letchworth, the first Garden City (founded in 1903 in the United Kingdom), which included some industry to support a local workforce, the homes of the varied social classes were carefully separated from each other. More significantly, only a few years later in Hampstead Garden suburb (begun outside London in 1907) there was not even a pretense of including industry or commerce, meaning the development was to be a commuter suburb from the start, dependant for its livelihood on the city. With few exceptions, that was to become the standard pattern of growth on the urban fringe in the decades to follow, especially in the United States.

Nonetheless the concept did have influence. Most famously it formed the basis for the British New Town program begun after the Second World War and exerted a strong influence on similar projects undertaken in Europe and even the United States in the 1960s (Hall 2002). While those developments did achieve some of Howard's goals of well-planned communities (self-sufficient in employment and housing), they were never large enough to accommodate the demand for growth in most cities. In the period following the Second World War, development more typically took the form of suburban bedroom communities, far from places of employment and shopping and increasingly automobile dependent. This was true in Europe, Japan, and the United States, though there was a noticeable lag as result of the time in which cars and trucks became commonplace in each nation.

In the 1960s and 1970s, patterns of urban growth in the developed world began to change radically. Cities were dispersed under the influence of suburbanization, and businesses and other functions followed both their workforce and their customers to the urban fringe. The early response to that change was to attempt to manage or limit growth, but by the 1980s focus shifted toward planning to accommodate it. At the same time awareness of environmental concerns was growing, culminating with publication in 1987 of the Brundtland Report, which provided the first modern definition of sustainability: "…development that meets the needs of the present without compromising the ability of future generations to meet their own needs" (WCED 1987).

It was in this context that urban planners and theorists began to search for policies and urban typologies that would allow them to create a sustainable urban form, but they were unsure how to translate that ambition into actual policies and plans. A number of research projects were begun by academics to test the possibilities, most focusing on the role of energy use in relation to urban form. Typical of research undertaken at that time was a seminal work by the Australian researchers Peter G. Newman and Jeffrey R. Kenworthy (1999), who undertook a global project that showed the least energy-intensive cities in the world were those that combined relatively high density with rail-based public transport. According to their criteria, Hong Kong and Tokyo were the most exemplary. European cities including Paris, Amsterdam, Copenhagen, and London performed well, with American cities, such as Houston and Phoenix, appearing to be the most serious wasters of both energy and land.

Based on these and similar insights, a number of new theories were advanced in the 1980s, many of them reviving and adapting the ideas of Howard's Garden City. In the United States, Peter Calthorpe proposed the *pedestrian pocket* (also called *pedestrian-oriented development* and *transit-oriented development*), a community that mixed both housing and commercial functions and located all homes within 400 meters (a quarter mile) of a transit stop and a commercial area. The careful mixing of land uses and easy access to public transit was intended to make communities more walkable and limit the need for automobiles in daily life. The concept was favorably received and implemented in several cities in the United States, most famously forming the basic structure for the master plan of the city of Sacramento, California.

At the same time the urban planners Andres Duany and Elizabeth Plater-Zyberk launched the New Urbanist movement (sometimes called a *neotraditional development*) with the development of Seaside, Florida (founded in 1979). New urbanism shares the same high-density mix of land use and easy access to public transportation as the pedestrian pocket. Additionally it advocates for the use of a traditional and clear civic structure in its plans and often mandates for traditional architectural styles and materials in its buildings. Seaside proved to be a commercial success, and new urbanism became a model for developments across the United States. In Europe the same movement is called *urban renaissance* and is strongly supported by Prince Charles, who advocated for creation of the new town of Poundbury (begun in 1988) in the county of Dorset, England, according to a master plan by the traditionalist planner Leon Krier. Similar examples were also built across Europe, including Val d'Europe (1995) outside Paris, and Kirchsteigfeld (1993), outside Potsdam, Germany.

The above examples are best understood as design-oriented developments. Policy-driven examples also exist. For example, from the 1980s onward, smart growth policies

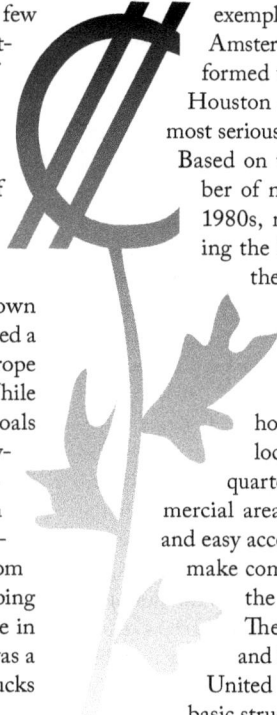

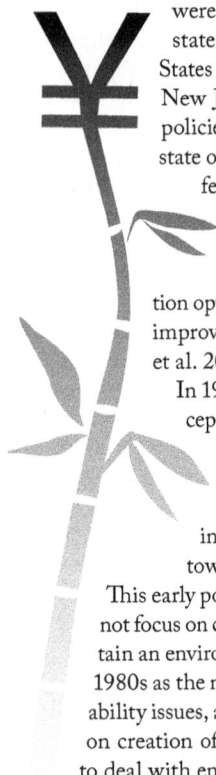

were officially adopted by several cities, states, and municipalities in the United States (most notably by the states of Florida, New Jersey, Oregon, and Maryland). As policies they are heterogeneous, and each state or city tends to work according to different priorities, but all are grounded in a desire to promote compact development, preserve environmental quality, provide transportation options, support affordable housing, and improve fiscal health of the area (Ingram et al. 2009).

In 1966 the Netherlands adopted the concept of *concentrated deconcentration* as the basis for urban growth for the entire country. It was used as a tool to channel development outside existing cities into relatively dense satellite towns, thereby preserving green space. This early policy for containing urban growth did not focus on curbing automobile use, nor did it contain an environmental agenda. This changed in the 1980s as the nation became more aware of sustainability issues, and policy shifted slightly by focusing on creation of compact cities that were more able to deal with environmental concerns such as reducing the use of automobiles and increasing access to public transportation. The compact city shares the same goals as the examples previously reviewed: high density, mixed land use, and ease of access to public transportation.

Japan too adopted the compact city model as a part of its urban renaissance policy in the 1990s. It is notable that the purpose of this planning policy is related to managing an aging population and is not primarily a tool to govern urban growth.

That smart growth was implemented so widely ensured the development of a number of practical experiments focusing on the creation of sustainable urban form. The focus for researchers since 2000 has been on measuring the successes and failures of those models and proposing alternatives and modifications.

Characteristics of Smart Growth

There are many varieties of smart growth, but most versions share the following characteristics:

- Mixed land use: Residential, commercial, and even some industrial activities are encouraged in close proximity, and even in the same buildings.
- Modal choice for transportation, public and private: Public transportation, in the form of rail or buses, is provided along with infrastructure that encourages cycling and/or walking.
- High residential and employment densities: Jobs and homes are close together.
- Continuous compact development: Leapfrog development is not permitted; growth occurs next to existing communities and without gaps. This ensures connectivity between communities and helps to protect open space, farmland, and other natural resources.
- Limits on growth and policies to encourage development in existing areas: Incentives supporting redevelopment of older sites in a city or town are combined with growth boundaries to set physical limits on expansion.
- Mixing of socioeconomic groups: Policies are used to encourage developments that mix housing types.

Collectively these elements are designed to improve access to the requirements of daily life, from employment and shopping to entertainment and community. There may also be a regional planning component that establishes growth boundaries and land-use restrictions to ensure municipalities tackle the issue of sustainability in a coordinated fashion.

The alternative to smart growth is urban sprawl—defined by leapfrog development (where development takes place noncontiguously, often jumping further and further from an existing city), by lack of control in terms of the direction and shape of urban expansion, and by strict separation of land-use functions. Patterns of this sort are assumed to be unsustainable.

Benefits of Smart Growth

Smart growth is ultimately a tool designed to encourage development of urban forms with a high degree of accessibility for all residents of a community to all the institutions and events in that community. This has environmental, social, and economic benefits.

Environmental Benefits

Studies indicate that smart growth can reduce the number of vehicle miles traveled by urban residents. This is significant because reduced dependence on automobiles (and simultaneous support for walking, cycling, and public transportation) logically leads to a reduction in energy use and a corresponding reduction in consumption of greenhouse gas–producing fossil fuels. Further, by ensuring that development is contiguous and undertaken at high densities, the costs of infrastructure and services can be reduced significantly and the consumption of resources curtailed. Some supporters also claim a health benefit that results from reduced car use and increased walking or cycling.

At the same time, open space and green areas including forests and farmland are preserved rather than consumed. In North America, perhaps the best-known example of smart growth can be found in Portland, Oregon, which uses a greenbelt to enforce a limit on urban growth, while simultaneously supporting a public transportation system. More progressive examples can be found in places such as the suburban community of Vauban (completed in 2006) in Germany, where cars are forbidden on most streets, and shops and streetcars are within walking distance of all homes. Residents walk or use bicycles to shop and commute by rail to work, thereby creating a lifestyle that does not require as much energy or resources to maintain or produce as much pollution.

Economic Benefits

Because urban economies are so complicated, isolating the economic benefits of even simple policies is difficult. Studies seem to show, however, that regions and cities that follow smart-growth policies in the United States can perform better economically than those that do not (Cervero 2000; Muro and Puentes 2004). Cities can also save significantly by avoiding the costs of investing in and maintaining inefficient infrastructure and services for low-density areas. The cost of roads, sewers and water lines, garbage collection, postal services, and schools are all affected by land-use patterns and density and can place a strain on municipal governments tasked with providing such services. Some scholars suggest that economic benefits might accrue in settings where businesses are able to trade more easily (because they are closer together) and where residents are attracted to a higher quality of life.

Social Benefits

The social consequences of smart-growth policies are different from country to country. In the United States and in Europe, smart growth is used to eliminate the segregation of social groups by mixing housing types for various economic levels in a single area. In Japan, the focus is instead on ensuring that elderly residents are able to maintain a high standard of living even if they are not able to drive. Encouraging patterns of mixed land use makes both of these ambitions possible.

Issues

Evaluating the impact of smart growth is difficult, first, because the concept is heterogeneous, and second, because agencies other than spatial planning can have a profound impact on urban development. Isolating causes and effects is not always straightforward. Research exists that both supports the claims of smart growth and refutes them. Where problems have been uncovered in most instances, the issue can be understood as a gap between the intent of the concept and its effect after implementation. In the Netherlands, for example, even though planners were able to mandate mixed land-use practices and provide public transportation alternatives, large numbers of Dutch people chose to drive rather than ride. To be fair, the policy was successful on many counts: populations in urban centers were largely maintained, growth on the urban fringe was controlled, and housing was developed in an orderly manner. Nonetheless, planning regulations were unable to stop development of employment centers along highways, and many residents today require a car to commute to work. At the same time a growing demand for lower-density housing has worked against the goals of the compact city, as this has a tendency to produce mono-functional housing areas (Bontje 2001). These developments suggest a failure of policy, but it has also been proposed that such patterns are actually the result of the substantial increase in real wealth of Dutch citizens in the 1980s and afterward (Van der Burg and Dieleman 2004). In response to these deficiencies the Dutch government expanded the scale of its urban planning policies in 2003 to ensure inclusion of the transportation corridors that connect communities in an urban network. While the compact city remains a planning goal, the need for a regional perspective has been acknowledged.

Similar problems can be found in both the United States and Europe. Ironically, in a study of the neotraditional town of Poundbury in the United Kingdom, it was found that car use was higher in the compact development than in the adjacent rural community (Watson et al. 2004). Similar outcomes have been found in other parts of the United Kingdom and in the United States, with the suggestion that compact development does not fit with modern household structure, in which it is now common for more than one family member to be employed, often in distant parts of the city, therefore requiring more than one car to accommodate everyone (Jarvis 2003).

The Future of Smart Growth

A significant amount of research is focused on measuring the effects of smart growth policies as applied to real urban situations around the world. (See, for example, Bontje 2001; Ingram et al. 2009; Jenks and Dempsey 2005.) Policies and theories will no doubt be adjusted as results from that work become available. In the Netherlands, as cited above, the focus has already shifted from the compact city to the urban network, which is intended to better reflect the behavior patterns of the country's urban residents.

Some theorists suggest that the best way toward sustainability is to combine the land-use policies of smart growth with financial disincentives to limit auto use, such as increased gasoline taxes and parking fees. These may well come to pass. Nevertheless, the lessons learned from research conducted in the field appear to be that policies need to be flexible, capable of adjusting to changing patterns of behavior as well as to the special needs of each community, wherever it is in the world. While there is little doubt that urban form affects sustainability, it seems likely that the evolution of smart-growth models will continue.

William GALLOWAY

frontoffice_tokyo; Department of Architecture,
Waseda University

See also in the *Berkshire Encyclopedia of Sustainability*: **Automobile Industry; Bicycle Industry; Building Codes, Green; Cement Industry; Development, Urban; Energy Efficiency; Facilities Management; Local Living Economies; Municipalities; Property and Construction Industry; Public Transportation**

FURTHER READING

Bogart, William. (2006). *Don't call it sprawl: Metropolitan structure in the twentieth century.* New York: Cambridge University Press.

Bontje, Marco. (2004). From suburbia to post-suburbia in the Netherlands: Potentials and threats for sustainable regional development. *Journal of Housing and the Built Environment, 19*(1), 25–47.

Bontje, Marco. (2001). Idealism, realism, and the Dutch compact city. *Town and Country Planning, 70*(12), 36–37.

Bruegmann, Richard. (2005). *Sprawl: A compact history.* Chicago: University of Chicago Press.

Burton, Elizabeth. (2000). The compact city: Just or just compact? A preliminary analysis. *Urban Studies, 37*(11), 1969–2001.

Calthorpe, Peter & Fulton, William. (2001). *The regional city: Planning for the end of sprawl.* Washington, DC: Island Press.

Cervero, Robert. (2000). Efficient urbanization: Economic performance and the shape of the metropolis. Cambridge, MA: Lincoln Institute of Land Policy.

Duany, Andres; Plater-Zyberk, Elizabeth; & Speck, Jeff. (2001). *Suburban nation: The rise of sprawl and the decline of the American dream.* New York: North Point Press.

Fulton, William; Pendall, Rolf; Nguyen, Mai; & Harrison, Alicia. (2002). *Who sprawls most? How growth patterns differ across the U.S.* Washington, DC: Brookings Institution.

Hall, Peter. (2002). *Cities of tomorrow: An intellectual history of urban planning and design in the twentieth century* (3rd ed.). Oxford, U.K.: Blackwell.

Hayden, Delores. (2003). *Building suburbia: Green fields and urban growth, 1820–2000.* New York: Pantheon Books.

Ingram, Gregory K.; Carbonell, Armando; Hong, Yu-Hung; & Flint, Anthony (Eds.). (2009). *Smart growth policies: An evaluation of programs and outcomes.* Cambridge, MA: Lincoln Institute of Land Policy.

Jarvis, Helen. (2003). Dispelling the myth that preference makes practice in residential location and transport behaviour. *Housing Studies, 18*(4), 587–606.

Jenks, Mike & Dempsey, Nicola. (Eds.). (2005). *Future forms and design for sustainable cities.* London: Architectural Press.

Muro, Mark, & Puentes, Robert. (2004). *Smart growth is smart business: Boosting the bottom line and community prosperity.* Washington, DC: National Association of Local Government Environmental Professionals.

Nelson, Arthur C., & Peterman, David R. (2000). Does growth management matter? The effect of growth management on economic performance. *Journal of Planning Education and Research, 19*(3), 277–285.

Neuman, Michael. (2005). The compact city fallacy. *Journal of Planning Education and Research, 25*(1), 11–26.

Newman, Peter G., & Kenworthy, Jeffrey R. (1999). *Sustainability and cities: Overcoming automobile dependence.* Washington, DC: Island Press.

Porter, Douglas. (2002). *Making smart growth work.* Washington, DC: Urban Land Institute.

Smart Growth Online. (2009). Retrieved September 1, 2009, from http://www.smartgrowth.org/Default.asp?res=1280

U.S. Environmental Protection Agency. (2009). Environmental benefits of smart growth. Retrieved September 1, 2009, from http://www.epa.gov/dced/topics/eb.htm

Van der Burg, A. J., & Dieleman, F. M. (2004). Dutch urbanization policies: From "compact city" to "urban network." *Tijdschrift voor Economische en Sociale Geografie, 204*, 108–166.

Watson, G.; Bentley, I.; Roaf, S.; & Smith, P. (2004). *Learning from Poundbury, research for the West Dorset District Council and the Duchy of Cornwall.* Oxford Brookes University.

World Commission on Environment and Development (WCED). (1987). *Our common future.* Oxford, U.K.: Oxford University Press.

Ye, Lin; Mandpe, Sumedha; & Meyer, Peter. (2005). What is smart growth—really? *Journal of Planning Literature, 19*(3), 301–315.

Green-Collar Jobs

The promise of an economy that creates good jobs while protecting and restoring the natural world is an alluring one. Depending on society's commitment to sustainability, between 8 and 40 million green-collar jobs—loosely defined as employment that contributes to environmental quality—could be created in the U.S. alone by the year 2030.

As more people recognize the need to address the multitude of threats to our environment, businesses are rethinking their core business models to reflect the shift in consumer preferences toward products that are less harmful to the environment. Likewise, entrepreneurs are rushing to develop new green products and services. Besides climate change, critical environmental issues facing business today include energy, water, biodiversity and land use, chemicals, toxics, heavy metals, air pollution, waste management, ozone layer depletion, oceans and fisheries, and deforestation (Esty and Winston 2009). The demand for innovative solutions to address these challenges has led many commentators to conclude that we are on the cusp of a "green wave" in terms of job growth and economic opportunity. Millions of new green jobs will be created, so the theory goes, ranging from renewable energy installers to mass transit employees, from sustainability analysts to water resource technicians. Because many of the jobs are blue-collar in nature, they may provide pathways out of poverty for low-skilled, low-income earners (Jones 2008).

Beyond job creation, the green economy promises to provide additional economic benefits. For example, households, businesses, and governments save money as they become more energy efficient. These savings are recycled into the local economy, creating opportunities for local businesses to grow. New markets for greener products and services also support new industries, potentially expanding the local tax base. A greener economy, with its emphasis on green buildings, also promises to improve worker productivity by creating healthier work environments where employees have greater access to fresh air, sunlight, and less exposure to toxins.

In addition to the economic benefits, the green economy will improve environmental quality as greener products and services are brought to market. Electric cars have lower carbon emissions. Green buildings use less water. Mass transit promotes denser development patterns lessening pressure to convert productive farm and forestlands.

Green-collar jobs provide communities with the opportunity to both strengthen the local economy and improve the health of the environment. As green-collar jobs become as commonplace as white- and blue-collar ones, we will be forced to rethink our current approach to economic development with its focus on unbridled growth and lack of concern for the environment. In a green economy, economic development and environmental quality go hand in hand. Businesses become much more efficient and waste as we know it is practically eliminated. Decision making is driven by the recognition that only a healthy environment can support a long-term, sustainable economy (Hawken, Lovins, and Lovins 1999).

Defining Green-Collar Jobs

There is no consensus in the literature on how to define green-collar jobs. A broad interpretation of green jobs includes all existing and new jobs that contribute to environmental quality. Probably the most concise, general definition is "well-paid, career track jobs that contribute directly to preserving or enhancing environmental quality" (Apollo Alliance 2008, 3). This definition suggests that green-collar jobs directly contribute to improving environmental quality, but would not include low-wage jobs that provide little job mobility. Most discussions of green-collar jobs do not refer to positions that require a college degree but to positions that typically involve training beyond high school. Many positions are similar to those held by skilled, blue-collar workers such as electricians, welders, and carpenters. Examples of green industries employing worker with such skills include smart-grid construction; expansion of freight and passenger rail; wind, solar, and biofuel production; and energy efficiency industries.

Estimating the number of existing and potential green-collar jobs is equally as difficult as defining exactly what a green job is. Thus far, research documenting the number of green-collar jobs has been quite varied. Conservative estimates that include only renewable-energy and energy-efficiency industries suggest about 8.5 million jobs in the United States. These estimates focus on specific activities rather than traditional job or industry characteristics (Pinderhughes 2007). According to the American Solar Energy Society, this figure could grow by as many as 40 million by 2030.

Differences in estimates of the number of green-collar jobs can be attributed to several issues. First, a few analyses include all jobs related to promote a green economy. Thus, they would include workers in the plastics and steel industry, for example, because these materials are used to construct products like wind turbines and solar panels. These reports tend to overestimate the number of green-collar jobs because most of these jobs would not be considered green. Second, even if these related jobs are considered, they probably should not be considered as full-time equivalents because much of their output, in most cases, may not go to green activities. A more accurate accounting method might try to take into consideration the proportion of their product that is used to promote environmental quality. Third, some analyses attempt to consider the multiplier effect of the green economy. These analyses assess the direct and indirect impacts on a regional economy by estimating the number of jobs and income that are created through investments in green-collar jobs (Pollin and Wicks-Lim 2008). These estimates typically include service-sector jobs that most people would not consider career-track jobs. Finally, data collected through the Census Bureau and other official sources do not collect information in a manner that would allow researchers to identify green-collar jobs.

Strategies for Promoting Green-Collar Jobs

Communities seeking to promote green-collar jobs first need to identify their goals. This does not have to be an extensive process, but it is essential to build on local strengths and opportunities (Green and Haines 2007). Next, localities need to identify appropriate public policies that will allow them to achieve their goals. Concurrently, it is essential to prepare the workforce for green-collar jobs. Programs should be linked to local opportunities and provide workers with skills that will allow them to move up the career-track (Apollo Alliance 2008). Finally, communities should monitor and evaluate their progress toward growing green jobs. Given the current economy and evolving technologies, it is likely that significant course corrections will be necessary as the green economy continues to take shape. By linking green job policies with environmental goals, communities may find broad-based support for the types of strategies discussed below.

Many of the green job strategies outlined are demand-driven. These types of strategies are seen as crucial to the successful development of the green economy because they provide a stable, secure funding environment in which companies can take root and grow. There are probably many more strategies than are discussed here, but these are the core considerations for most communities.

Energy Efficiency and Green Buildings

A report by The American Council for an Energy Efficient Economy (ACEEE) found that significant energy efficiency potential remains available in the United States. For example, across all sectors, studies show a median technical potential of 33 percent for electricity (Nadel, Shipley, and Elliot 2004). In addition, approximately 40 percent of our energy use is associated with buildings. Energy efficiency is seen as a powerful strategy to grow green-collar jobs because of the potential demand for energy audits and retrofits that exists in neighborhoods, schools, and businesses across the entire United States. Communities can drive green-collar job creation that is tied to efficiency and green building by crafting policies to improve their own facilities. The jobs related to energy efficiency are often concentrated in traditional building trades and construction industries. The jobs related to green buildings not only include green construction jobs but sustainability analysts, urban planners specializing in brownfield redevelopment, and other development professionals with experience in green design. Estimates suggest that about ten jobs are created per $1 million investments in high-performance buildings (Center on Wisconsin Strategy 2007). Jobs are created through the economic activity associated with retrofitting buildings and green construction, and also through the energy savings that result from these activities (Goldstein 2007).

Renewable Energy

Renewable energy is growing rapidly as an alternative to fossil fuel usage. It is seen as a significant generator of green-collar jobs both in terms of manufacturing and in terms of design, installation, and servicing of the systems themselves. Communities can promote renewable energy development through conventional means such as offering tax incentives, credits, and other mechanisms to encourage renewable energy manufacturing in their own backyards. They can also develop creative financing mechanisms that incentivize homeowners and businesses to deploy renewable energy on site. Many countries, states, and even some cities are effectively mandating renewable energy development by passing renewable energy portfolio standards (RPS) requiring that a certain percent of energy purchased be derived from renewable sources. Worldwide, the largest number of jobs in this sector is in biomass. Three countries (Brazil, the United States, and China) account for the vast majority of jobs in biomass. Jobs in solar industries are the second highest, with most of those jobs located in China. Overall, renewable energy sources are growing rapidly, especially in developed countries (Renner, Sweeney, and Kubit 2008). Varied job opportunities appear throughout the renewable energy industry including biomass, solar thermal, wind, solar panels, hydropower, and geothermal. A few of the renewable-energy job types include electrical and mechanical engineers to design solar components, solar installers, and geothermal and heat pump system engineers, installers, and operators.

Transportation

Transportation accounts for about one-fourth of the world's energy use. Green-collar jobs in this sector are most often associated with fuel efficiency and public transportation. There are few reliable estimates of the number of jobs in the transportation sector. The discussion tends to focus on improvements made through green vehicle manufacturing and through public transportation. Green vehicles include electric hybrids, compressed natural gas, low sulfur diesel vehicles, and vehicles capable of running on various biofuel blends. As of 2009 the number of jobs in manufacturing green vehicles is relatively small, with most of the jobs concentrated in Europe. Public transportation, however, is a significant employer in many developed countries. Many of these counts, however, include employment with traditional petroleum-based bus systems.

Smart Grid

The current electrical grid is widely seen as a barrier to achieving significant improvements in both energy efficiency and renewable energy growth. The system prevents the full deployment of wind, for example, because the transmission lines simply do not exist to connect our nation's largely rural high-plains wind resource to our urban population centers. The grid is also highly localized and disjointed, which prevents the effective movement of power throughout the country when demand exceeds supply in a given region. A newer, more modern smart grid can take advantage of recent improvements in information technologies to better manage electrical loads. An industry estimate of jobs associated with investments in a smart-grid system for the United States claim that 280,000 jobs potentially could be created (The Gridwise Alliance 2009). These jobs would likely encompass a broad range of occupations including system designers, project developers, marketers, public relations, supply chain managers, and several types of field technicians.

Environmental Management

This strategy is often not equated with green-collar jobs, but it is so broad that it has tremendous potential to grow them. Included in this category would be many technologies that directly benefit the natural environment, including water, solid and hazardous waste, and air quality technologies among others. We are reluctant to include the recycling industry, although many states and localities have been very successful in promoting recycling programs. Most of the jobs in this sector, however, are low-wage positions with few opportunities for mobility. Recycling markets also appear to be quite sensitive to economic conditions. One of the lessons learned is that green industries will still be market-driven and may experience many swings as they mature. It also shows that not all green industries will produce good jobs for workers. It is difficult to estimate the number of green-collar jobs in this area because the category is so broad. Job types might include air quality specialists, greenhouse gas managers and accountants, and water resource specialists (Lewellyn, Hendrix, and Golden 2008).

By adoption of these broad strategies, communities may be able to achieve multiple goals including environmental quality and green job creation. Many of these strategies are particularly appealing because they are demand driven, meaning locally elected officials can create the demand for green industry by simply shifting their regulatory and purchasing policies to achieve their green job and environmental goals. Communities that can weave together a policy framework with broad-based support will likely be at a significant advantage in terms of creating a business environment that encourages green industry development.

Challenges and Solutions

There are many challenges to green-collar job creation including workforce development, policy development, technological barriers, geography, environmental issues, and financial constraints. Many of the solutions to the challenges facing green job growth are policy related. For example the lack of a coherent federal policy has led to a very chaotic growth in the wind industry. Tax credits that make wind financially competitive have only been reauthorized for two years at a time. Thus the industry is in a constant state of flux between rapid project growth and dramatic reductions in investments depending on the biennial whims of federal policy makers. The challenge for local governments is to focus on those areas over which they have control while seeking to minimize the negative impacts of state and federal policies over which they have little control.

Workforce development is a key challenge. Many green-collar jobs do not require major changes in training programs because they can build on programs in the trades and advanced manufacturing industries. These programs still face some of the same obstacles that workforce development efforts have experienced in the past. It is difficult to recruit youth into these programs even though they tend to be good-paying jobs with opportunities for income mobility. In addition, it may be too costly for small communities to develop specialized training programs for emerging green-collar jobs. A more likely strategy is that green-collar jobs will require more intensive use of apprenticeships and school-to-work programs to provide on-the-job training. Another solution may be to develop green entrepreneurship programs for youth.

Many jobs in the renewable energy sector will be tied in the short run to geographical regions that have considerable sources of renewable energy, such as biomass, wind, and even solar. For example, the Midwest has a large concentration of biomass that could be used for biofuels; over 80 percent of biofuel facilities currently are located in the Midwest. Many coastal communities can harness wind energy. The Southwest has a significant potential for solar energy. These regions are likely candidates for renewable energy production and manufacturing. But geography need not be a constraint for communities pursuing renewable energy job creation. A very strong predictor of green-collar job growth is local renewable energy policy. Those states with strong incentives, including New Jersey and California, have leapt to the lead in renewable energy deployment. Not surprisingly, they have also benefited from new green industry creation, especially in sales, servicing, and installation of renewable systems. Communities can enact policies that increase demand for residential, business, and government renewable energy projects.

There are several technical challenges to green-collar job creation. For many reasons, it is likely that the renewable energy sector will be more decentralized and based in smaller units than our current system is. This technical challenge will likely be overcome through development of a smart-grid system that will create many more opportunities to develop locally distributed renewable energy resources that can feed into the grid. Overcoming this challenge will take considerable public and private investment and will not happen overnight.

Financial constraints are another challenge to green job creation. For example, green buildings include both energy efficiency and renewable energies. There is general agreement that retrofitting existing buildings and improving energy efficiency offer the greatest potential for the environment and jobs, at least in the short run. Yet this may be the most challenging sector with which to grow jobs. The cost of retrofitting will be prohibitive for low-income residents in most countries and will require substantial government subsidies (Jones 2008). Cost is also a major challenge for individuals to install renewable energy at their home including solar PV (photovoltaic), hot water, and solar space heating. Americans are extremely mobile and may be reluctant to pay for these technologies because they are concerned they will not get their investment back before they sell their homes. One solution to this problem is being adopted in communities across the country: Local governments are bonding and then using the funds to lend to homeowners at very low interest rates for installation of renewable energy systems. These systems are then paid off over a ten- to twenty-year period through the property tax bill. If the homeowner moves, the payment stays with the home and the new homeowner continues payment.

Green vehicles continue to draw a great deal of interest among environmentalists. Only a very small percentage of the workforce, however, is now employed in automobile manufacturing that would be considered green. There have been important breakthroughs in automotive technology that may significantly increase the potential for green vehicles. Moving this new technology to mass production, however, could take many years and significant capital investment. A major hurdle to green vehicle growth is battery technology: Without adequate storage, the concept of plug-in vehicles is limited. Efforts are underway to reduce the size of battery storage. With improved batteries, green vehicles may be charged at night to take advantage of lower electricity rates; the batteries' energy then is used during the day for driving or for powering household appliances. When combined with renewable energy sources, such as solar power, green vehicles could have a significant impact on carbon emissions.

Finally, there are a number of environmental issues that may constrain green-collar job growth in areas such as biofuels. Much of the current literature focuses on the dilemmas associated with corn ethanol (i.e., trade-offs between food costs and fuel costs). Research focusing on cellulosic ethanol offers the potential of avoiding the trade-off between food and fuel and overcoming many of the economic and environmental costs associated with corn ethanol. Other solutions include the development of algae as a biofuel and utilizing other types of nonfood feedstock for biofuel production.

The Future

Green-collar job growth will be dependent on sustained societal commitment to addressing climate change and other threats to the environment. If commitment is long-lasting, then our current economic system will have to be transformed in a way that puts focus on other metrics (i.e., measurements) beyond just gross domestic product and unbridled growth. Environmental factors will need to be considered as well. This will create a huge opportunity across all sectors of the economy as new and existing businesses look for ways to become greener in terms of product and service delivery. The transition toward a green economy will be difficult for many regions. Promoting green industries will lead to job loss in some traditional industries. It will require more investment in workforce development to help workers make this transition.

In summary, green-collar jobs are expanding, but not rapidly enough. Worldwide, green jobs tend to be concentrated in a few developed countries. The United States has not invested as much in research and development in the green sector as many western European countries. Investments in research will be critical to the growth of green-collar jobs over the next decade. Government support for the public and private sector to adopt new technology will also be an essential factor in the transition to this new economy. Finally, educational programs have been proven to be an important element in increasing the public's awareness of environmental issues and in changing attitudes and behavior.

Gary Paul GREEN
University of Wisconsin, Madison/Extension

Andrew DANE
University of Wisconsin-Extension

See also in the *Berkshire Encyclopedia of Sustainability*: **Education, Business; Education, Higher; Energy Industries—Overview of Renewables; Investment, CleanTech; Natural Capitalism; Social Enterprise**

FURTHER READING

Apollo Alliance. (2008). *Green-collar jobs in America's cities: Building pathways out of poverty and careers in the clean energy economy.* Retrieved January 20, 2009, from http://apolloalliance.org/downloads/greencollarjobs.pdf

Audirac, Ivonne. (Ed.). (1997). *Rural sustainable development in America.* New York: John Wiley and Sons.

Center for American Progress. (2008, September). *Green recovery: A program to create good jobs and start building a low-carbon economy.* Retrieved January 28, 2009, from http://www.americanprogress.org/issues/2008/09/pdf/green_recovery.pdf

Center on Wisconsin Strategy. (2007). *Milwaukee retrofit: Capturing home energy savings in Milwaukee.* Retrieved January 20, 2009, from http://www.cows.org/pdf/bp-milwaukeeretrofit_050807.pdf

Esty, Daniel C., & Winston, Andrew S. (2009). *Green to gold: How smart companies are using environmental strategy to innovate, create value, and build competitive advantage.* Hoboken, NJ: John Wiley and Sons.

Friedman, Thomas. (2008). *Hot, flat, and crowded: Why we need a green revolution—and how it can renew America.* New York: Farrar, Straus, and Giroux.

Goldstein, David B. (2007). *Saving energy, growing jobs: How environmental protection promotes economic growth, competition, profitability and innovation.* Berkeley, CA: Bay Tree Publishing.

Green, Gary Paul, & Haines, Anna. (2007). *Asset building and community development* (2nd ed.). Thousand Oaks, CA: Sage Publications.

The Gridwise Alliance. (2009). *The U.S. smart grid revolution: KEMA's perspectives for job creation.* Retrieved February 10, 2009, from http://www.gridwise.org/pdf/KEMA_SmartGridJobsCreation_01-13-09ES.pdf

Hawken, Paul; Lovins, Amory; & Lovins, L. Hunter. (1999). *Natural capitalism: Creating the next Industrial Revolution.* New York: Back Bay Books.

Jones, Van. (2008). *The green collar economy: How one solution can fix our two biggest problems.* New York: HarperCollins Publishers.

Lewellyn, A. Bronwyn; Hendrix, James P., & Golden, K. C. (2008). *Green jobs: A guide to eco-friendly employment.* Avon, MA: Adams Media.

Mazmanian, Daniel A., & Kraft, Michael E. (Eds.). (1999). *Toward sustainable communities: Transition and transformations in environmental policy.* Cambridge, MA: MIT Press.

McKibben, Bill. (2007). *Deep economy: The wealth of communities and the durable future.* New York: Henry Holt and Company.

Nadel, Steven; Shipley, Anna; & Elliot R. Neal. (2004) *The technical, economic and achievable potential for energy-efficiency in the U.S.—A meta-analysis of recent studies.* Proceedings of the 2004 Summer ACEEE Summer Study on Energy Efficiency in Buildings. Retrieved February 9, 2009, from http://www.aceee.org/conf/04ss/rnemeta.pdf

Ong, Paul M., & Patraporn, Rita Varisa. (2006, June 30). *The economic development potential of the green sector.* Retrieved January 20, 2009, from http://repositories.cdlib.org/lewis/pb/Policy_Brief_06-06/.

Pinderhughes, Raquel. (2008). *Green collar jobs: An analysis of the capacity of green businesses to provide high quality jobs for men and women with barriers to employment: A case study of Berkeley, California.* Retrieved January 20, 2009, from http://www.greenforall.org/resources/An-Analysis-of-the-Capacity-of-Green-Businesses-to/

Pollin, Robert, & Wicks-Lim, Jeannette. (2008, June). *Job opportunities for the green economy: A state-by-state picture of occupations that gain from green investments.* Retrieved March 8, 2009, from http://www.bluegreenalliance.org/atf/cf/%7B3637E5F0-D0EA-46E7-BB32-74D973EFF334%7D/NRDC_report_May28.pdf

Renner, Michael, Sweeney, Sean., & Kubit, Jill. (2008). *Green jobs: Working for people and the environment.* Worldwatch Paper 177. Washington, DC: Worldwatch Institute.

Shuman, Michael H. (2000). *Going local: Creating self-reliant communities in a global age.* New York: The Free Press.

Speth, James Gustave. (2008). *The bridge at the edge of the world: Capitalism, the environment, and crossing from crisis to sustainability.* New Haven, CT: Yale University Press.

Public–Private Partnerships

The public sector—government—has not always been successful in providing adequate services, especially in poorer, more remote areas. Since the 1990s, the private sector has been used to deliver financing opportunities and improve services in conjunction with the public sector through public–private partnerships. Water and sanitation has been one sector addressed globally through different types of these contractual agreements.

Throughout the world, the public sector is principally responsible for water and sanitation services, operating more than 90 percent of the piped networks in developing countries. On the whole, however, the public sector has not succeeded in improving water and sanitation access and quality in many parts of the world, especially for poorer people, and in more remote areas. Such operators typically suffer from various problems, including low service coverage and quality of service, artificially low tariffs, billing and collection difficulties, lack of capacity, lack of capital investment, lack of operation and maintenance and poor consumer relations. In the 1990s, public–private partnerships (PPPs) began to be promoted as a means to deliver financing for investments and efficiency improvements. Infrastructure (telecommunications; electricity generation, transmission, and distribution; natural gas transmission and distribution; transport; and water) accounted for half of privatization/PPP proceeds in developing countries in 1990–2003 (ADB 2008). By 2000, private operators were serving 93 million people in developing countries (Marin 2009); high profile projects were undertaken in Latin America as well as in megacities including Buenos Aires, Argentina; Manila, the Philippines; and Jakarta, Indonesia.

What Is a Public–Private Partnership?

While there is a large volume of literature relating to public–private partnerships, there appears to be no hard and fast definition. The predominant understanding of public–private partnerships is a general one: public–private partnerships serve to implement projects in which there is some form of collaboration between the public and private sectors; they also finance or otherwise increase resources for the sector (resources include people, skills, expertise, knowledge, technology, equipment, facilities, and spare capacity) in order to expand capabilities.

In general, public–private partnerships have a number of common features:

- A formal or informal agreement. The majority of PPPs are governed by a formal contract, which is generally understood to be a legally binding written agreement. But public–private partnership is also used to describe other types of less formal agreements between governments and private organizations. These "agreements" spell out the responsibilities of each party but stop short of being legally binding arrangements.
- A public- and a private-sector entity. There is a lack of consensus over the definition of what constitutes the private sector in the context of PPP arrangements. For example, a private partner might be a private company (international or local), an informal service provider (international or local), a nongovernmental organization (NGO), or a community-based organization (CBO). The partnership may be a bilateral contractual arrangement or a multiparty arrangement.
- An outcome. PPPs are intended to ensure that services are provided in the most efficient and effective ways possible and usually through joint realization. For

example, the private sector typically contributes design, construction, operation, maintenance, finance, and risk management skills while the government is responsible for strategic planning, regulation, and so on. This sets PPPs apart from other forms of public–private interaction, such as when a private-sector operator or an NGO has essentially been subcontracted to provide a service (or services) independently.

• A degree of risk borne by the private-sector entity. Most definitions of PPPs usually refer to the degree of risk borne by the private sector. There is a distinction between models of PPP with low private-sector risk, such as service and lease contracts, and those with significant private-sector risk, such as concession contracts (Sohail 2003).

PPP Models

There are a number of different types of PPPs in existence. The following is a typical categorization of different contractual arrangements for private-sector participation, but several hybrid arrangements are also possible.

Service Contracts

Under a service contract, the government pays a private entity to perform specific tasks. Service contracts are a long-established practice used for routine operations (meter reading or leak detection), engineering works, and the laying of pipelines.

Management Contracts

Management contracts are contractual agreements between the government and a private partner under which the private partner is given the responsibility for day-to-day management of an enterprise in exchange for a fee; the government, however, retains financial and legal responsibility for delivery of services. These are arrangements in which a municipality or local government purchases management services from a company.

Leasing or Affermage

Under this model, the government delegates management of a public service to a company in return for a specified fee, commonly based on the volume of water sold, while ownership of assets remains with a holding company operating for the government.

Concessions

This arrangement usually gives the concessionaire (the owner or operator) a monopoly service provision for a fixed period of time, during which the concessionaire also assumes any significant investment risk. The model of large concessions has worked in some places, but its suitability to most developing countries has been questioned.

Why Use PPPs?

Public–private partnerships are pursued as a way to leverage knowledge, resources, and capabilities to achieve public goals. PPPs are often used to address non-revenue water reduction (reducing the amount of water "lost" before it reaches the customer and is paid for), billing collection, and labor productivity. While the early models of partnerships focused on the gains from private financing, the most successful PPPs in the water and sanitation sector have largely been based on public financing (leases or hybrid programs) combined with private-sector efficiency. Thus rather than improve access to private financing, PPPs have been used to improve the financial viability of the water and sanitation operators through service quality, access expansion, and increasing cash flow for investment and creditworthiness. In the long term these improvements should translate into broader, more equitable, efficient, affordable, and effective delivery of services. Nevertheless, PPPs may not be selected as an option to improve service delivery on ideological grounds or the basis of public service ethos (Sohail 2002a).

Innovative Solutions

Access has improved by expanding the water network to poor neighborhoods that were previously unserved, as in Queenstown, South Africa; La Paz–El Alto, Bolivia; Manila; and Buenos Aires. In Queenstown, a much smaller PPP covering a population of 22,000 was amended to include an extra 170,000 inhabitants of predominantly low-income areas (Sohail 2005). The renegotiation of existing concession contracts operated in Manila and Buenos Aires led to affordable connection charges for lower-income consumers—benefiting 400,000 in Manila and 260,000 in Buenos Aires. Connection-fee cross-subsidies were used in Buenos Aires; reduced connection costs through distant meter locations and the use of community labor led to 90 percent cost reductions in water tariffs for the poor in Manila (Nickson and Franceys 2001). Nonetheless, there is little evidence of coverage extended to the urban poor as a result of

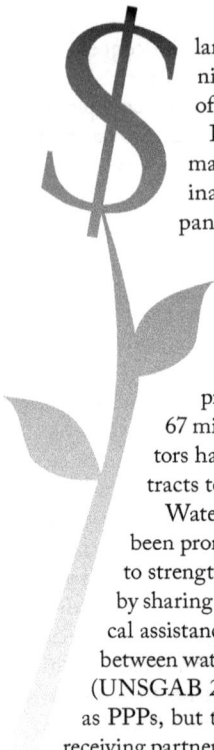

larger scale, formal private-sector companies in PPPs, at least in the initial stages of the contract (Sohail 2004).

In 2000, 80 percent of the water PPP market in developing countries was dominated by five international water companies. Since 2001, however, most new contracts have been signed by private operators from developing countries (these account for 90 percent of the growth in the number of people served by PPP projects). By 2007, local private water operators served more than 67 million people; some international operators have also transferred their existing contracts to local investors (Marin 2009, 9).

Water operator partnerships (WOP) have been promoted by the U.N. since 2006 as a way to strengthen local water and sanitation services by sharing expertise through training and technical assistance. WOPS are defined as "cooperation between water operators," on a "not-for-profit" basis (UNSGAB 2006, 3). Some may not classify them as PPPs, but they are partnering arrangements: the receiving partners are always public undertakings (water and sanitation utilities, drainage and sewerage companies, or wastewater organizations), but their collaboration partners may be well-performing public (foreign public utilities or local public utilities) or private operators (international private operators or local private operators), small-scale water and sanitation service providers, or community-based organizations.

Small, often informal service providers play a significant role by filling in the gaps in service delivery. These service providers, however, are often not officially recognized or involved in PPPs. The potential for these small service providers in PPPs has not been accurately assessed.

Controversies

In developing countries, PPPs haven't met initial expectations: there have been a series of highly publicized contract cancellations, mostly in Sub-Saharan Africa, and in Latin America among concession programs. Doubts still remain over the suitability of PPPs both for improving the performance of water utilities and extending access to water and sanitation to the unserved in developing countries.

Cherry-picking is a particular danger with PPPs, that is, the sites that are most attractive to private investors—large cities in countries with large economies and a large middle class—will be selected rather than areas with the greatest

need. Poor areas and people are often seen as unprofitable and difficult to serve, which means that connections and extension of services are typically not made to residents with insufficient funds, insecure tenure, and those living in difficult-to-reach locations such as rural areas (Sohail 2002b).

The pricing of services in general and the design of tariffs for service provision in particular is a significant issue. In most cases, PPP projects have been accompanied by tariff increases (due to more realistic pricing or greed, depending on one's point of view) that put services beyond the reach of the poor. PPPs may also be accompanied by massive lay-offs, depending on extent of "over-staffing."

Some services are less attractive for private-sector involvement due to their more complex nature; neglect in the area of sanitation is a significant trend that has been noted with PPPs. This could be the case for many reasons: sanitation facilities are often more complex and expensive than water facilities; the demand for the service often does not exist; there is an unwillingness by users to pay; or there may be unnecessary bureaucracy or regulation that constrains service delivery (Sohail 2002c).

PPPs require significant government capacity to be effectively managed, however, such capacity is often lacking. Local government officials need to learn not just how to strategically manage PPPs, but also how to renegotiate and implement them to achieve their objectives.

Successes of PPPs

PPPs haven't always worked, but successes have often received much less publicity than failures. PPPs tend to work best for those who can pay and who live in places where the overall demand makes the provision of services a viable option. If a PPP is to improve access and service delivery for the poor, then this has to be specified in the contract documents that will ultimately be the basis for engaging the private sector. Very few PPP contracts contain explicit pro-poor references. Bidding procedures and contract design should allow sufficient flexibility for innovative solutions to water and sanitation supply, such as lower-cost or alternative technology (for example, pipes at lower depth or condominium sewerage), and flexible billing arrangements as well as payment options, particularly with respect to poor neighborhoods (Hemson and Batidzirai 2002). Multipurpose contacts, such as the combined water and electricity concession in Casablanca, offer opportunities to optimize the demand and sources and should be explored further. In Casablanca the larger electricity side of the services was subsidizing investment in the smaller water division (Hall, Bayliss and Lobina, 2002).

Developing a long-term business model for PPPs to work within a given context is a challenging activity and requires further exploration.

M. SOHAIL and Sue CAVILL
WEDC (Water, Engineering and Development Centre), Loughborough University

See also in the *Berkshire Encyclopedia of Sustainability*: **Development, Sustainable; Development, Rural—Developed World; Development, Rural—Developing World; Development, Urban; Health, Public and Environmental; Municipalities; Public Transportation; Water Use and Rights**

FURTHER READING

Asian Development Bank (ADB). (2008). Recent experience with infrastructure privatization and PPPs. In *Public–private partnership (PPP) handbook*. Retrieved November 2, 2009, from http://www.adb.org/Documents/Handbooks/Public-Private-Partnership/Chapter2.pdf

Gassner, Katharina; Popov, Alexander; & Pushak, Nataliya. (2009). *Does private sector participation improve performance in electricity and water distribution?* (International Bank for Reconstruction and Development / The World Bank Trends and Policy Options No. 6). Retrieved November 2, 2009, from http://www.ppiaf.org/documents/trends_and_policy/PSP_water_electricity.pdf

Hall, David; Bayliss, Kate; & Lobina, Emanuele. (2002). Water in Middle East and North Africa (MENA)—trends in investments and privatisation. Retrieved November 2, 2009, from http://www.psiru.org/reports/2002-10-W-Mena.doc

Hemson, David, & Batidzirai, Herbert. (2002). *Public private partnerships and the poor. Dolphin Coast water concession: Case study: Dolphin Coast, South Africa*. Retrieved January 11, 2010, from http://www.ucl.ac.uk/dpu-projects/drivers_urb_change/urb_infrastructure/pdf_public_private_services/W_DFID_WEDC_HemsonPPP_and_Poo_Dolphin_Coast.pdf

Marin, Philippe. (2009). *Public–private partnerships for urban water utilities: A review of experiences in developing countries* (International Bank for Reconstruction and Development / The World Bank Trends and Policy Options No. 8). Retrieved January 5, 2010, from http://www.ppiaf.org/documents/trends_and_policy/PPPsforUrbanWaterUtilities-PhMarin.pdf

Nickson, Andrew, & Franceys, Richard. (2001). Tapping the market. Can private enterprise supply water to the poor? Retrieved January 11, 2010, from http://www.eldis.org/id21ext/insights37Editorial.html

Sohail, M. (Ed.). (2002a). *Public private partnerships and the poor. Private sector participation and the poor, part 1: Strategy*. Longborough, U.K.: WEDC, Loughborough University.

Sohail, M. (Ed.). (2002b). *Public private partnerships and the poor. Private sector participation and the poor, part 2: Implementation*. Loughborough, U.K.: WEDC, Loughborough University.

Sohail, M. (Ed). (2002c). *Public private partnerships and the poor. Private sector participation and the poor, part 3: Regulation*. Loughborough, U.K.: WEDC, Loughborough University.

Sohail, M. (Ed.). (2003). *Public private partnerships and the poor: Pro-poor longer term contracts*. Loughborough, U.K.: WEDC, Loughborough University.

Sohail, M. (Ed.). (2004). *Tools for pro-poor municipal PPP*. Weikersheim, Germany: UNDP, Margraf Publishers.

Sohail, M. (Ed). (2005). *Public private partnership and the poor. Case study: Revisiting Queenstown, South Africa*. Loughborough, U.K.: WEDC, Loughborough University.

United Nations Secretary General's Advisory Board on Water and Sanitation (UNSGAB). (2006). Hashimoto action plan: Compendium of action. Retrieved November 2, 2009, from http://www.unsgab.org/docs/HAP_en.pdf

Community Capital

Community capital comprises the economic, cultural, and social resources that communities must access to foster their sustainable development. Emerging from nineteenth-century social thought, community capital financial networks such as cooperatives, credit unions, and local alternative currencies benefit both individuals and businesses, while social networks support feelings of well-being and belonging. Corporate social responsibility in community capital extends the corporate sector's focus beyond profit margin toward sustainable and pro-community activities.

Community capital is the sum of the various elements of capital upon which a community relies and from which it benefits. It draws on all the areas underpinning community life: human, social, environmental, economic, and cultural. In addition, community capital includes indigenous resources, regional amenities, and a local skills base; these, combined with corporate and civic forms of philanthropy and volunteerism, are necessary to make a community sustainable in its most extensive aspects. Community capital comprises the significant forms of capital outlined by the theorist Pierre Bourdieu (1986) in "The Forms of Capital": economic, cultural, and social. At the center of this understanding of community capital, Bourdieu outlined a series of "relationships of mutual acquaintance and recognition." Within this context, community capital can be understood as the kinds of economic, cultural, or social capital that link social groups who provide due concern for the well-being of their counterparts, and who do so without immediate recourse to the usual concerns about profit or other compensation.

Community Capital and Networked Finance

One significant outcome of the global economic downturn that began in late 2007 was the emergence of community capital networks to replenish flows of finance to local businesses. A number of initiatives have extended community capital in local or regional contexts over time. These enterprises have included cooperatives, credit unions, and local alternative currencies. Community capital may also include those assets that can be held in common by a community for their mutual benefit. Such assets may include the provision of labor, technologies, equipment, factory space, or land banks that could be used in commonage. While the reasons for this pooling of resources may vary, ultimately programs that create flows of community capital are devised to have universal benefits for society.

The Cooperative Movement

The cooperative movement emerged during the Industrial Revolution to facilitate the economic plight of workers exposed to the vagaries of nascent capitalism. One of the earliest exponents of the cooperative movement was Robert Owen (1771–1858), who developed the concept of utopian cooperative villages in Britain and the United States. The ethic of pooled labor and resources was common in agrarian societies, and the cooperative movement developed these concepts by establishing a framework for mutual cooperation in a planned community. Throughout the eighteenth and nineteenth centuries, cooperatives, intentional communities, workers' collectives, and religious communes were developed through the promotion of an ethic of community capital. Owen founded the rationalist cooperative in New Harmony, Indiana, in 1825. The

Brook Farm experiment of the 1840s in Massachusetts was frequented by utopians, transcendentalists, and intellectuals such as Nathaniel Hawthorne, Ralph Waldo Emerson, and Henry David Thoreau, under the influence of Charles Fourier (Leonard 2007).

Credit Unions

Credit unions represent another form of community capital. One key idea underpinning the credit union is that ownership remains in the hands of the group membership. In addition, credit unions extend financial services such as loans to their members at reasonable rates without the emphasis on profits that characterize the mainstream banking sector. The role of credit unions in maintaining access to credit and direct finance has been an important aspect of localized responses to the economic challenges that have emerged since the collapse of the corporate banking sector.

In the United States credit unions are classified as nonprofits, while in Canada credit unions are free to return a profit from their enterprise. In the United Kingdom, "mutual friendly societies" were established to extend credit to poorer sectors of society, while "building societies" were created to extend credit for housing to the same sector. Credit-union directors are volunteers and are democratically elected by members without an emphasis on their assets. Credit unions also provide a microfinance service based on the provision of financial services to low-income clients who may not have access to mainstream banks. Corporate credit unions provide a clearinghouse service for the wider corporate sector.

Both cooperatives and credit unions continue to play a significant role in contemporary society. In many countries, cooperatives and credit unions have contributed to alternative economic activity since the onset of the global "credit crunch" and subsequent downturn. Cooperatives continue to play a significant role in rural development, while credit unions are expanding their influence, with new credit unions opening across the world at a rapid rate.

Alternative Currencies

Alternative currency movements are often conceptualized as an object of protest or a tool for constructing alternative communities, economies, and societies. Contemporary alternative-currency networks have attempted to use new forms of money as a tool for building more fair and balanced economies and societies. Traditionally, community capital initiatives have included concepts such as social credit or the paying of a dividend to equalize incomes in free societies. Since the homestead movement of the Great Depression, supporters of alternative currencies have advocated a supply of credit based on principles of bartering or exchanging goods and services (North 2007). In contemporary society, the Local Exchange Trading System (LETS) in North America, or local currencies such as "favours" in the United Kingdom, promote local self-sufficiency. Greens have advocated replacing welfare with a program that would guarantee recipients a basic income and allow them additional earnings, whether in local or traditional currencies, and thereby provide an incentive to work.

The Role of Business

One further area of community capital is witnessed in the moves to engage business with sustainable and pro-community activities. Writers such as Fritjof Capra and Gunter Pauli (1995) have outlined the significant role business plays in creating more sustainable pathways for communities and their environments. The active role played by businesses in developing community capital is best understood though an examination of the concept of corporate social responsibility (CSR). Essentially, corporate social responsibility extends the corporate sector's focus beyond mere concerns with profit margins and allows for recognition of the world beyond the business–customer relationship.

As multinationals increase their presence across the globe, this move toward increased integrity in the relationship between corporations and communities has become more significant. Corporations have also moved toward contributing to communities through increased charitable philanthropy. This process of making donations to help communities develop has been described as "cause marketing." Jocelyne Daw (2006) described the emergence of the cause-marketing phenomenon in international business. Representing a market worth $1.4 billion, Daw outlined the manner in which cause marketing has become a sophisticated contemporary trend that creates deeper links between the corporate sector, communities, and the groups or foundations that enhance the lives of others.

Community Culture

Community culture emerges from a process of socialization whereby inhabitants are indoctrinated with distinct values by social institutions including parents, schools, peers, work colleagues, religious groups, media, and state apparatus. The creation of these bonds of socialization lies at the heart of community capital. For Bourdieu, the local characteristics that underpin socialized community cultures are part of that region's "habitus," or the identity born of shared forms of local experiences and environments. Community capital is then derived from a system of mutual exchange built from what Bourdieu describes as "all the goods, material and symbolic, without distinction, that present themselves as rare and worthy of being sought after in a particular social formation" (Harker, Mahar, and Wilkes 1990, 1).

According to Robert Putnam, author of *Bowling Alone: The Collapse and Revival of American Community* (2000), the social version of capital "refers to the collective value of all *social networks* and the inclinations that arise from these networks to do things for each other." In his study of American community, Putnam set out two main components of social capital: bonding capital and bridging capital. Bonding capital refers to the value attributed to the social networks that exist within homogeneous communities, while bridging capital refers to the social networks that exist between socially heterogeneous groups. Relevant examples are utilized by Putnam to demonstrate the consequences of the existence or nonexistence of community capital. For instance, adolescent gangs may create forms of bonding social capital with negative consequences, while sports groups such as the bowling clubs referred to in Putnam's title may create bridging forms of social capital with positive outcomes. Bridging social capital may be beneficial for society in a number of ways; democratic deficit and social breakdown can be addressed as participatory activity is enhanced in the civic sector. Alternatively, the absence of community capital may lead to the further eroding of civil rights and the loss of public amenities, creating negative consequences for wider society and the environment.

The formation of community capital is dependent on the existence of a "sense of community," which is a shared psychological experience of community rather than its tangible or structural frameworks. Such experiences are multifaceted and interwoven with the experiences of others, and it is within this "imagined community" (Anderson 1983) that community capital emerges in its nascent form. This sense of community engenders shared feelings of belonging that are supported by a mutual respect and sense of commitment. Ultimately this sense of social cohesion can be understood by examining the social relations found within a neighborhood, where socialized forms of influence are crucial to the formation of norms and values. The shared values, both imagined and acted upon, form the social cohesion (or "glue") that binds communities. Internet communities have developed the imagined community further, with the technological capital that has emerged from such innovations central to the contemporary concept of community diffusion.

From a social psychological perspective, David McMillan and David Chavis (1986) set out a theory within the field of community psychology; it argues that a prevailing "sense of community" comprises the following four key elements:

- membership that includes boundaries, emotional safety, a sense of belonging and identification, personal investment, and a common symbol system
- influence that is reciprocal because participants have some influence over the wider group and the group has influence on participants in order to maintain wider cohesion
- integration and fulfillment of needs that occurs when participants attain benefits or rewards for their contribution to the group
- a sense of shared emotional connection that includes shared histories and experiences borne from participation and engagement with the group

Classical Theory and Community Capital

Further understanding of community capital can be gained from the works of classical social theorists. The philosopher, social scientist, and revolutionary Karl Marx (1818–1883) extolled a concept of collectively pooled "species being," or the group-based aggregate of skills passed on within a community from the skilled exponents of communal-based crafts. The social theorist Max Weber (1864–1920) outlined an understanding of "status and association" whereby social networks and mobility could be derived from the groups with which a person associated, with status being bestowed by the community for contributions rather than earnings or profit. Credited by many to be the father of sociology, Émile Durkheim (1858–1917) identified the central role of "organic and social solidarity networks" in the development of society, as different types of social solidarity came to correlate with different types of society. Durkheim divided these into mechanical and organic solidarity in his seminal study *The Division of Labour in Society* (1893). Mechanical solidarity comes from the homogeneity of individuals connected by shared location or common goals and is an attribute of traditional societies. Organic solidarity emanates from the interdependence that arises from specialized activities in modern societies. This interdependence is therefore based on the sum of a community's component elements. In modern societies, social solidarity develops through the interaction

COMMUNITY CAPITAL • **133**

stemming from the complexities and interdependence of the industrial age.

The sociologist Ferdinand Tönnies (1855–1936) contrasted social groups formed through personal and social ties—in families, villages, and towns, for instance—that link like-minded individuals sharing values and belief systems (*gemeinschaft*) with the impersonal, formalized, and engaging links, such as economy and industry, that exist across society (*gesellschaft*). The pluralism set out by the French political thinker Alexis de Tocqueville (1805–1859) in *Democracy and America* (2000) depends on the creation of public space for such forms of community capital to exist. Community capital is formed through the tapping of reservoirs of key elements and resources in and around the community by those who comprise the community, and through the value placed on this process. This value is supported by the public-spirited impulse that survives without recourse to preexisting alignments or alliances, avoiding what de Tocqueville described as "the tyranny of the majority." From the work of the historian and philosopher Michel Foucault (1926–1984), community capital can be understood through the nodes of "local governmentality" that emerged from regional forms of power.

Key Indicators

The conditions that point to whether sufficient degrees of community capital exist in a social group include levels of pluralistic activism within participatory democracy and an active civil society with associated nongovernmental organizations (NGOs) and community-foundation groups with access to Internet resources. Economic capital augments community capital in the form of credit unions and cooperative movements, corporate social responsibility movements engaged with cause marketing, and alternative financial networks. Cultural-capital contributions to community capital incorporate "the engaged campus" with enhanced opportunities for volunteerism, knowledge sharing and pooling of existing educational resources, smaller school sizes with literacy programs, and equal access to education for all sectors in society. Particularistic elements within a region such as pedestrian access to commercial, residential, and public structures, as well as the availability of park benches, sports facilities, woodlands, and cycle lanes, play a significant role in the development and retention of levels of community capital. Therefore, spatial planning for public spaces and amenities becomes a crucial part of community-capital projects. Due to the costs involved, public/private partnerships have emerged around community projects, enhancing corporate engagement with the public sector and local municipalities.

Ecological capital is provided through the establishment of sustainable practices such as recycling, community farming, cooperative markets, pooled labor, and alternative or green-living practices. The corrosive results of poor urban planning and neglect were outlined in David Harvey's book *Spaces of Hope* (2000). He presented the significance of good planning practice and the development of the public space as an antidote to the urban breakdown that has become characteristic of major cities such as Baltimore. The development of social ecology and ecological capital is also a significant element of the concept of sustainable development. End-of-pipe solutions are replaced with green processes that incorporate sustainable practices into the chain of production, from the product-planning stage through to recycling of used parts, with integrated forms of management and production being utilized for the benefit of the environment and wider community.

Various forms of mutual engagement create community capital that can be measured through a series of indices to quantify quality of life, happiness, health, longevity, optimism about the future, employment and wealth, civic engagement, and neighborliness. Religious participation and family interaction may also be measured as part of a community-capital index. These indices can be referenced during societal upheavals, such as economic downturns, demographic shifts, increased ethnic diversity, and spatial developments, or in wider events such as climate change, to create better understandings of community-capital reservoirs. The creations of horizontal public networks are at the core of the quest to enhance or retain levels of community capital. Public-spirited concepts such as civic leadership, egalitarian volunteerism, philanthropy, and social responsibility are crucial to this initiative. Once sufficient levels of these civic virtues are attained, the subsequent civic engagement provides an effective bridging function between nonlinear and nonaffiliated networks and the wider population. This connectivity between social networks and community capital has provided a local and interpersonal response to the anomie, or the social instability and personal uncertainty, formed from trends in globalization and accelerated change that is a characteristic of the post-modern condition.

In Chinese culture, the concept of *guānxi* is used to describe the interpersonal networks that exist between two people whereby one person is able to rely on another for assistance, favors, or other forms of community benevolence, regardless of preexisting levels of social status. *Guānxi* can also be used to describe a network of prevailing contacts that can be mobilized within the community. In addition, influence for the common good can

be maintained in this way. This form of community capital can become an unspoken norm, part of the manners or etiquettes of what the sociologist Norbert Elias (1897–1990) called *The Civilizing Process (2000)*. Ultimately a key component of sustainability is derived from the sharing of practice and knowledge that emerges from community discourse, as when innovative solutions and best practices evolve from such flows of knowledge.

Recent discussions of community capital have dealt with demographic diversity. Ethnic diversity is on the increase across developed nations. The imparting and learning of new languages and cultures is an important aspect in the development of community capital. Multicultural-based community capital creates opportunities for new forms of economic and development entrepreneurialism. This is the basis for the study *Better Together: Restoring the American Community* (Putnam and Feldstein 2003), which explores social cohesion and civic engagement within the context of shifting demographics and increased migration. Community capital is built as different cultures merge to form new identities based on the exchange of cultural norms and values, and as they develop bonds through institutions and practices such as educational pursuits and volunteerism.

Using Civic Intelligence to Address Issues

Another element in the formation of community capital is civic intelligence, or the pooled expertise devoted to addressing public or civic issues by organizations, public bodies, or individuals. Within the framework of the community, civic intelligence is the understanding that there is a value in the contribution made by all members of the community regarding the decisions affecting the community. According to the sociologist Jared Diamond in his study *Collapse: Why Some Societies Choose to Fail or Succeed* (2005), significant levels of civic intelligence are required for humankind to solve the planet's major problems such as climate change or the energy crisis.

Community capital can be seen in a range of social engagements and interactions, from community-development initiatives to intentional communities, to credit unions, cooperatives, and the social responsibility

of the corporate sector. The shared experiences and values formed from community capital create a pool of human and natural resources that can be drawn upon to meet the many challenges facing neighborhoods, societies, and nations on this ever-changing planet.

Liam LEONARD
Institute of Technology, Sligo

See also in the *Berkshire Encyclopedia of Sustainability*: **Corporate Citizenship; CSR and CSR 2.0; Development, Sustainable; Ecological Economics; Municipalities; Public Transportation; Smart Growth; Social Enterprise**

FURTHER READING

Anderson, Benedict. (1983). *Imagined communities: Reflections on the origin and spread of nationalism*. London: Verso.

Bourdieu, Pierre. (1986). The forms of capital. In John G. Richardson (Ed.), *Handbook of Theory and Research for the Sociology of Education* (pp. 241–258). New York: Greenwood Press.

Capra, Fritjof, & Pauli, Gunter. (Eds.). (1995). *Steering business towards sustainability*. New York: The United Nations University Press.

Daw, Jocelyne. (2006). *Cause marketing for non-profits: Partner for purpose, passion and profits*. Hoboken, NJ: John Wiley & Sons.

Diamond, Jared. (2005). *Collapse: Why some societies choose to fail or succeed*. New York: Viking.

Durkheim, Émile. (1893). *The division of labour in society*. New York: Free Press.

Harvey, David. (2000). *Spaces of hope*. Berkeley: University of California Press.

Harker, Richard; Mahar, Cheleen; & Wilkes, Chris. (1990). *An introduction to the work of Pierre Bourdieu*. London: Macmillan.

Leonard, Liam. (2007, Winter). Sustaining ecotopias: Identity, activism and place. *Ecopolitics Online Journal 1*(1), 105–122. Galway, Ireland: Greenhouse Press.

McMillan, David W., & Chavis, David M. (1986). Sense of community: A definition and theory. *Journal of Community Psychology, 14*(1), 6–23.

North, Peter. (2007, Winter). Alternative currencies as localised utopian practice. *Ecopolitics Online Journal 1*(1), 50–64. Galway, Ireland: Greenhouse Press.

Putnam, Robert. (2000). *Bowling alone: The collapse and revival of American community*. New York: Simon & Schuster.

Putnam, Robert, & Feldstein, Lewis M. (2003). *Better together: Restoring the American community*. New York: Simon & Schuster.

Tocqueville, Alexis de. (2000). *De la démocratie en Amerique* [Democracy in America]. (Harvey C. Mansfield & Delba Winthrop, Trans. & Eds.). Chicago: University of Chicago Press (Original work published 1835) .

Local Living Economies

Essential building blocks of a socially, environmentally, and financially stable global economy, local living economies are rooted in smaller, more accountable local businesses instead of transnational conglomerates and superstores. Locally owned, independent businesses enable communities to prosper through higher economic multipliers, greater self-reliance, and stronger labor, ecological, and social standards.

The nonprofit organization Business Alliance for Local Living Economies (BALLE), formed in late 2001, popularized the term *local living economies*. BALLE is currently the leading organizer of local business alliances in North America, with more than sixty official networks in existence (as of early 2009) and dozens of others in formation. In the words of the BALLE (n.d.) mission statement, a local living economy "ensures that economic power resides locally, sustaining healthy community life and natural life as well as long-term economic viability."

Contours

The term *local living economy* emerged from two intellectual currents. The first was the writings of David Korten, a leading thinker about the challenges of globalization and author of numerous books, including the best-selling *When Corporations Rule the World* (1995). Korten believes we now depend on a "suicide economy," which is sowing the seeds of its own destruction through unsustainable economic growth, environmental disruption, inequality, social unrest, repression, militarism, and war. A core problem, he argues, is the emergence of powerful global corporations that are unaccountable to communities and ecosystems. He calls for an alternative "living economy" rooted in smaller, more accountable local businesses.

The second intellectual current concerns localism, expounded in such early works as E. F. Schumacher's *Small Is Beautiful* (1973) and Jane Jacobs's *Cities and the Wealth of Nations* (1985). The writings of Michael Shuman, including *Going Local* (1998) and *The Small-Mart Revolution* (2006), make the case that local ownership of business and community self-reliance are key requirements of prosperous local economies. Local ownership means that majority control of a company exists in close geographic proximity to its operations. Examples of locally owned businesses include small family-owned companies, nonprofits, cooperatives, and municipally owned utilities. National or global companies, such as chain retailers or multifactory producers, are usually not regarded as local, and consequently the term *independent* is often paired with local.

Local businesses are usually synonymous with small but not always. Zingerman's in Ann Arbor, Michigan, started as a small delicatessen, but has since grown into more than a half-dozen sister businesses employing more than 500 people. It is regarded as one of the premiere examples of a local living economy business.

Mission

Underlying the concept of local living economies are three major goals: local ownership of business, community self-reliance, and high social performance.

Local Ownership

Local ownership of business matters for community prosperity. One key reason is that locally owned businesses spend more of their revenue locally than do nonlocal businesses. This contributes to the economic multiplier, the benefits that flow from a dollar circulating many times in a community. In 2002, the economic consulting firm Civic Economics analyzed the relative impact of a proposed non-local Borders bookstore in Austin, Texas, as compared to two local bookstores the chain was gunning to put out of business. The researchers found that one hundred dollars spent at Borders would circulate thirteen dollars in the Austin economy, while the same one hundred dollars spent at either of the two local bookstores would circulate forty-five dollars (Civic Economics 2002, 14). Roughly speaking, the study suggested that every dollar spent at the local store contributed three times the jobs to the local economy, three times the boost to income, and three times the tax benefits (Civic Economics 2002, 4).

Subsequent work has confirmed these results. In 2004, Civic Economics improved its methodology by expanding research to include analysis for additional business types and completed another study of Andersonville, a neighborhood in Chicago (Civic Economics 2004, 2 and 8). The principal finding was that a dollar spent at a local restaurant generated 25 percent more economic multiplier than a chain. The local advantage was 63 percent more for local retail, and 90 percent more for local services. In 2007, Civic Economics did its most in-depth study yet, encompassing the city of San Francisco and neighboring communities of South San Francisco, Colma, and Daly City. Looking at books, toys, sporting goods, and fast food, the researchers found that if San Franciscans shifted just ten cents of every dollar of their spending from chain stores to local retailers, they could add nearly 1,300 more jobs and $200 million more in annual output to the city's economy (Civic Economics and San Francisco Locally Owned Merchants Alliance 2007, 27).

An economy made up largely of locally owned businesses confers other advantages on community economies as well. While the exit of absentee-owned businesses moving to Mexico or China may throw the community into an economic tailspin, businesses anchored locally through ownership stay and produce wealth for many years, often many generations. Because local businesses tend to stay put, a community with primarily local businesses can raise labor and environmental standards with confidence that its businesses will adapt rather than flee. The stability of local businesses also tends to contribute to greater social stability and higher levels of political participation. And the small-scale, unique, and dynamic features of local businesses make them better equipped to promote smart growth, draw tourists, attract talented young people, and seed a self-reinforcing entrepreneurial culture.

The broad, popular perception that all local businesses are inefficient, mom-and-pop retailers is incorrect. All retail stores, in fact, make up only 7 percent of the entire economy, and small businesses in all sectors (under the definition of the U.S. Small Business Administration) constitute

roughly half the entire private sector. Small businesses—those with less than 500 employees—moreover, produced almost twice as many new jobs between 1993 and 2008 and thirteen times as many patents per employee as large businesses (SBA 2009).

More serious doubt about local businesses concerns competitiveness. Are we not in an era when bigger businesses can better achieve economies of scale? In fact, in all but seven of the thousand-plus sectors of the roughly 1,100 industrial categories of the North American Industrial Classification System (NAICS), there are more examples of competitive small-scale enterprise in each sector than large-scale enterprise. Put another way, the U.S. economy is full of models of small-scale success that could guide entrepreneurial activities in even very small communities.

Mindful of all these advantages and opportunities, advocates of a local living economy seek to maximize the number and competitiveness of local enterprises, and to increase their relative presence in a community economy.

Community Self-Reliance

A second feature of a local living economy is a higher degree of economic self-reliance, effected through a strategy known as import substitution. *Degree* is an important qualifier here, since few advocates envision or desire a community withdrawing from the national or global economy altogether into a state of autarky. But increasing the relative percentage of the economy focused on local markets is important for several reasons.

Every time a community imports a good or service that it might have cost-effectively produced for itself, it "leaks" dollars and loses critically important multipliers associated with them; this is known as import leakage. Unnecessary imports—of petroleum, for example—also subject a community to risks of major price hikes and disruptions outside local control. They deny a community a diversified base of businesses and skills needed to take advantage of unknown (and unknowable) future opportunities in the global economy. And unnecessary dependence on outside shipments of food or other easy-to-produce goods increases the burdens that distribution systems—transportation, packaging, refrigeration, middle people, and advertisers—impose on the environment, especially with each step consuming energy and releasing climate-disrupting carbon dioxide into the atmosphere.

Some economists disparage import substitution, pointing out that such policies in Latin America in the 1960s and 1970s tended to mean higher tariff and nontariff trade barriers that increased domestic prices, choked foreign technology and investment, and generally stifled economic development. But import substitution can also mean educating consumers (citizen, business, and governmental purchasers) about cost-effective local buying opportunities and encouraging them to take advantage of these. So reconceived as demand driven rather than trade restrictive, import substitution actually turns out to the most effective way to develop export-oriented businesses, as Jane Jacobs long argued.

Jacobs's argument was essentially this: suppose North Dakota wished to replace imports of electricity with local wind-electricity generators. Once it built windmills, it would be self-reliant on electricity but dependent on outside supplies of windmills. If it set up its own windmill industry, it would then become dependent on outside supplies of machine parts and metal. This process of substitution never ends, but it does leave North Dakota with several new, strong industries—in electricity, windmills, machines parts, and metal fabrication—that are poised to meet not only local needs but also export opportunities.

The strongest local economy, in theory, will be one in which its businesses saturate local markets and maximize global markets. To local living economy advocates, a mistake of mainstream economic development has been to focus on global markets and expect trickle-down benefit to local businesses. A growing body of evidence suggests that the causality works in the opposite direction. Instead of putting all of the community's eggs in one export-oriented basket, a community should develop myriad small businesses, grounded (initially at least) in local markets, with confidence that many will naturally graduate into exporters. Ultimately, having a local economy with multiple points of connection with the global economy, rather than just one "comparative advantage," provides better insurance against the natural ups and downs of global markets.

Social Performance

A final goal for local living economies is to increase performance of local businesses in noneconomic areas. These goals are expressed in terms like *social responsibility*, *the three E's* (efficiency, equity, environment), and *the triple bottom line* (profit, people, planet). In fact, there are far more than three dimensions to social performance when all the stakeholders of a business are considered: workers, suppliers, consumers, contractors, owners (passive and active), plant neighbors, local charities, and so forth.

The local living economy movement seeks to find exemplary companies with respect to each stakeholder and spread these models of success to other companies and communities. The Sustainable Business Network, the BALLE affiliate in Philadelphia, Pennsylvania, is trying to improve the social performance of each sector of the local economy through exemplary "building block" organizations in food, energy, finance, clothing, housing, and so forth.

While advocates of local living economies believe there is much local businesses can learn from the performance of exemplary nonlocal businesses, like the Ben & Jerry's and the Benettons of the world, they also believe that kinder, gentler, friendlier, and greener nonlocal businesses can only go so far in reforming themselves before the brutal logic of globalization undoes their progress. How much credit do you get if you give your workers better wages and health care benefits this year but shut down the plant the next? Or if you reduce your energy use, like Walmart, while encouraging millions of purchasers to skip nearby downtown stores and drive literally billions of additional miles per year to the supercenters? At the end of the day, argue local living economy activists, any business that sacrifices its bottom line in the name of responsibility leaves itself vulnerable to a hostile acquisition by another global firm that has the mettle to make such "hard choices." That's what happened to the organic yogurt maker Stonyfield Farms, which was acquired by the Danone Group and has since become a major supplier to Walmart, the bête noire of localization advocates. These dynamics underscore the rationale for believing that social responsibility must include local ownership.

Implementation

One cornerstone of the local living economy movement is to end what are regarded as counterproductive practices by most economic developers. The conventional paradigm today is that a locale should attract and retain globe-trotting companies that expand clusters of existing business and allow a community to achieve one or two global comparative advantages. While economic developers often praise local business, the majority of their spending—some believe well over 90 percent—aims to attract or retain nonlocal businesses through public "incentives." The best estimate of the annual cost of these subsidies by state and local governments is $50 billion per year, and federal agencies contribute at least as much. A growing body of evidence suggests that this kind of economic development is ineffectual at best and a huge waste of local resources and opportunities at worst.

Advocates of local living economies seek to focus scarce public and private money on a series of initiatives that tend to be minimized or ignored altogether by economic developers. There are several key questions currently receiving scant attention:

- Local Planning—Where are significant import leaks in the local economy that could be plugged with new or expanded local enterprises?

- Local Entrepreneurship—How can a new generation of entrepreneurs be nurtured and trained to lead local firms?
- Local Business Organizing—How can existing local businesses work together (through, for example, purchasing cooperatives) to improve their competitiveness?
- Local Investing—How can local savings, whether currently in banks or pension funds, be redirected to support new or expanded local businesses?
- Local Purchasing—How can local businesses achieve greater success through "Local First" purchasing by consumers, businesses, and government agencies?
- Local Public Policy Making—How can the myriad biases that exist against local businesses, such as security laws that have all but made it impossibly expensive for "unaccredited investors" (98 percent of the U.S. public) to invest in local businesses, be overhauled so that they can compete on a level playing field against nonlocal businesses?

These questions have unleashed a new generation of economic development initiatives in the sixty communities in which BALLE is active—and in many more. These programs include leakage studies, local business incubators, farm-to-school collaborations, local stock markets, and business-to-business purchasing networks.

Overall the local living economy movement remains relatively new and small, but there is scarcely a community where its influence cannot be seen in signs that read Local Bank, Local Food, and Local Crafts. In March 2007, the cover of *Time* proclaimed, "Forget Organic, Eat Local." Many economic trends, such as the rising price of oil and the shift of family spending from global goods to local services, almost guarantee that this movement will grow in the foreseeable future.

Michael H. SHUMAN

Business Alliance for Local Living Economies

See also in the *Berkshire Encyclopedia of Sustainability*: **Agriculture; Community Capital; Corporate Citizenship; CSR and CSR 2.0; Fast Food Industry; Investment, Socially Responsible (SRI); Municipalities; Smart Growth; Triple Bottom Line; True Cost Economics**

FURTHER READING

Alperovitz, Gar, & Faux, Jeff. (1984). *Rebuilding America: A blueprint for the new economy*. New York: Pantheon.

Business Alliance for Local Living Economies (BALLE). (n.d.) Mission, vision, and principles. Retrieved May 20, 2009, from http://www.livingeconomies.org/aboutus/mission-and-principles

Civic Economics. (2002). *Economic impact analysis: A case study—Local merchants vs. chain retailers*. Retrieved November 18, 2009, from http://www.liveablecity.org/lcfullreport.pdf

Civic Economics. (2004). *The Andersonville study of retail economics*. Retrieved November 18, 2009, from http://www.civiceconomics.com/Andersonville/AndersonvilleStudy.pdf

Civic Economics & San Francisco Locally Owned Merchants Alliance. (2007). *The San Francisco retail diversity study*. Retrieved November 18, 2009, from http://www.civiceconomics.com/SF/SFRDS_May07.pdf

Daly, Herman E., & Cobb, John B., Jr. (1989). *For the common good*. Boston: Beacon.

Douthwaite, Richard. (1996). *Short circuit*. Devon, U.K.: Resurgence.

Florida, Richard. (2002). *The rise of the creative class*. New York: Basic Books.

Gunn, Christopher, & Gunn, Hazel Dayton. (1991). *Reclaiming capital: Democratic initiatives and community development*. Ithaca, NY: Cornell University Press.

Hawken, Paul. (1993). *The ecology of commerce*. New York: HarperCollins.

Imbroscio, David L. (1997). *Reconstructing city politics*. Thousand Oaks, CA: Sage.

Jacobs, Jane. (1985). *Cities and the wealth of nations: Principles of economic life*. New York: Vintage Books.

Kinsley, Michael. (1996). *Economic renewal guide: A collaborative process for sustainable community development*. Snowmass, CO: Rocky Mountain Institute.

Korten, David C. (2001). *When corporations rule the world* (2nd ed.). Bloomfield, CT: Kumarian Press.

LeRoy, Greg. (2005). *The great American job scam*. San Francisco: Berrett-Koehler.

Mitchell, Stacy. (2006). *The big box swindle: The true cost of mega-retailers and the fight for America's independent businesses*. Boston: Beacon Press.

Peters, Alan, & Fisher, Peter. (2004). The failures of economic development incentives. *Journal of the American Planning Association, 70*(1), 28.

Polanyi, Karl. (1944). *The great transformation*. Boston: Beacon Press.

Power, Thomas Michael. (1998). *Environmental protection and economic well-being*. Armonk, NY: M. A. Sharpe.

Sale, Kirkpatrick. (1980). *Human scale*. New York: J.P. Putnam.

Schumacher, Ernst Friedrich. (1975). *Small is beautiful: Economics as if people mattered*. New York: Harper & Row.

Shuman, Michael H. (2000). *Going local: Creating self-reliant communities in a global age*. New York: Routledge.

Shuman, Michael H. (2006). *The small-mart revolution: How local businesses are beating the competition*. San Francisco: Berrett-Koehler.

Small Business Administration Office of Advocacy (SBA). (2009, September). Frequently asked questions. Retrieved November 18, 2009, from http://www.sba.gov/advo/stats/sbfaq.pdf

Williamson, Thad; Imbroscio, David; & Alperovitz, Gar. (2003). *Making a place for community: Local democracy in a global era*. New York: Routledge.

Social Enterprise

Social entrepreneurs pursue both social and environmental objectives in addition to economic returns on business investments. The resulting social enterprises are not limited to nonprofit businesses; in fact current emphasis is placed on the involvement of the public and private sectors as well. Underdeveloped countries often are ready markets for these social enterprises.

Tackled in the right way, today's economic, energy, and climate crises will lead to tomorrow's solutions, and the size of the potential market opportunities for solutions is staggering. There are an estimated 4 billion low-income consumers, constituting a majority of the world's population, and they make up what increasingly is called the base of the (economic) pyramid, or BOP. A growing body of research is exploring how to use market-based approaches to "better meet their needs, increase their productivity and incomes, and empower their entry into the formal economy" (Hammond et al. 2007, 3). BOP markets are far from small: it is estimated, for example, that the BOP market in Asia (including the Middle East) is made up of 2.86 billion people with a total income of $3.47 trillion, while in Eastern Europe it is estimated at $458 billion; in Latin America, $509 billion; and in Africa, $429 billion. In total, these markets are thought to be worth some $5 trillion.

But how can mainstream business, financial, and political leaders best come to grips with these emerging BOP trends in value creation? Three answers immediately spring to mind. First, they can experiment with new business models, as much of the BOP literature suggests. Second, as leading business thinkers have long argued, a can-do attitude is much more likely to succeed than don't-do, won't-do, or can't-do mindsets. And, third, it makes sense to find, study, and work alongside can-do and we-can-work-out-how-to-do-it innovators and entrepreneurs

already hard at work developing real-world solutions. In the process, we need to define our terms—particularly the term *social enterprise*. Social enterprises, to quote Social Enterprise London (2009), are "businesses which exist to address social or environmental need. . . . Rather than maximising profit for shareholders or owners, profits are reinvested into the community or back into the business."

When the Seventh Social Enterprise Conference was held at Harvard University in 2006, co-chair Caitrin Moran spotlighted the accelerating convergence between private, public, and nonprofit sectors in this field. "More than ever, social problems are being addressed not just by nonprofits, but by people and organizations in all sectors," she noted. "Involvement in social enterprise is not limited to those who pursue nonprofit careers. It includes those who work in big corporations, in government, and in nonprofits" (Harvard Business School 2006).

Business Models for Social Change

Anything like global sustainability will be impossible without the engagement—and radical restructuring—of business and markets. As the entrepreneur and philanthropist Pierre Omidyar put it, "I have learnt that if you want to have a global impact you can't ignore business. I don't mean corporate responsibility programs, but business models that provoke social change" (Byrne 2006). So where to look for such change and its agents? Time and again in periods of extraordinary volatility, disruption, and change, it turns out that the best place to look for clues to tomorrow's revolutionary business models is at the fringes of the current, increasingly dysfunctional system. In *Out of Control*, a groundbreaking book on twenty-first-century business models, author Kevin Kelly says, "In economic, ecological, evolutionary, and institutional models, a healthy fringe speeds adaptation, increases resilience, and is almost always the source of innovations" (1994, 468).

Although there is new momentum, this is not a new field of inquiry. Among the books already published are excellent works with titles like *How to Change the World*, *Profits with Principles*, and *Untapped* (which is subtitled *Creating Value in Underserved Markets*). It is clear that there is no standard-issue version of the entrepreneur, but there is a reasonable consensus on what entrepreneurs do. Through the practical exploitation of new ideas, they establish new ventures to deliver goods and services not currently supplied by existing markets. In recent years, however, there has been a growing recognition that there is a spectrum of enterprise, from the purely charitable to the purely commercial. Social and environmental entrepreneurs operate right across that spectrum, though—because of the immaturity of the markets they address—they currently tend to be skewed toward the nonprofit end.

On the purely charitable side, "customers" pay little or nothing, capital comes in the form of donations and grants, the workforce is largely made up of volunteers, and suppliers make in-kind donations. At the purely commercial end of the spectrum, by contrast, most transactions are at market rates. Interestingly however, many of the most noteworthy experiments these days are happening in the middle ground, where hybrid organizations pursue new forms of "blended value"—a combination of social, environmental, and economic value—and where less well-off customers are subsidized by better-off customers.

Against this backdrop, so-called social entrepreneurs develop and operate new ventures (social enterprises) that prioritize social returns on investment. They think in terms of—and aim to measure—social return on investment (SROI). They aspire to improve the quality of life for marginalized populations in terms of poverty, health, or education. One key reason why mainstream business needs to pay attention is that these people try to achieve higher leverage than conventional philanthropy and most nongovernmental organizations (NGOs), often aiming to transform the systems whose dysfunctions help create or aggravate major socioeconomic, environmental, or political problems.

Pursuing the Ideal

While entrepreneurs come from all sorts of geographical, cultural, educational, and religious backgrounds, they share certain characteristics that are immediately apparent the more one gets to know them. These common characteristics color their motivations and influence the kinds of organizations they establish. Social and environmental entrepreneurs share the same characteristics as all entrepreneurs—namely, they are innovative, resourceful, practical, and opportunistic. They delight in coming up with new products or services, or new approaches to delivering them to existing or undiscovered markets. But what motivates the social and environmental entrepreneur is not doing the deal but achieving the ideal. And because the ideal takes a lot longer to realize, these entrepreneurs tend to be in the game for the long haul, not until they can sell their venture to the highest bidder.

One of the burning questions that invariably comes up, particularly when successful business entrepreneurs meet successful social entrepreneurs, is, what motivates you? The implication behind the question is, if you have been so clever in achieving what you have accomplished, why haven't you applied your talents to making money? In response to that question, David Green—one of the world's outstanding examples of entrepreneurial genius involved in creating financial models that deliver quality health technologies to the world's poor—quipped:

> My reasons are purely selfish. I figure I have been put on this earth for a very short period of time. I could apply my talents to making lots of money, but where would I be at the end of my lifetime? I would much rather be remembered for having made a significant contribution to improving the world into which I came than for having made millions. (Elkington and Hartigan 2008, 4)

As interest grows in trying to solve the world's great social, environmental, and governance challenges, definitions—and the boundaries between fields—increasingly blur. In the process, the field of social entrepreneurship has become "a truly immense tent into which all manner of socially beneficial activities may fit," as two board members of the Skoll Foundation (dedicated to supporting social entrepreneurship)—Roger Martin, dean of the University of Toronto's Rotman School of Management, and Sally Osberg, the Foundation's president and CEO—recently put it. Instead, they argue, the real measure of social entrepreneurship is "direct action that generates a paradigm shift in the way a societal need is met" (SustainAbility n.d., 1). What such people do, in effect, is to identify an "unsatisfactory equilibrium" (Martin and Osberg 2007, 32).

Unreasonable People

Any proposed solutions seem improbable given the current consensus that the problems are to all intents and purposes beyond resolution. As a result, many people continue to see

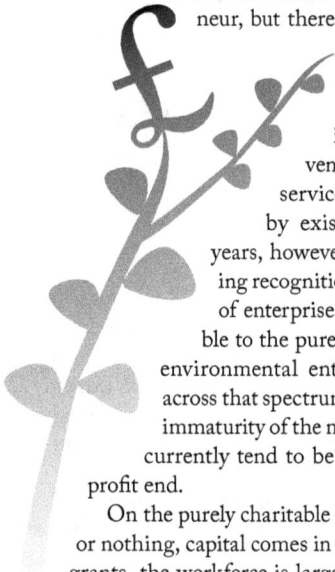

the world's leading social entrepreneurs—and, to a degree, those who invest in them—as unreasonable. In fact, a few years ago Muhammad Yunus, the world's leading social entrepreneur, best known as founder of the revolutionary Grameen Bank and winner of the 2006 Nobel Peace Prize, wryly described his breed as "70 percent crazy." (The Grameen Bank, or "village bank," was founded in 1976 and offers small loans to help impoverished people in Bangladesh achieve economic independence through self-employment; in January 2008 the bank opened a branch in the borough of Queens, New York.) It's extraordinary how often these entrepreneurs have been called crazy by the media, by colleagues, by friends, and even by family members. But they are crazy like the proverbial fox. They look for—and often find—solutions to insoluble problems in the most unlikely places.

Many are pioneering and helping map out future markets where most people would see only nightmare problems and risk. Think of it this way: whatever they may intend, these entrepreneurs are doing early market research on some of the biggest opportunities of the century. But they cannot tackle market failures alone. Instead their efforts need to be supported by all levels of government, by business, by the financial markets, and, crucially, by civil society organizations and ordinary citizens—by each and every one of us.

John ELKINGTON
SustainAbility and Volans Ventures

The author wishes to thank Pamela Hartigan, director of the Skoll Centre for Social Entrepreneurship at Oxford University's Said Business School.

See also in the *Berkshire Encyclopedia of Sustainability*: **Base of the Pyramid; CSR and CSR 2.0; Development, Sustainable; Investment, CleanTech; Investment, Socially Responsible (SRI); Natural Capitalism; Performance Metrics; Poverty; Sustainable Value Creation; Triple Bottom Line; United Nations Global Compact**

FURTHER READING

Ashoka. (n.d.) Retrieved June 11, 2009, from http://www.ashoka.org/

Baderman, James, & Law, Justine. (2006). *Everyday legends: The ordinary people changing our world, the stories of 20 great UK social entrepreneurs.* York, U.K.: WW Publishing.

Bornstein, David. (2004). *How to change the world: Social entrepreneurs and the power of new ideas.* Oxford, U.K.: Oxford University Press.

Byrne, Fergal. (2006, March 24). Dinner with the FT: Auction man. Retrieved November 10, 2009, from http://www.omidyar.com/about_us/news/2006/03/24/dinner-with-ft-auction-man

Dees, J. Gregory, & Anderson, Beth Battle. (2006). Framing a theory of social entrepreneurship: Building on two schools of practice and thought. In Rachel Moser-Williams (Ed.), *Research on social entrepreneurship: Understanding and contributing to an emerging field* (pp. 39–66). ARNOVA Occasional Paper series, Vol. 1, No. 3. Washington, DC: The Aspen Institute.

Elkington, John, & Hartigan, Pamela. (2008). *The power of unreasonable people: How social entrepreneurs create markets that change the world.* Boston: Harvard Business School Press.

Hammond, Allen L.; Kramer, William J.; Katz, Robert S.; Tran, Julia T.; Walker, Courtland; World Resources Institute; & International Finance Corporation. (2007). *The next 4 billion: Market size and business strategy at the base of the pyramid.* Retrieved November 10, 2009, from http://www.wri.org/publication/the-next-4-billion

Harvard Business School. (2006). 2006 Social Enterprise Conference: Convergence across sectors. Retrieved December 22, 2009, from http://www.hbs.edu/socialenterprise/newsletter_archives/2006spring_5.html

Kelly, Kevin. (1994). *Out of control: The new biology of machines, social systems, and the economic world.* Reading, MA: Perseus Books.

Martin, Roger, & Osberg, Sally. (2007, Spring). Social entrepreneurship: The case for definition. *Stanford Social Innovation Review*, 28–39. Retrieved June 12, 2009, from http://www.skollfoundation.org/media/skoll_docs/2007SP_feature_martinosberg.pdf

Schwab Foundation for Social Entrepreneurship. (n.d.) Retrieved June 11, 2009, from http://www.schwabfound.org/sf/index.htm

Skoll Foundation. (n.d.). Retrieved June 11, 2009, from http://www.skollfoundation.org/

Social Enterprise London. (2009). Social enterprise: Definition. Retrieved December 22, 2009, from http://www.sel.org.uk/definition-of-se.aspx

SustainAbility. (n.d.). The business case for engaging social entrepreneurs. Retrieved January 7, 2010, from http://www.sustainability.com/downloads_public/BusinessCaseforEngagingSocialEntrepreneurs.pdf

Weiser, John; Kahane, Michele; Rochlin, Steve; & Landis, Jessica. (2006). *Untapped: Creating value in underserved markets.* San Francisco: Berrett-Koehler.

Editors and Editorial Advisory Board

Editors

The following people served as Editors for the source of these articles, *The Business of Sustainability*, Volume 2 of the *Berkshire Encyclopedia of Sustainability*.

General Editor:
Ray Anderson, *Interface, Inc.*

Volume Editors:
Chris Laszlo
Case Western Reserve University

Karen Christensen
Berkshire Publishing Group

Daniel S. Fogel
Wake Forest University

Gernot Wagner
Environmental Defense Fund

Peter Whitehouse
Case Western Reserve University

Editorial Advisory Board

Lester Brown, *Earth Policy Institute*; Robert Costanza, *University of Vermont*; Luis Gomez-Echeverri, *United Nations Development Programme*; John Elkington, *SustainAbility*; Daniel Kammen, *University of California, Berkeley*; Ashok Khosla, *International Union for Conservation of Nature*; and Christine Loh, *Civic Exchange, Hong Kong*

Author Credits

Accounting
by **Doug Cerf, Kate Lancaster, and Arline Savage**
California Polytechnic State University, San
    Luis Obispo

Base of the Pyramid
by **Mark B. Milstein, Erik Simanis, Duncan Duke,** and
    Stuart Hart
Johnson Graduate School of Management, Cornell
    University

Climate Change Disclosure
by **Steve Rhyne**
K&L Gates LLP

Community Capital
by **Liam Leonard**
Institute of Technology, Sligo

Consumer Behavior
by **Tim Jackson**
University of Surrey

CSR and CSR 2.0
by **Wayne Visser**
CSR International

Energy Subsidies
by **Joshua P. Fershee**
University of North Dakota School of Law

Equator Principles
by **Herman Mulder**
Independent ESG Advisor & Board Member

Fair Trade
by **Rachel Denae Thrasher**
Pardee Center for the Study of the Longer-Range Future,
    Boston University

Financial Services Industry
by **Daniel S. Fogel**
Wake Forest University; EcoLens

Free Trade
by **Rachel Denae Thrasher**
Pardee Center for the Study of the Longer-Range Future,
    Boston University

Global Reporting Initiative (GRI)
by **Elizabeth F. R. Gingerich**
Valparaiso University College of Business
    Administration

Green Taxes
by **Janet E. Milne**
Vermont Law School

Green-Collar Jobs
by **Gary Paul Green**
University of Wisconsin, Madison/Extension and
    Andrew Dane
University of Wisconsin-Extension

Green GDP
by **Jianguo Wu**
Arizona State University
and **Tong Wu**
Northern Arizona University

Investment Law, Energy
by **Peter Cameron** and **Abba Kolo**
University of Dundee

Investment Law, Foreign
by **Kate Miles**
University of Sydney

Investment, CleanTech
by **Peter Adriaens**
Ross School of Business, University of Michigan

Investment, Socially Responsible (SRI)
by **Jacob Park**
Green Mountain College

Local Living Economies
by **Michael H. Shuman**
Business Alliance for Local Living Economies

Public–Private Partnerships
by **M. Sohail** and **Sue Cavill**
WEDC (Water, Engineering and Development Centre), Loughborough University

Risk Management
by **Tamara Bekefi**
Daedalus Strategic Advising
and **Marc J. Epstein**
Rice University

Smart Growth
by **William Galloway**
frontoffice_tokyo; Department of Architecture, Waseda University

Social Enterprise
by **John Elkington**
SustainAbility and Volans Ventures

Sustainable Value Creation
by **Chris Laszlo**
Case Western Reserve University; Sustainable Value Partners

Transparency
by **Aarti Gupta**
Environmental Policy Group, Wageningen University

Triple Bottom Line
by **John Elkington**
SustainAbility; Volans Ventures

True Cost Economics
by **William E. Rees**
University of British Columbia

World Bank
by **Marisa B. Van Saanen**
Yale Law School

Image Credits

The illustrations used in this book come from many sources. There are photographs provided by Berkshire Publishing's staff and friends, by authors, and from archival sources. All known sources and copyright holders have been credited.

Bottom front cover photo: Fireflies (*Pyractomena borealis*) on an Iowa prairie. Photo by Carl Kurtz. Top photo: Shanghai skyline. Photo by Tom Christensen.

Photo used with the Author Credits and Index: *Design in Nature*. Photo by Carl Kurtz.

Money-plant illustrations by Anna Myers. Engraving illustrations of plants and insects by Maria Sibylla Merian (1647–1717). Dragonfly illustration by Lydia Umney.

Pages 1, 2, 6, 19, 99, *General view of the city and the Atchison, Topeka, and Santa Fe Railroad, Amarillo, Texas; Santa Fe R.R. trip*. Photo by Jack Delano. Library of Congress.

Pages 10, 34, 121, *Windmills*. Photo by Jusben. Morguefile.com.

Pages 13, 38, 110, 130, *Pink sedum*. Photo by Anna Myers.

Page 20, *Autumn azalea*. Photo by Anna Myers.

Page 23, *Landscape, northeast Utah*. Photo by John Vachon. Library of Congress.

Pages 25, 29, 66, *Kongenog Dronningen, Bispen, Norway*. Library of Congress.

Page 43, *Minnows in Jordan's Pond, Acadia National Park, Maine, USA*. Photo by Amy Siever.

Page 48, *Cotswold Hills in autumn, Gloucestershire, UK*. Photo by Amy Siever.

Pages 55 and 60, *Prickly pear cacti and flowers, Red Rocks State Park, Sedona, Arizona, USA*. Photo by Amy Siever.

Pages 76 and 82, *Bamboo*. Photo by Anna Myers.

Page 86, *Yellowthroat female*. Photo by Carl Kurtz.

Page 88, *Ailsa Craig, Scotland*. Library of Congress.

Page 93, *Evening thunderheads*. Photo by Carl Kurtz.

Page 126, *Basilicata, Italy*. Photo by Gianfranco Franci. Morguefile.com.

Page 135, *Bands of sheep on the Gravelly Range at the foot of Black Butte, Madison County, Montana*. Photo by Russell Lee. Library of Congress.

Pages 104, 116, 139, *Longqing Gorge, China*. Photo by Thomas Christensen.

Index

A

Accounting, 68, **93–98**. *See also* **Climate Change Disclosure; Global Reporting Initiative (GRI); Green GDP; Transparency; Triple Bottom Line; True Cost Economics**
emission credits, 95
and environmental liabilities, 95-96
external reporting, 93
full cost accounting, 96–97
greenhouse gas (GHG), 94–95
sustainability reporting and **Global Reporting Initiative**, 93–94
sustainable practices and assets, 96
and **Triple Bottom Line**, 93
AIDS, 86
airline industry. *See also* energy efficiency
emission reduction regulations, 95
Alliance of Religions and Conservation (ARC), 87
antiwar activism, 82

B

Base of the Pyramid, 23–24, 84, 139. *See also* **Investment, Socially Responsible (SRI)**; poverty
layers or levels of, 23–24
benefit-cost analysis (BCA), 4–5

bilateral investment treaties, 62, 63
biofuel, 77
biotechnology industry, 76
Bourdieu, Pierre, 130
Bowen, Howard Rothmann, 13
Brundtland Report, 117
Business Alliance for Local Living Economies (BALLE), 135

C

Canada
North American Free Trade Agreement (NAFTA), 26, 55–58, 62
cap-and-trade, 53
vs. carbon tax, 52–53
cap-and-trade carbon trading system, 4
carbon dioxide, 50, 51
emissions, 51
Carbon Disclosure Project (CDP), 69–70
carbon footprint, 77
Carbon Offset Provider Evaluation Matrix (COPEM), 95
carbon productivity, 68
carbon tax, 48, 51–52
climate change and, 51
in practice, 52
vs. cap-and-trade, 52–53
China
biomass jobs in, 123

Bold entries and page numbers denote articles in this volume.

Bold entries and page numbers denote articles in this volume.

This **BERKSHIRE** *Essentials* book was distilled from the

Berkshire Encyclopedia of Sustainability Volumes 1–10

Knowledge to Transform Our Common Future

In the 10-volume *Berkshire Encyclopedia of Sustainability*, experts around the world provide authoritative coverage of the growing body of knowledge about ways to restore the planet. Focused on solutions, this interdisciplinary print and online publication draws from the natural, physical, and social sciences—geophysics, engineering, and resource management, to name a few—and from philosophy and religion. The result is a unified, organized, and peer-reviewed resource on sustainability that connects academic research to real world challenges and provides a balanced, trustworthy perspective on global environmental challenges in the 21st century.

Ray C. Anderson

General Editor

Sara G. Beavis, Klaus Bosselmann, Robin Kundis Craig, Michael L. Dougherty, Daniel S. Fogel, Sarah E. Fredericks, Tirso Gonzales, Willis Jenkins, Louis Kotzé, Chris Laszlo, Jingjing Liu, Stephen Morse, John Copeland Nagle, Bruce Pardy, Sony Pellissery, J.B. Ruhl, Oswald J. Schmitz, Lei Shen, William K. Smith, Ian Spellerberg, Shirley Thompson, Daniel E. Vasey, Gernot Wagner, Peter J. Whitehouse

Editors

10 VOLUMES • 978-1-933782-01-0
Price: US$1800 • 6,084 pages • 8½ × 11"

"The call we made in *Our Common Future*, back in 1987, is even more relevant today. Having a coherent resource like the *Encyclopedia of Sustainability*, written by experts yet addressed to students and general readers, is a vital step, because it will support education, enable productive debate, and encourage informed public participation as we join, again and again, i the effort to transform our common future

—Gro Harlem Brundtland, chair of the World Commission on Environment and Development and three-time prime minister of Norway

"This is undoubtedly the most important and readable reference on sustainability of our time"

—Jim MacNeill, Secretary-General of the Brundtland Commission and chief architect and lead author of *Our Common Future* (1984–1987)

Praise for Berkshire's "This World Of Ours" series

This Is America: A Short History of the United States is the latest in Berkshire's "This World Of Ours" series, acclaimed by some of the world's leading scholars. *This Fleeting World: A Short History of Humanity,* the first in the series, was praised by Bill Gates, founder of Microsoft and author of *The Road Ahead.* The books tackle big subjects such as China, America, Islam, sports, environmental history, and Africa—even the universe—in about a hundred pages. Each book is designed to be read in one or two sittings.

This Is China

"It is hard to imagine that such a short book can cover such a vast span of time and space. *This Is China: The First 5,000 Years* will help teachers, students, and general readers alike, as they seek for a preliminary guide to the contexts and complexities of Chinese culture."

> Jonathan Spence, professor of history,
> Yale University; author of
> *The Search for Modern China*

This Fleeting World

"I first became an avid student of David Christian by watching his course on DVD, and so I am very happy to see his enlightening presentation of the world's history captured in *This Fleeting World.* I hope it will introduce a wider audience to this gifted scientist and teacher."

> Bill Gates, founder of Microsoft

This Is Islam

"*This Is Islam* provides interested general readers and students with a concise but remarkably comprehensive introduction to Islam. It is a clearly presented guide that provides both a broad overview and important specifics in a way that is easy for both experts and non-specialists to use."

> John Voll, professor of Islamic history,
> Georgetown University

Forthcoming titles in the series include *This Good Earth: A Short History of Human Impact on the Natural World, This Sporting World,* and *This Is Africa.*

www.ingramcontent.com/pod-product-compliance
Lightning Source LLC
Chambersburg PA
CBHW080554220326
41599CB00032B/6478